Praise for *As by Fire*

'The dysfunctional interactions of poorly impoverished students, insurgent nationalists, short-sighted govern-ments and corrupted states – all poorly interpreted by weak mass media – erode the foundations of university systems operating amidst perva-sive economic and social injustice. Exposing the nervous system of such deep-seated misery requires a rare combination of surgical skill, courage and compassion – qualities that Jonathan Jansen, easily the country's leading expert on education at all levels, has in abundance. Anyone wanting to know why South Africa's best universities are now set to become indistinguishable from the worst simply *has* to engage with this chilling – superb – study.' **Charles van Onselen**

'#Feesmustfall but what must rise? This pre-eminent educationist and thinker shines a light on higher education and the student protests that rocked SA. A must read by Jonathan Jansen.' **Ferial Haffajee**

'This is *what* really happened, told with the clarity and compassion of a brilliant insider.' **Don Pinnock**

AS BY FIRE

The end of the South African university

Jonathan Jansen

Tafelberg

Tafelberg, an imprint of NB Publishers,
a division of Media24 Boeke Pty (Ltd),
40 Heerengracht, Cape Town, South Africa
www.tafelberg.com

Set in 12 on 15 pt Garamond Premier Pro
Cover by Fuel Design
Book design and typesetting by Purple Pocket Solutions
Edited by Lisa Compton
Proof read by Russell Martin
Commissioning editor: Gill Moodie

Printed by **novus print**, a Novus Holdings company

First edition, first impression 2017

ISBN: 978-0-624-08030-5
Epub: 978-0-624-08031-2
Mobi: 978-0-624-08032-9

for grace

Contents

Preface

On 9 March 2015, a postgraduate student at the University of Cape Town (UCT) poured human waste over the campus statue of the colonialist Cecil John Rhodes. In the weeks and months that followed, a series of student demonstrations erupted across the historically English university campuses of South Africa, such as Rhodes University and the University of the Witwatersrand (Wits). Shortly after the dousing of Rhodes, on 26 March 2015, a statue of King George V was defaced at the University of KwaZulu-Natal's Howard campus, the home of the original University of Natal.

The main focus of this first phase of student protests was against the colonial character and content of the old, long-established universities, and the general failure of transformation evident in indicators such as the very small numbers of black professors in these former white institutions. In time the call for transformation, a term associated with the increasingly unpopular ruling party, the African National Congress (ANC), was replaced with the more radical demand for decolonisation of the universities, including their 'colonial' curricula.

A protest moment in the long history of student activism in South Africa became a movement which, by May 2015, would spread to the historically Afrikaans universities, where the demand of the protestors was the dropping of Afrikaans as a major language of instruction. The release of a video titled *Luister* (Listen), in August 2015, captured the deep discontent among black students at the University of Stellenbosch as one student after another recited his or her experiences of racism and exclusion within the university. These sentiments spread quickly to the University of Pretoria (UP), where again Afrikaans was targeted as the primary instrument for the marginalisation of black students in this large urban university.

Then things started to fall, consistent with the protestors being labelled 'the Fallists' as they promoted and made use of the hashtag #RhodesMustFall. On 9 April 2015, the gigantic bronze statue of Cecil John Rhodes was removed from the UCT campus exactly a month after the protestors' first action against what they saw as a symbol of their alienation and exclusion on former white university campuses. A month later, on 27 May 2015, the University of Stellenbosch removed a campus plaque honouring the notorious apartheid prime minister Hendrik Verwoerd and replaced it with the flag of the new South Africa.

Over the next few months, buildings would be renamed and institutional policies changed as university leaders scrambled to accommodate the incessant demands of the Fallists during 2015. Processes of renaming already under way – such as at the University of the Free State (UFS), where a men's residence named after the racial ideologue JBM Hertzog had already been renamed after struggle hero Beyers Naudé – were accelerated. Policies already under review, such as changes to the parallel-medium (English and Afrikaans) language policies of the universities of Pretoria and the Free State, were now claimed as Fallist victories by the growing student movement for change at former white institutions. University councils rushed to approve complex measures that would make English the primary medium of instruction at these universities – a trend already under way given the growing majority of black students at some former Afrikaans universities (UFS) and gradual changes in favour of English at others (UP). The new language policies would be challenged in the courts by conservative Afrikaans bodies, such as AfriForum, but gradually the law came down on the side of changes in favour of English-language instruction.

The student protest movement did not, however, start at UCT. In response to #RhodesMustFall, students at the historically black universities expressed frustration around the fact that they had been protesting for years about financial exclusion, but were never taken seriously until the protests began at the former white universities. Indeed, in the months preceding the attack on the Rhodes statue, there were continuing protests at institutions such as the Tshwane University of Technology (TUT) and the Durban University of Technology (DUT). These protests were not about transformation (or decolonisation) but about financial exclusion. It is true that student discontent only made the headlines with the outbreak of protests at the former white universities in March 2015. But financial exclusion was about to become the next major rallying point for student activism.

As the first phase of the student movement appeared to fizzle out, a new wave of protests started at Wits University, this time focused on leaked information that the Johannesburg university was about to increase its 2016 fees by 10,5 per cent. On 14 October 2015, this second phase of the student protest movement was promptly dubbed with the enduring hashtag #FeesMustFall. On the day this protest started, Blade Nzimande, the minister of higher education and training, was hosting the Summit on Transformation in Higher Education in Durban with university stakeholders, including students. There were clear signs of trouble ahead with regard to the financial affordability of higher education for poor students. Those present reported a rather dismissive attitude towards students on the part of the minister and his senior bureaucrats when these concerns were raised. At Wits, in the meantime, the protests were gaining steam and the vice-chancellor, Adam Habib, hastily left the summit to meet with students.

The focus of the student protest movement had largely shifted from transformation and the affordability of higher education, and would gradually evolve into more radical demands for decolonisation and free higher education for all. By this time the higher education minister, and indeed President Jacob Zuma, had realised that what they now faced was much more serious than #RhodesMustFall. While universities were the sole targets of symbolic reparation, the purse strings that determine financial inclusion lay within the state.

Small steps were taken to try to alleviate the pressure. The minister thought he was being responsive by capping the fee increase at 6 per cent for all institutions – an illegal act, since only university councils could make that determination. That decision seemed to inflame the protestors. The president then stepped in and, under huge pressure, declared a zero per cent fee increase for 2016. As the 2015 academic year drew to a close, there was a lull in protest activity. But a realignment in student politics for the new academic year led to an eruption of the most violent protests on university campuses in the country's history.

For the rest of 2016, university leaders were literally fighting fires. The student protestors, however small their numbers, took fire to lecture theatres, cars, libraries, computer laboratories, statues, university paintings, administration buildings, residences, and the offices of vice-chancellors.

What was once a largely peaceful and broad-based student protest movement had become increasingly disruptive, violent and even racist in its character and demands.

As the 2016 academic year came to an end, leaders in government, universities, the private sector, and civil society scrambled once again to find ways of meeting the demand for free higher education without creating a serious financial crisis for the country and its public institutions. The general thinking in these quarters was to fully fund poor students, provide aid to middle-class students who fell between the cracks (the so-called missing middle, not rich enough to pay their way and not poor enough to qualify for state funding), and to require the wealthy to pay their keep. To many student leaders this was playing games. The demand was for free higher education, period.

Soon it became clear that for some of the more vocal and violent elements in the protest movement, the radical change agenda went far beyond the demand for free higher education to include the destruction of 'colonial institutions' and even a change of government.

What is going on?

I wrote this book for two related reasons. As the student protests escalated on South African campuses starting in early 2015, there were many questions in university quarters such as why, why now, and why in some institutions and not others. What was going on? It did not help that in the print and online media, everyone *seemed* to know exactly what was going on and what needed to be done. On every campus there were seminars, workshops, and conferences which almost without exception hailed the student voice and extolled the protest movement. Any university event convened outside the authority of the protestors was interrupted and condemned. The problem was clear and the remedies straightforward. The first academic books on the crisis emerged within record time even as the protests were still gathering steam. The line between victim and villain was drawn clearly and quickly.

Working inside the turbulence, I was not at all certain that we had a deep enough understanding about what at root was driving the increasingly violent protests of students and, later, workers on our public university campuses. The quest to understand more deeply the origins, character, and consequences of the student protest movement of 2015–2016 is my first reason for writing this book.

Writing about student activism is inevitably a political activity. This book charts, even applauds, the direction of a movement or institution or nation, but also warns of consequences. My approach to the student protests is therefore both empathetic and critical. It is empathetic in that I recognise the two main fault lines in the attack on public universities after apartheid: cultural alienation and financial exclusion. I appreciate the power and the authenticity of student voices, especially in the 2015 period, and the need for leaders to listen and attend to what is being expressed by courageous student leaders.

At the same time my approach is critical in that I question and interrogate some of the main lines of attack on the public university, especially in 2016 – from simple untruths that billions of rands are being hoarded away by the state and universities, to the more dangerous position that violence against individual persons and public property can be justified by some theory of revolution, or by the logic of justified retaliation, or by no theory at all.

The account of leadership in this book does not accept the outright dismissal of student protests nor does it condone the unconditional celebration of student behaviour. If anything, the leadership stories that emerge from the interviews I held with vice-chancellors draw attention to the complexity in trying to explain these sustained and destructive protests. What the voices of leaders in this book reveal is that the solutions to the complex crisis appear to be quite simple in a rational world. But the operational world for higher education leaders, as will be demonstrated, is hardly rational. Thus, an engagement with the political dimensions of the student protests takes centre stage in this account.

What we do not know

My second reason for writing this book is to address a gap in the literature on university leadership by providing the perspectives of sitting vice-chancellors in the context of nationwide crises in higher education. There are, of course, retrospective accounts of the general experiences of retired university leaders in South Africa, and ample biographical accounts of the lives and ambitions of vice-chancellors on the job.[1] But none of these publications captures the ambition and anxiety of leadership practice during a period of sustained crisis. That is what this book offers.

The paucity of relevant research is also evident in the international scholarship on leaders and crisis. Over the past two decades there has been an explosion of literature on education leadership, but that work is focused largely on the work of school principals and superintendents. Studies of university presidents (as the leaders are called in the US) or vice-chancellors (the title used in the UK and its former colonies) are less common. And even in these rare studies, research on the heads of universities in times of crisis is often reported by those at a distance from institutional calamities. There is, of course, a burgeoning literature on business leaders in times of crisis, but this tradition focuses almost entirely on the role of chief executives.[2] Moreover, it is a literature that is largely descriptive, often autobiographical, and almost always prescriptive in nature.

What constitutes a 'crisis' in much of the literature outside of Africa is also in question. Scholars write about 'tragedies as crisis', such as a mass shooting on a campus (Virginia Tech, for example),[3] the crashing of a plane carrying campus citizens (Oklahoma State University),[4] the uncovering of a serial child molester among the football coaching staff (Pennsylvania State University),[5] allegations of sexual assault by members of a campus sports team (Duke University),[6] or the torture and killing of a gay student (University of Wyoming).[7] This first category of crisis is typically a single, tragic event requiring an emergency reaction or a disaster management response and for which the immediate responsibility lies with a small group or even a single individual.

The second category of crisis, the kind that this book focuses on, includes those cases in which the institution turns on itself; that is, when students mobilise to disrupt university operations through both peaceful and violent means over lengthy periods of time. In this category of crisis, there is no single individual to call to account, but rather an often amorphous mass of protestors priding themselves on the fact that there is no one leader.

In the first category, the critical incident is short-lived, intensive, and contained, even though institutional and personal effects may last well into the future. In the second case, the incidents are many, complex, and open-ended,[8] so that the institutional leadership finds itself perpetually stressed and drained as the crisis continues over days, weeks, months, and even years. It is therefore reasonable to conclude that two very different kinds of leadership persona are required, and that different leadership effects emerge from each of the two crisis scenarios.

In any case, the higher education literature desperately needs a base of knowledge on crisis leadership. In particular, we need to know how university leaders are affected by and respond to crises in a sphere of work that, in the post-independence context, has become known for its chronic instability. The stakes are high. A serious crisis can be cataclysmic for both individuals and the university as a whole. 'One event,' holds an authoritative source on the matter, 'can change the course of a campus, alter the reputation of a leader, and forever change the external perception of an institution.'[9]

The negative impact on university leaders can be devastating for institutions as leaders resign or find themselves effectively fired for mismanaging a crisis. Trust relationships between students and staff or staff and management can break down irrevocably in a stand-off protest. The academic credibility of an institution can go downhill rapidly when, for example, there is evidence of graduate certificate fraud. Donors might reconsider funding, with lasting reputational damage to a university. Prospective students might look elsewhere when extreme initiation practices result in injury or death. Both the public and university leaders therefore have a vested interest in understanding what a crisis means, how to manage it, and, ideally, how to prevent it from happening in the first place. On the positive side, effective leaders can teach us much about how to turn crisis into opportunity. Either way, we need to know about the relationship between leaders and crises, and especially the effects of crisis on this most valuable and often well-paid resource, the university principal.

Insider research

The period covered by this study of university leaders and campus crisis is roughly March 2015 through September 2016. Between June and August 2016, I met with eleven vice-chancellors from South Africa's most troubled universities and interviewed them in depth. The objective was to ascertain their understanding of the university crisis, their managerial and personal responses on their own campuses, and their view of the future of the country's higher learning institutions. As the rector of the University of the Free State since 2009, I am therefore the twelfth vice-chancellor in this study of the origins, meanings, and longer-term effects of the crisis on universities. In writing this book, I have interspersed my own leadership experiences among those of my eleven colleagues. Based on my direct experiences with students, I bring in the relational aspects of the university leader and students in the years leading up to the crisis and in the period of turmoil up until I resigned as vice-chancellor at the end of September 2016.

Of course I am emotionally and intellectually invested in this study. I do not stand outside the turmoil of 2015–2016. I approach the inquiry with empathetic commitment to my fellow vice-chancellors but also to my students. I am not unaffected by what I hear both from poor students as well as from struggling university leaders. Like all vice-chancellors, I recognise that the students have a point to their struggle, although my own sense of how to achieve their goals is very different from theirs. Clearly I do not enter this study as the detached, clinical, independent outsider; the book will reveal my own passions and commitments, and my 'being implicated' within the research process. And yet truth matters, not simply experimental truth but narrative truth: the heart-and-mind accounts of real leaders in crisis situations in which their very lives, and those of their followers, are on the line. This book is not the whole truth – there is no such thing – but a perspective on the truth, and an important one from the rare and relatively unstudied vantage point of the university leader.

Following the approach I took in writing my book *Leading for Change*,[10] I decided to dispense with unnecessary jargon and to focus on communicating what are sometimes complex ideas in everyday language. The crisis in and future of South African universities is too important a topic to cloud or conceal important issues behind the shroud of academic pretence. The use of everyday language does not make research less scholarly; it makes it more accessible, and helps contribute towards public scholarship as well as academic debate.

The sample

All but one of the sample of eleven vice-chancellors were men, of which only two were white. There are too few women leaders of South African universities, and among the few approached for inclusion in this study only one responded positively or at all. The institutions themselves are richly diverse in terms of age, origins, region, racial demographics, politics, and resource profiles. And as indicated in the table on the next page, the status of these university leaders was changing even before this study was completed.

None of the traditional black universities were included in the sample since the purpose of this study was not to investigate those institutions where routine protest cycles were well established and which were bypassed, for the most part, by the violent protests of 2015–2016. For example, the issue of decolonisation would not come up in any serious and sustained manner on the historically black campuses. What happened at the sampled institutions was that their leaders were confronted for the first time by a scale and intensity of protest not seen before and which required extraordinary leadership and management responses. This is not, however, a study of the institutions themselves, but of the leaders of those universities and how they managed and led within their particular environments.

Although the vice-chancellors themselves represent a variety of personality types and a range of leadership styles, they all carry a deep concern and a heavy personal burden in relation to the future of South Africa's 26 public universities. This concern prompted the vice-chancellors' engagement with questions such as the following: What does this analysis of the student protests foretell about the prospects for vibrant and viable institutions of higher education in the southernmost region of the continent? Given that so many African universities lost their intellectual vibrancy and social value in the post-colonial period, can South Africa expect to be different? South Africa is home to some of the world's leading research and teaching universities, attracting more and more African students from north of the Limpopo. Will the student protests destroy or enhance these institutions of higher learning? That is the key question that should be kept in mind in the course of reading this book – and to which the final chapter hazards a response.

University and leader	Total enrolments (2014)	Black*	White
Cape Peninsula University of Technology (CPUT) Professor Prins Nevhutalu (placed on leave)	33 186	29 024 (87,5%)	4 162 (12,5%)
Durban University of Technology (DUT) Professor Ahmed Bawa (resigned)	26 472	25 707 (97,1%)	765 (2,9%)
Nelson Mandela Metropolitan University (NMMU) Professor Derrick Swartz (stepping down, 2017)	26 510	20 162 (76,1%)	6 348 (23,9%)
North-West University (NWU) Professor Dan Kgwadi	63 135	45 354 (71,8%)	17 781 (29,2%)
Rhodes University Professor Sizwe Mabizela	7 519	4 830 (64,2%)	2 689 (36,8%)
Tshwane University of Technology (TUT) Professor Lourens van Staden	56 785	54 027 (95,1%)	2 758 (4,9%)
University of Cape Town (UCT) Dr Max Price (end of term, 2017)	26 357	18 120 (68,7%)	8 237 (21,3%)
University of the Free State (UFS) Professor Jonathan Jansen (resigned)	31 032	22 040 (71,0%)	8 992 (29,0%)
University of Johannesburg (UJ) Professor Ihron Rensburg (stepping down, 2017)	49 789	44 427 (89,2%)	5 362 (10,8%)
University of Pretoria (UP) Professor Cheryl de la Rey	56 376	32 215 (57,1%)	24 161 (42,9%)
University of the Western Cape (UWC) Professor Tyrone Pretorius	20 582	19 473 (94,6%)	1 109 (5,4%)
University of the Witwatersrand (WITS) Professor Adam Habib	32 721	25 152 (76,8%)	7 569 (23,2%)

Source: Enrolment data from Department of Higher Education and Training (DHET) Higher Education Management Information System (HEMIS). Available at: http://chet.org.za/data/sahe-open-data.

*'Black' includes African, coloured, and Indian students. The total enrolments include students in distance education, almost exclusively black, offered by institutions such as NWU (47% contact white in 2012) and UP (52% contact white in 2012) in which the contact numbers are more white. The racial distribution of students also does not reflect campus-specific racial numbers or dynamics. For example, the Potchefstroom campus of NWU is largely white, and the Bloemfontein campus of UFS is more integrated than its virtually all-black Qwaqwa campus; such differences relate to the 1990 mergers and incorporation of former black and white colleges and universities.

Acknowledgements

I am grateful to the following people, who helped make this book possible:

My family: Grace Jansen, Mikhail Jansen, Kathryn Jansen, and Sara-Jane Jansen.

My tireless research assistant, Nicoleen Snyman; my selfless director of office, Rhoda Grobler; and my survey assistant, Sinoxolo Gcilitshana on the Bloemfontein campus, as well as Teboho Manchu and his assistant on the Qwaqwa campus.

My colleagues at the Center for Advanced Studies in the Behavioral Sciences (CASBS) at Stanford University, especially Margaret Levi, Sally Schroeder, Terry Maroney, Ruth Chang, Barbara Schneider, Batja Gomes Mesquita, Fenrong Lui, Donald Chi, Marie Chevrier, Arnold Rampersad, Jesse Ribot, Eitan Wilf, and Barry Zuckerman. The two library specialists at CASBS, Jason Gonzales and Darin Spelber were exceptional in their support by linking ideas to resources for all four books completed during the Fellowship.

My former Stanford professors Hans Weiler, Joel Samoff, Martin Carnoy and Chiqui Ramirez – who still teach me – as well as Jim Ferguson, Ann Lieberman, Jim Campbell, Laura Hubbard, Jonathan Berk; Stanford students Jess Auerbach and Monde Nkosi; and friends in the Stanford, CASBS and Bay Area community David Christie, Nancy Christie, Carla King, Ernie Lieberman, Marvina Rampersad, Rachel Samoff, Frauke Weiler, Luisa Lopez, Benny Carle and Iris Wilson.

My South African friends in the academy, especially Jeremy Seekings and Brenda Schmahmann as critical commentators on specific chapters; as well as Nico Cloete, Jacqui du Toit, Andre Keet, Lis Lange, Lacea Loader, Simon Morilly, Ian Phimister, Neil Roos, Helene Strauss, J.C. van der Merwe, Charles van Onselen, Dionne van Reenen, Melanie Walker, and Corli Witthuhn.

The eleven vice-chancellors whose experiences and insights are the foundation of this study: Ahmed Bawa, Cheryl de la Rey, Adam Habib,

Dan Kgwadi, Sizwe Mabizela, Prins Nevhutalu, Tyrone Pretorius, Max Price, Ihron Rensburg, Derrick Swartz, and Lourens van Staden.

My editor at NB Publishers, Gill Moodie, and Lisa Compton for their professional guidance and meticulous editing of the long and unwieldy version of the manuscript. And the external reviewers of the book whose comments also improved the final product.

Interviewed vice-chancellors

Ahmed Bawa	Durban University of Technology (DUT)
Cheryl de la Rey	University of Pretoria (UP)
Adam Habib	University of the Witwatersrand (Wits)
Dan Kgwadi	North-West University (NWU)
Sizwe Mabizela	Rhodes University (RU)
Prins Nevhutalu	Cape Peninsula University of Technology (CPUT)
Tyrone Pretorius	University of the Western Cape (UWC)
Max Price	University of Cape Town (UCT)
Ihron Rensburg	University of Johannesburg (UJ)
Derrick Swartz	Nelson Mandela Metropolitan University (NMMU)
Lourens van Staden	Tshwane University of Technology (TUT)

Abbreviations and acronyms

ANC	African National Congress
BFLF	Black First Land First
CHE	Council on Higher Education
CPUT	Cape Peninsula University of Technology
DA	Democratic Alliance
DASO	Democratic Alliance Student Organisation
DHET	Department of Higher Education and Training
DUT	Durban University of Technology
EFF	Economic Freedom Fighters
FMF	#FeesMustFall
IFP	Inkatha Freedom Party
LGBT	lesbian, gay, bisexual, and transgender
LGBTQI	lesbian, gay, bisexual, transgender, queer or questioning, and intersex
NDP	National Development Plan
NEHAWU	National Education, Health and Allied Workers' Union
NGO	non-governmental organisation
NMMU	Nelson Mandela Metropolitan University
NSC	National Senior Certificate
NSFAS	National Student Financial Aid Scheme
NUSAS	National Union of South African Students
NWU	North-West University
PAC	Pan Africanist Congress
PASMA	Pan Africanist Student Movement of Azania
RMF	#RhodesMustFall
SACP	South African Communist Party
SADC	Southern African Development Community
SADESMO	South African Democratic Students Movement
SALDRU	Southern Africa Labour and Development Research Unit
SASCO	South African Students Congress
SASO	South African Students Organisation
SRC	Student Representative Council

SU	Stellenbosch University
TRC	Truth and Reconciliation Commission
TUT	Tshwane University of Technology
TVET	Technical and Vocational Education and Training
UCT	University of Cape Town
UFS	University of the Free State
UJ	University of Johannesburg
UKZN	University of KwaZulu-Natal
UNISA	University of South Africa
UP	University of Pretoria
USAf	Universities South Africa
UWC	University of the Western Cape
WITS	University of the Witwatersrand
WSU	Walter Sisulu University

Introduction

The Perfect Storm

*All waves, no matter how huge, start as rough spots –
cats' paws – on the surface of the water.*
– Sebastian Junger, The Perfect Storm, *1997*

The student protests of 2015–2016 caught South Africans by surprise. In a relatively short period of time, the defilement of a campus statue in Cape Town and a complaint about student fee increases in Johannesburg melded into a powerful protest movement that affected almost every one of the 26 public universities in the country. Even during the long, dark days of apartheid, no university had ever experienced this level of student protest in terms of scale, scope, intensity, and, in the course of time, violence.

The African National Congress (ANC), South Africa's ruling party, was caught off guard, resting in an unmerited assurance that it enjoyed political dominance on most campuses through its student affiliates. The government was surprised, given its expanding pro-poor investments in student welfare, particularly through the national bursary aid scheme. Much of the broader community was shocked, in light of the widely accepted understanding of education as the key to personal and social mobility. The universities themselves were caught napping, unprepared for the sudden backlash for which they had neither the resources to meet student demands, the skill to negotiate the new politics, nor the security to protect campus lives and property.

One group was not surprised: the university leaders, variously called rectors (at the Afrikaans-origin universities) or principals (at the English-origin universities) but commonly designated vice-chancellors of their institutions. Over the course of the protests, one after another university leader would say something like, 'We tried to warn the government for more than a decade that a perfect storm was brewing.' The 'perfect storm' metaphor would be heard again and again above the din of the protests to refer to the twin dangers of the decline in government subsidies and the steady increase in student fees. At some point these two planes would cross each other in foul weather with costly and potentially catastrophic consequences. And they did so with a vengeance in March 2015 and especially in October 2016. Yet even these vice-chancellors could not predict the intensity of the student revolt on their campuses and around the country. A seasoned veteran of campus politics as a student activist, one vice-chancellor would say repeatedly: 'I was profoundly shocked by what was happening.' What in the world was going on?

This book attempts to answer three difficult questions about the crisis in South Africa universities in 2015–2016:

- *What in fact happened?* Neither claims of some incipient political revolution nor an easy dismissal of protests as social pathology answers this question. What at first seems to be the obvious answer – angry students were upset with universities and reacted through peaceful and sometimes violent protests – clearly does not capture the many different faces of the revolt expressed in different ways on diverse campuses with varied consequences. Conclusions made at first glance are often too simple and cannot be read off the headlines in a newspaper or in an instant missive by a 750-word-limit columnist. This unprecedented disruption of public universities needs a clearer and deeper narration organised around an informed understanding of exactly what was taking place.

- *Why did it happen?* As the protests broke out in earnest, there were thoughtful people who immediately opined that the desecration of the monument honouring Cecil John Rhodes at the University of Cape Town (UCT), and its eventual removal from a prominent position on Upper Campus, were not about the statue. Then what was it about? Here was a liberal university that had long ago opened its doors to black students under constant threat from the apartheid government. It had a proud tradition of anti-apartheid protest, freedom lectures, and critical centres for intellectual thought, as well as two black vice-chancellors in recent history. More than one scholar warned that the protests were not about student fee increases per se; rather, they expressed a much larger grievance against a grossly unequal society. Still, why would the liberal universities – including Nelson Mandela's alma mater, the University of the Witwatersrand (Wits) – become the special targets of such fervent and sustained protest? Or were the protests about these very universities in the first place?

- *What does the protest crisis mean for the future of South African universities?* The duration and intensity of the protests invariably raised questions about the long-term effects of the crisis on universities. In particular, the recognition of the unmanageability of the crisis in both financial and political terms cast doubt on the sustainability of public institutions. Protests on university campuses are certainly not unusual, but this streak did not seem to end. Countless attempts inside and outside higher education to resolve the impasse ended without success. Hours, days, and even weeks of negotiations would come to an abrupt end when protestors shifted the goalpost at the eleventh hour and disruptions continued, including heavy damage to university property and buildings. No interdict could stem the tide of protests, and no amount of private security or riot police could contain the assault on buildings and the disruption of classes. Eventually students and academics with options began signalling their plans to depart to private universities or institutions overseas. At this juncture we must ask: Under what conditions does the downward slide of public universities become irrevocable? What can we learn from post-independence universities in other African countries? And, most critically, can South African universities survive the present calamity?

An insider view of the crisis

The more reports and opinion pieces on the student protests that I read, the more I realised that what was missing in these many accounts from researchers, journalists, students, and general commentators was an insider's view of the crisis from the perspective of those charged with leading public universities.[1] These university leaders were women and men who had to balance budgets to sustain universities and engage students to ascertain budgetary priorities. Whether they liked it or not, they stood between the government, which required accountability, and the students, who demanded accessibility. These leaders had to ensure living-wage increases for their academics and workers but at the same time engage with students' demand to insource contract workers, which threatened to collapse personnel budgets. As vice-chancellors, they had to reassure their senates that the academic project would not be compromised even while making adjustments to the academic calendar and examination timetable forced on them by relentless protest actions. They had to convey confidence and assure parents and alumni that their children were safe, and yet bring in added security that made some students feel unsafe. The vice-chancellors were easy targets for those needing a punching bag to alleviate their frustrations with the constant protest actions, campus instability, and the unpredictable teaching and examination schedules that resulted from the chronic disruption. As leaders, vice-chancellors had to reassure their own families about their safety even as the social media raged with abuse and sometimes even death threats against them and their loved ones.

As an insider myself, a fellow vice-chancellor, I wanted to know from my colleagues what they saw and heard, what they felt and feared, in their efforts to manage the crisis. And so I sent each of them an email invitation to a one-on-one dialogue, a relatively unstructured interview session in which I would probe their understandings of and emotions around the three broad questions that this book tries to answer. The interviews were conducted in their offices, at hotels, in restaurants, or in my own campus office, in the period between June and August 2016. Eleven vice-chancellors of the most troubled universities agreed to meet with me, and in fact were exceptionally generous with their time.

These university leaders were so clear and articulate in responding to the three framing questions of the study that I decided to let their words speak for themselves rather than edit, paraphrase, or interpret what they had to say. Hence this book includes extended passages from the interview transcripts, which have been only lightly edited for clarity and readability. What you will read are the perspectives and emotions of university principals inside the turbulence of an unprecedented crisis that most of them worked eighteen hours a day and over weekends to resolve.

I began the interviews by asking a single broad question and then allowed the vice-chancellor to take the response in any direction he or she wished to go. This explains the unevenness of responses to different trigger questions since respondents chose to spend varying amounts of time on particular aspects of the crisis. Each vice-chancellor was asked to respond from the vantage point of his or her own institution. Under the ambit of the three broad research questions, additional interview probes included the following:

- Why did the crisis happen in the first place?
- What explains the shift from a broad-based and generally peaceful movement in early 2015 to a black-based and increasingly destructive movement from October 2015 onwards?
- What do the protestors really want?
- What are the kinds of student political formations involved and how do their interests shape the protest movement on each campus?
- What has been the role of the Student Representative Council (SRC) in the student movement, and how did its standing change, if at all, over the course of the protests?
- Was the 2016 protest moment different, as some claim, from the 2015 moment?
- Did the vice-chancellor's relationship with student leaders change or stay the same over time?
- How did this national movement express itself within the political ecology of the campus or campuses (for multi-campus institutions)?

What leaders actually do

There is a long-standing debate in the literature about the real influences of leaders in complex organisations such as universities.[2] Are universities in effect 'leaderless organizations' in which 'the [university] presidency is an illusion ... [and] the president's role more commonly sporadic and symbolic than significant'?[3] Or are university leaders in fact 'strong and effective', with the power to make important symbolic, political, intellectual, and administrative decisions?[4]

Neither of these views completely captures the leadership influence of South African vice-chancellors in the twenty-first century. These are indeed influential figures in different ways. Some are charismatic leaders whose persuasive powers and political instincts carry considerable authority within their institutions; others are hamstrung by interfering councils and dominating senates that may steer the university in a direction that goes against the desires of their vice-chancellor.

Institutional conditions matter in enabling or limiting the authority of a university leader at different times. And yet all of the vice-chancellors are senior managers, directors of the institutional budget, and leaders of the academic estate. On a day-to-day basis they can and do make critical decisions that affect the direction of their universities. But they are not all-powerful, and something as simple as the appointment of a female or black colleague that also advances transformation can easily be undermined in one of a multitude of academic departments that no vice-chancellor, however powerful, can influence or direct 24 hours a day.

It is precisely this circumscribed authority of the vice-chancellor that drew me to these leaders. How do they actually negotiate their authority in a crisis? What is the leadership practice – what leaders actually do and what they cannot do – in severe and sustained institutional crises such as in the 2015–2016 period? When the general public rages against the local university vice-chancellor, they do so with little knowledge of the intricacies of power and powerlessness that inform a leader's decision making in a time of crisis. Through the direct approach of the one-on-one interviews, this book attempts to shed light on leadership practice from the perspective of sitting vice-chancellors in South African universities.

Since this is an account given in the words and from the vantage point of university leaders, it obviously cannot be the only view of the crisis. A student, a worker, a protestor, a non-protestor, a parent of a first-year student, or an alumnus would each see the university crisis from his or her own vantage point. Yet the perspective of university leaders is undoubtedly unique and valuable. My main objective has been to weave together the vice-chancellors' stories in the hope of conveying a fuller account of what happened (narration), why (explanation), and with what possible effects (prediction).

Overview of *As by Fire*

As my fellow vice-chancellors and I pursued the main questions guiding this study, other issues were addressed along the way, and the ten chapters in this book capture those themes and concerns.

Chapter 1 deals with the problem of *university leadership in crisis situations*. It briefly surveys what we know about leaders, and university leaders in particular, when they are called on to lead when a crisis breaks. The focus in this chapter is less on what textbooks say university leaders are *supposed* to do than on what they actually do when major crises envelop campuses. While each of the stakeholders, such as alumni or students or workers, makes particular demands on the vice-chancellor, this chapter draws attention to the delicate balancing act that the university leader must perform to steady and steer a large and often unwieldy institution in difficult times. The chapter concludes with a discussion of the global context of student protests, in which the crisis of South African universities is certainly not exceptional.

The next two chapters should be read in tandem since they present the foundations on which the 2015–2016 protest movement was launched – the one financial and the other cultural.

Chapter 2 traces the *financial origins* of the 2015–2016 protests. It explains how the decline in government subsidies and the increase in student fees brought on the October 2015 protests, and describes the nation-wide consequences of what followed. The impact of the financial impasse is illustrated through stories of the lives of poor and desperate students under funding constraints. The logic of the crisis is explained from a financial point of view by the eleven vice-chancellors, whose voices are heard throughout the chapter. These leaders must manage budgets constrained from the outside and manage discontent inflamed from the inside of the university campus. Although their views are expressed in individual one-on-one interviews, the striking resonance of diverse leader voices on the subject of the financial crisis is telling.

Chapter 3 recounts the *cultural origins* of the crisis. It delves into the social, cultural, and intellectual alienation that black students claim to experience on former white liberal campuses in South Africa, the most prominent institutional case for this exploration being UCT. Why would black middle-class students, who had experienced racial integration in top public and private schools, react so vehemently against 'white symbols' at UCT and similar English-origin campuses such as Rhodes and Wits? Much time is given in this chapter to the voice of Max Price, the vice-chancellor of UCT, where the first of the two revolts happened, and where the statue of the imperialist Cecil John Rhodes became the focus of a broader grievance against white dominance in the curriculum, campus artworks and symbolism, and the professoriate itself.

Chapter 4 locates the crisis inside universities in the broader context of the *failure of democratic consolidation*, both political and economic, following the end of apartheid. The promise of 1994 and the high hopes for democracy were unrealised for the poor. After more than two decades, students came to understand that poverty was still a lived reality for their parents and communities, and that inequality had in fact worsened. The unexpected anger on the streets and on the campuses against 'the deals Mandela made' was now being expressed openly among a new generation of youth who rejected with contempt their designation as 'born frees'.[5] They did not feel free, and the vice-chancellor voices explain how that sense of betrayal shows up on campuses even though the broader origins of the crisis lie within the state.

Chapter 5 describes the *leaderless revolution*, unravelling the mystery of who 'the students' or 'the protestors' are. The protestors have been depicted in the media as a large, homogeneous, like-minded group of activists fitting comfortably under the conceptual umbrella of 'the Fallists'. Who do vice-chancellors actually see around them as they negotiate for hours with one group of students, only for that group to be sidelined and replaced by another group, even on the same day of a meeting with management? This chapter explains how small and disparate groups of protestors form, split apart, and re-form in another image, disappearing and reappearing in what has become known as a leaderless movement.

Yet each campus is different, and the combination of student organisations in and out of power would differ from one university to the next, making management of the crisis nearly impossible. This explains why the body selected by students, the SRC, would lose its standing and authority on most campuses as new organisations and new student leaders jostled for position. It would become the most tiring task of the vice-chancellors: negotiating an end to the crisis with small and changing groups of students who had no intention of ending what they had started.

Chapter 6, dealing with the *personal costs of crisis leadership*, is perhaps the saddest in the book. Here the eleven vice-chancellors open up about the personal stress, fear, disappointment, and anger generated by the crisis. It reveals the human face of leaders and the real distress that they as individuals had to work through every day. It was not only the protesting students that brought grief upon vice-chancellors in these difficult times; it was also some of their staff. And it was not only their personal safety that weighed on the vice-chancellors' minds, but also that of their families. Behind the required projection of confidence and direction-giving stances in public, the private lives and thoughts of university leaders during periods of crisis are expressed in deeply moving ways. I found these moments very disturbing, for I knew from personal experience how incredibly lonely one could feel in those times of fear and anxiety, even in the presence of supportive staff and loving family members. These personal feelings and anxieties are not known to the general public, nor to those dishing out a relentless battering of the individual vice-chancellors in the media.

Chapter 7 deals with the vexed demand for *decolonisation*. What does it mean and for whom, and what are its consequences for the academic project of universities? This chapter draws on the anti-colonial literature produced by the heroes of South Africa's contemporary student protestors, such as Frantz Fanon, Albert Memmi, and Aimé Césaire, but also postcolonial authors such as Ngũgĩ wa Thiong'o who gave meaning to the concept of decolonising the curriculum of African universities. The chapter describes the ways in which protestors and scholars alike speak of the 'decolonisation of curriculum', drawing on research about subjugated minorities such as the indigenous communities of North America. The chapter wrestles also with the racial essentialism associated with the decolonisation demanded by black protestors, and the anachronism of old, lived-out binaries such as 'black–white' in a globalised, integrated, multimedia world where knowledge no longer 'belongs' to race or ethnicity or nation. This is the only chapter with a minimal input of vice-chancellors' voices, since it is a later addition to the book inspired by persistent queries about the meaning of decolonisation in South Africa's constitutional democracy.

Chapter 8 takes on the sensitive subject of the *welfarisation of South Africa's universities*. As the number of poor students enrolled at universities trebled over a decade, the institutions were starting to sink under the weight of social demands from the new entrants to higher education. Government-funded bursaries were no longer sufficient to finance students' expenses, and many of the recent new students are among the first to have been raised in welfare-supported families primarily through the government's child support grant. On entering university, many poor students from communities on welfare brought with them the expectation that they would be cared for beyond tuition fees. They also held the understanding that if the university – in their minds an extension of government services – did not deliver on their needs, then protests, even violent ones, were a perfectly rational strategy for extracting those demands from 'management', even when management said they lacked the resources called for.

Chapter 9 examines how *social media* allowed protests that started at UCT and Wits to accelerate like flames following a petrol trail across the country's campuses. The new social media communicated in real time a grievance expressed here or an incipient protest under way there. This phenomenon posed a special challenge to university leaders – how to stay ahead of the protest narrative in a context where virtually every student has a mobile phone. Yet it was not only the new social media that sent the university communications offices into scramble mode; it was also the traditional media, which, with few exceptions, took the side of the student protestors even as buildings went up in flames. And in some cases, the local newspaper would make the vice-chancellor the target of sustained personal attacks even as it offered legal and other material support to student leaders.

Chapter 10 asks what the unending campus disruption and instability mean for *the future of South African universities*. The three forces acting together – underfunding, interference and instability – spell doom for top-quality research institutions. The fragility of the universities, and of the liberal institutions in particular, makes them vulnerable to ongoing violence in the face of a built-in ambivalence towards any form of state or private security on campuses. But there is one last chance of recovery, and the book ends with a few words of hope.

Chapter 1

The Leader and the Crisis

---

*When you're up to your ass in alligators, it's easy to forget
that the initial objective was to drain the swamp.
– Popular saying among consultants and crisis managers*

It was about 2:30 am, on 23 February 2016, when the buzzer on my WhatsApp signalled that a group message had been received. I woke up with a start, and anxiously reached for my cellphone on the bedside cabinet. This must be serious. The seven members of my senior leadership team, as well as the head of campus security, the director of communications, and the dean of students, would instantly and simultaneously receive notice of a crisis via the WhatsApp texting service. The emergency could be anything – a residence roof collapsing, a student suicide, a foiled kidnapping attempt, or a spontaneous protest action under way. We all had our assigned roles: information gathering (as in 'establish the facts as soon as possible'), personal counselling, monitoring, facilities protection, external and internal communication, hospital transfers, police notification, and media management. When any one of us notified the group of an emergency situation, the management machinery kicked into action as regular updates filtered through this handy messaging system. But this was half past two in the morning, which could mean only one thing. Something extremely serious had just happened.

We were in the middle of a horrible week at the University of the Free State (UFS). Without warning, a small group of students and outsourced workers had disrupted a rugby game in progress. After some of the spectators pleaded with them to leave the field so that the game could continue, a larger group of those in the stands ran onto the rugby field and attacked the protestors. The confrontation spread across the campus as right-wing whites from outside the university joined the fray, while black protestors, some of them non-students, attacked university property and threatened white and non-protesting students and staff. None of us on the university management team slept much that week as we tried to contain the retaliatory violence. Nerves were constantly on edge, and at that time we simply did not have the security resources in place to deal with this paroxysm of violence. In this context, a WhatsApp message in the dead of the night was not a good sign at all.

I seldom panic, and staff or students throwing tantrums in my office are asked to leave and come back when they're ready to talk. Staying calm is something I learnt from my father; in the worst of situations, even at the death of his youngest child, he would enter a zone of placidity and call the family to prayer. That humble man – the one-time laundry driver, fruit-and-veg hawker, messenger, and missionary – taught me how to remain calm in a crisis. But for the first time in years, I panicked as I reached for my cellphone. The first question that ran through my mind was, 'Are the children safe?' By 'children', I mean the more than 30 000 students on our three campuses, for whose safety and security I found myself taking personal responsibility. There was no difference in the level of concern I had for my own daughter, who studies on the main campus, from that for the sons and daughters of any other parent – and for good reason.

When a parent brings a child to the university's Open Day (recruitment) and eventually to Welcoming Day (registration), I would often be confronted by a mother and father with their first-year student in tow. In the Afrikaans-speaking community in particular, there would be an unspoken 'handing over' of the new undergraduate fresh from high school. The parents' feelings are reminiscent of the sentiment expressed in *'Juffrou, ek bring jou my kind'* (Teacher, I bring you my child), a warm and charming recollection of many teachers and principals on receiving a new learner in traditional public schools.

I would come to understand that the principle of *in loco parentis* still applied for many parents even when they bring their children, now budding adults, to a university campus. The words on their minds might very well be, 'I am bringing you my child and you are responsible for him or her as if you were the parent.' Of course, there is ample room here for debate on the social meanings and cultural appropriateness of such understandings of a young adult entering higher education, but nonetheless I assumed that caretaker responsibility for all students regardless of any personal misgivings about being a parent of sorts to other people's children.

The message was from the head of security. A small group of protestors, possibly including a few non-students, was on the move around the campus trying to outwit campus security. A package looking like a petrol bomb was found at the door of one of the lecture halls; a small fire had started but was quickly extinguished. Everything was under control, said the security chief, and they were 'keeping a close eye' on the mobile group. More updates would follow if necessary, and there would be a full debriefing with management in the morning.

By now I was sweating, and that 2:30 am electronic message had just confirmed a decision I had made earlier. It was time for me to leave the university.

With this 2016 academic year I was approaching the end of seven wonderful years of an effective ten-year contract as UFS vice-chancellor and rector, but I had told my senior colleagues and the chairman of the council that I had no intention of staying for the two full terms. It is my long-held belief that in a high-intensity leadership assignment such as a university principal on divided campuses in an angry country, you work flat out to transform the organisation and then you leave so that others can continue the work. Seven years of working eighteen hours a day, weekends included, was enough. I had even placed a tweet to that effect in my 2012 book *Letters to My Children*: 'If you stay in the same job for longer than seven years, you lack imagination.'[1] Now it was crystal clear that the time had come for me to move on.

As I put the phone back on the table, I looked towards the other side of the bed. There was a good chance my wife was awake, but she would not show it. Grace and my children carried the brunt of the stress and tension I brought home, even though I hardly spoke about campus crises so as not to alarm them. But they would hear about it elsewhere – at the hairdresser's, or in the shopping mall, or from the lamppost where newspapers jockeyed for headline space – and what they heard was always half the truth and sensationalised with suggestions of impending doom.

That was another reason why the decision to leave was confirmed at that early hour. Yes, it was a time of crisis as increasingly intense and then violent protests spread across the campuses of South Africa's 26 public universities, including UFS. But this was not going to stop anytime soon, and so whether I left in 2016 or in 2019, there would still be crises to manage. For every analyst of higher education knew that what had started in 2015 as a national uprising of students had also launched a new normal – chronic and system-wide instability and disruption in South Africa's higher education system.

I recall now that as I left my farewell dinner at UFS, a colleague stepped from the shadows, grabbed my arm, and said this: 'Boss, thank you for leaving in the upright position.' I gave him a knowing hug. He was the brother-in-law of Russel Botman, the beleaguered principal of the University of Stellenbosch who faced criticism and controversy in his efforts to transform the institution, and who said farewell to the university in a funeral casket.[2]

A wide-angled view of the crisis

What does a campus crisis look like from the office of the university principal? When students take the leader of the university hostage, or occupy a major administration building for days on end, or burst into a council meeting and prevent the governors of the university from leaving, or set fire to university property, what does the head of the university experience? What is it like for university leaders when crises such as these become endemic, paralysing institutional functions and setting off alarm bells among parents, donors, alumni, faculty, the general student body, prospective students, and the public even as the media demand official responses against tight publishing deadlines?

Much of what has been written and debated in the media tells the story of the campus protests from the perspective of students agitated about fees, or through the voices of workers concerned about outsourcing, or the lament of staff decrying low salaries and unacceptable working conditions. When yet another protest rocks a university campus, the media rush dutifully to the scene, often on an invitation sent prior to a routine march or a spectacular event, to record the complaints, condemnation, and concerns of students in particular. Aided and abetted by new communication technologies, the media often prod spectators from a distance for assistance on the scene of a protest or a burning building: 'Were you there? Please send us your stories and photos.'

The public has rightly heard student voices, which were often very compelling, distressed, and anger-filled, but the reporting has been partial, one-sided, and sometimes dangerously misleading. The news also carried heart-rending stories of outsourced workers demanding an end to their exclusion from the benefits of tenure, pension, and other rights that accrue to those directly employed by the university. And there have been regular features in the media on academic and administrative staff who, in the considerations of annual salary increases, would complain bitterly about below-inflation increases in their compensation. These voices of students, workers, and academics remain critical in the democratic space. But what about those who stand between declining revenues from the state and incessant demands for 'more' from students, staff, and workers?

In other words, what would a fuller account of the 2015–2016 crisis look like if it included the voices of senior university leaders? What do these university principals witness from their offices in the main administration building? Are they, as activist student leaders often portray, self-serving bureaucrats operating as mere state functionaries, extensions of an oppressive 'system' who themselves need to fall? Is it the case that they do not 'listen' to students and workers, thereby sparking disruption and destruction as a last resort of frustrated protestors? Are they effective in their leadership or 'utterly powerless ... subject only to the gravitational pull of history'?[3] And how do the leaders themselves view the causes of the crisis and the future of the South African university?

My sample of university principals includes men and women, white and black, single and married, new and experienced, scientists and humanities scholars, rural and urban university leaders, executives in charge of relatively well-resourced universities as well as those running institutions which for many years have merely survived from one salary payout to the next, and not a few activists from the anti-apartheid days. This diversity is limited, of course. Most principals are men. Several universities, the poorer ones, have been in crises of instability long before the period under consideration (2015–2016). And while all universities in South Africa struggle with budgetary pressures, their capacities for managing crises, in financial terms, vary between the better-endowed former white universities and the historically disadvantaged institutions. Who these vice-chancellors are matters in leadership, especially in times of crisis.

Leadership in times of crisis

Research indicates that a number of factors contribute to a leader's effectiveness in crisis management. First, a leader's personality matters.[4] In this study, the personalities of the interviewees cover the range, from outspoken media personalities who often appear as talking heads on radio, television, and in print, to quiet, soft-spoken leaders who consciously stay out of the media limelight. Some speak too much, say some of their critics;[5] others are not present, and are therefore saying more, claim their opponents. Some are thoughtful and laid-back, even conceding in interviews that 'I simply do not know'. Others readily offered 'two or three things' to virtually any question. Yet across these very different personality types there was, as we will see, a common thread of understanding, of concern, and of genuine fear for the future of universities in South Africa's fragile democracy.

Experience, of course, also matters in leadership,[6] and this is reflected in the interviews with the vice-chancellors. Those with years of experience managing universities either as the principal or in a less senior capacity have encountered student protests and demonstrations before; they are familiar with the repertoires of protest management, from anticipation of the crisis to its immediate containment and the aftermath of the unrest. Newer principals found the crisis situations particularly stressful; while they might have served as senior executives elsewhere, managing unruly protestors was a new challenge that took its toll on them. Experience as a scholar mattered little in a turbulent political environment where reason and logic were not going to win an argument as easily as in the seminar room. And yet none of the principals had ever experienced the intensity and longevity of the 2015–2016 crisis, and it was beginning to wear them all down.

Institutional readiness matters in crisis management.[7] Yet none of the university leaders had ever felt it necessary to equip their campuses with the levels of surveillance, equipment, and personnel that the new crisis demanded. Situations had become life-threatening, and the only surprise was that between March 2015 and August 2016 no one had been killed, even as buildings were torched and a petrol bomb was lobbed through one vice-chancellor's office window.

In September 2016, however, a worker at Wits University was hospitalised and died, apparently after inhaling smoke from a campus fire-extinguisher set off by protestors. The normal security plans, sufficient before 2015, were clearly no longer adequate and, as we shall see, the gap between the pre-crisis state of security and the in-crisis security needs was exploited by the more violent of the student protestors. For the crisis now gripping universities was something very deep, 'a disruption that physically affects a system as a whole and threatens its basic assumptions, its subjective sense of self, and its existential core'.[8]

Organisational ideology also matters in crisis management.[9] What and how much a leader can do depends on what environmental conditions allow. UCT, for example, is a liberal university that strongly upholds the right to protest inside an 'open university' campus where scholars baulk at the notion of an on-site police presence. The University of Pretoria (UP), by contrast, emerges from a very conservative historical tradition in which certainty and control are primary commitments, and for which security and police are readily summoned onto campus. The older universities are unlike the newer ones, for 'institutions shaped by history channel and constrain leaders'[10] in very different ways.

In the older, former white universities, the polemic of race invariably surfaces in any conflict or protest. By contrast, on the historically black campuses race and ethnicity never feature because it is primary needs that fuel revolt, such as accommodation, transport, and food quality. On some campuses, aggressive student protests are routine and campuses are often closed. In others, the intensity of recent protests is new. And in some universities, the ANC as the ruling party has a firm grip on campus politics and enjoys support all the way up to the governing body; in the former white universities, independence and autonomy from external politics are fundamental commitments. How leaders navigate their universities through these contexts depends very much on complex environmental conditions. Thus effective leadership requires a good dose of strategic knowledge about where the political minefields lie.

Moreover, a university leader's academic specialty also affects the way he or she leads.[11] One vice-chancellor, a medical scientist, described his university at the outset of his tenure as 'a patient in good health'. Another vice-chancellor, a natural scientist, is bewildered by the lack of order, control, and predictability on his campus. Still another vice-chancellor, a curriculum specialist, sees a knowledge problem: the lack of a deeper, critical education to arm the protestors for thoughtful engagement on the crisis. And yet another vice-chancellor, this one a political scientist, sees the crisis through the competing interests of rival groups, and links what happens on campus to what happens in cabinet, student politics, and party politics. Yet no one disciplinary perspective can fully come to grips with the depth, intensity, and uncertainty of this crisis, as the interviews will reveal.

Beyond these things that matter (personality, experience, prepared-ness, environment, and academic discipline), all leaders carry similar identities and position themselves in particular ways. How, then, should these leaders be framed? In the business world they would be called CEOs, a tag most vice-chancellors instinctively resist because of their unease with and even criticism of reducing universities to business enti-ties in an age of neoliberalism. If you want to sting a scholarly minded vice-chancellor, tell him or her that a university is nothing more than a corporate organisation in which students are merely clients, where research amounts to maximising subsidy-generating outputs, and in which teaching is nothing more than preparing young people to meet the demands of a market economy. It is for this reason that some univer-sities deliberately frame the principal as 'the academic leader of the university', while others, leaning towards the language of the state bureaucracy, are content with 'the administrative head of the university'. It will become clear from this book that what university leaders actually do is often far removed from the formal duties and responsibilities out-lined in the institutional statute required of each higher education institution.

The position and authority of vice-chancellors

But why the focus on the singular leader, the university principal? Surely research and experience show that leadership *collectives* steer organisations, from schools to companies to government departments. In fact, some of the most exciting advances in leadership studies point to 'stretched-over leadership' and 'distributive leadership' to make a point that is both empirical (research informed) and normative (desirable).[12] No university principal, no matter how confident his or her personality, runs a complex institution alone; that is simply impossible. And yet the focus and target of much of the student protests was against one person, the man or woman in the principal's office. That is no accident, as I will show later, but a determined strategy to run down the head of the university. It makes sense, therefore, to understand the heart and mind of the chief executive, so to speak, as well as the role of the vice-chancellor in the university as an organisation.

Every vice-chancellor is appointed by and responsible to the council, the highest decision-making body of a South African university. While council is responsible for the governance of the university – such as setting broad policies for the institution – the vice-chancellor is charged with implementing those policies. Perhaps the most important function of a council is the oversight of the finances of the university for which the vice-chancellor is held strictly accountable. For example, council approves the annual budget of a university, and the vice-chancellor and his or her executive team are responsible for the management of that budget within the available resources and constraints of the institution.

The vice-chancellor is also the chairperson of the university senate, which has responsibility for the academic mandate of the institution – such as teaching, research, and curriculum. The chancellor of a university holds a largely ceremonial position and officiates at important functions such as the annual graduation ceremonies.

It is, however, the vice-chancellor alone who carries responsibility for the management of the institution on a day-to-day basis. In the mantra of a healthy university, council governs and management manages the institution. When either of those two functions interferes with the mandate of the other, there is always trouble. What this means is that in the course of a major crisis, a vice-chancellor would inform the council through its chairperson, and even consult when necessary, but is expected to make the critical management decisions as head of the university. On the other hand, if the financial demands of student protestors means going outside the budget parameters set by council, a vice-chancellor can only proceed with the approval of the governing body.

Thus, the running of a university is left to the vice-chancellor and the executive team. In American-speak, the buck stops with the university principal. And as I know from hard experience, when everyone else has left, you are alone, in your office or your home, contemplating the meaning of a difficult day or week of crisis, and planning how to respond to the multiple stakeholders who call the university head to find out what exactly is going on, and going wrong. There is merit, therefore, in a closer, detailed examination of what exactly happens in the lives of university leaders who, in critical moments, are solitary figures alone with their ambitions and emotions inside the turbulence of a never-ending crisis.

Yet what exactly is the positional advantage of the university leader in relation to student protests? In the words of one of the principals interviewed, student leaders speak for students, unions for workers, academic staff associations for lecturers, but who speaks for the university? This is a crucial point. The university leader in a crisis has that job of defending the university – to his bosses, the council, about accountability for operations; to alumni fretting about what is happening to their cherished institution; to major and minor donors concerned about their investments; to government worried about the effective management of the university; to parents concerned about the safety of their children and the costly disruption of their education; to the senate for the integrity of the disrupted academic programme; and to employers of degreed students who constantly complain about the lack of 'oven-ready' graduates coming out of universities.

This is complex terrain. For example, not all alumni are the same, and this is more markedly so in the former white universities. There are those more conservative alumni who remember a pristine, white, settled (*sic*) institution which carried their values, and demand that it stays that way even if some black students are accommodated. But there are others who support the protests and demand a deeper 'transformation' that they were denied as students. Then there are the politicians, constantly seeking advantage from a crisis. When a crisis hits, they descend like vultures on the principal's office. The more radical parties align with the students and put pressure on the university leader. The more liberal parties seek to counter the dominant or more radical parties, and will attack or defend the principal depending on the position taken relative to the ruling party. The more conservative politicians want immediate action taken against revolting staff or students and a restoration of 'law and order' at any costs.

In the midst of this noise, the university principal has to remain composed and reasonable, adjusting the main message for varying emphasis from one constituency to the next. The leader should, above all else, be visible.[13] His or her face should convey calm and restraint, and yet also empathy and resolve, for 'in a crisis, everybody watches what you do'.[14] This brings enormous pressure to bear on the leader and, whatever happens, he or she has to come across in the media as stable and informed. The leadership task is almost impossible – keeping all the constituencies more or less on board throughout the crisis, even as the media take a position for or against the leader depending on which media house is concerned with the crisis. In other words, the principal speaks for the university as a whole.

What makes the task of the university principal most unenviable is that he or she sits between the impending crisis of diminishing state funding and uncertain revenues from student income. Put bluntly, the government says it has no money and the students insist they will not pay any increases in tuition. Here's the problem: South Africa is not a well-endowed nation with large numbers of private funders, wealthy families, established trusts, and flourishing foundations which together can pour billions of dollars into higher education (as in the US, for example). If the money does not come from government, it has to come from either tuition or what the locals call third-stream (non-state and non-student sources) income.

Third-stream income is extremely limited in South Africa, except in the case of those few universities that can leverage professional schools such as engineering or nursing to deliver short courses or consultancies to bring in millions of rands in additional income. But even those sources of funding are dependent on the state of the economy, fluctuate wildly from one financial cycle to the next, and hardly provide for the historically black universities at all. The only other viable source is tuition fees, which, for most universities, come not directly from students but through loans and grants made by the government's massively funded if poorly administered National Student Financial Aid Scheme (NSFAS). So if the tap of tuition fees is shut off, that crisis lands on the vice-chancellor's desk, with very damaging consequences.

What, then, does the university principal do? His responsibility, in cold terms, is to keep the lights on. To maintain ageing buildings and facilities, knowing that the failure to do so on schedule will multiply the costs, and risk, in future years. To upgrade and secure computers and software in all the student laboratories. To increase staff remuneration every year or lose talented academics. To pay rates and taxes to the same government that reports, regularly, that there is no money. To fund, out of institutional budgets, the additional costs of more and more students who need funding but cannot find those resources within NSFAS because of the problem of adequacy. That is, while NSFAS funding has increased dramatically, it is still not enough for the growing numbers of students in general, and especially for students without any resources to access and succeed within higher education.

And the responsibilities of the vice-chancellor continue. To fund crises such as when the municipal water taps run dry, as in the small, dilapidated city of Grahamstown, which houses one of the nation's prestige institutions, Rhodes University. To finance new student demands, such as the additional accommodation, after-hours transport, study locks on campus, extended library hours, and many others. To fund development programmes that increase student graduation rates and staff research performance, since these two sources of revenue, from the subsidy, can make or break an already fragile budget. To keep some funds in reserve to be able to prevent poaching of top scholars, especially black and women academics, by other universities, and to attract new talent into the academy. To create opportunities for international partnerships and exchange for staff and students. To secure the holdings of the library, and update journals and books purchased mainly from overseas and against a declining currency. To improve the security of the campuses and residences against the infiltration of crime and criminal networks onto the *relatively* resource-rich and self-contained environment called the university.

Every year the seasoned university principal sees the money declining and the demands accumulating and getting more serious, even violent – and the campus crisis is compounded. One year of no fee increases, according to the misinformed decree from the president in 2015, placed almost every university on the edge of collapse. And still the demands increase. The students do not want to pay a fee increase; in fact, they want no fees at all. Outsourced workers want to be made part of the staff establishment immediately – an arrangement that will sink any university if done recklessly. And in the meantime, the cost of everything escalates, from library books to computer software to electricity accounts. Something has to give. As usual in such a stalemate, retrenchments might be the only option. Yet, when institutions resort to offering early retirement to academics, the best ones leave, secure in the knowledge that they can be hired elsewhere. At this point, the university principal starts to panic as the *academic* future and financial sustainability of the institution begin to look very, very bleak.

The problem is, nobody wants to listen to the university principal. He or she is at once the recalcitrant bureaucrat that stands in the way of the revolution, according to the protesting students, and the only remaining bulwark against institutional collapse, according to those who know from close quarters what is at risk. The pressure is unrelenting and begins to take a toll on the university leader. A populist would succumb to every demand, with the result that the university has to apply to the government for overdraft facilities from the banks or, in utter desperation, pay salaries out of NSFAS funding intended for student fees. Most university principals are not populists, as this book will show, and they understand all too well the fate of post-independence African universities elsewhere under these conditions of incessant demands and declining revenue streams.

Is it even reasonable to expect any university leader to manage such complex and compounded crises? South Africa's vice-chancellors are natural scientists, sociologists, physicians, medical scientists, psychologists, curriculum theorists, physicists, biochemists, political scientists, and engineers. In most cases, they were chosen as leaders because of their academic prestige and their basic leadership competences. None of them received training in crisis management, crowd control, or political strategy. Some had experience of protests from their days as student activists, but many were not schooled in the rough-and-tumble of anti-apartheid political strategy. Even if they were, they now face a different kind of confrontation demanding a new skill set for which none of these leaders was prepared.

The South African university crisis in a global context

The South African student uprising of 2015–2016 did not occur in a vacuum. To begin with, the movement is part of a long and unbroken line of university student protests around the world over more than a century, as described in Mark Boren's historical account of 'the unruly subject' since the origins of the university.[15] But in recent years there has been a striking resemblance between student protests in the US and in South Africa, suggesting copycat tactics in each locale.

In November 2015, students at Princeton University, New Jersey, occupied the university president's office for 32 hours, demanding that the name of former US president Woodrow Wilson be removed from university buildings since he was a known segregationist who supported the Ku Klux Klan. In September 2015 at the University of Missouri, a series of rolling protests began that included students building a tent city on the campus, while one protestor staged a hunger strike against a racially segregated and unwelcoming university environment (e.g. a swastika made with faeces appeared in a residence toilet). In the same year a group called Royall Must Fall protested the racist environment at Harvard University by calling for the removal of the law school seal, which included the family crest of Isaac Royall Jr, a violent slave-owner. Meanwhile, students from Brown University in Rhode Island protested against racial discrimination on campus and, with students from another college, stood in solidarity with their peers at the University of Missouri. Across the US, protests broke out in some 60 colleges and universities, often against acts of racism and alienating symbols, with students demanding a more welcoming environment for blacks and other minorities at institutions such as Yale University (Connecticut), Ithaca College

(New York), Claremont McKenna College (California), the University of Cincinnati (Ohio), and Amherst College (Massachusetts).[16]

Once again something had stirred in the student heart around the world, including South Africa. Issues were similar – Rhodes, Wilson and Royall were symbols of racial offence, social exclusion, and cultural alienation on the part of black and other minority students. Tactics and strategies diffused across campuses and countries. Some protest actions were reminiscent of the 'shantytown' protests through which US students demanded that their universities divest from companies doing business with apartheid South Africa.[17] Across time and space, students would express a deep discontent with their universities as a reflection of problems in the broader society.

There are, however, important differences between the student protests in the US and what is happening in South Africa. In the US the protests were seldom violent, even under police provocation. There protests were focused and brief, and ended when the university leadership officially responded to demands. If some demands were not met through the official response, students accepted the leadership dispensation on other demands and vowed to return to fight another day. In none of the US protests did the students disrupt university classes or events in the course of making their demands; they respected the rights of others. And in the US institutions mentioned, none of the protests was concerned with financial exclusion per se, even though affordability of university education was a major issue and the problem of student debt would feature in the 2016 presidential primaries, championed by the Democratic Party contender Bernie Sanders.

It will be the task of scholars of comparative history, politics, and sociology to explain more fully the differences between the US and South African student protests. But what we do know is that the South African protests have been violent and persistent, with student organisations often aligned to external political parties and making their demands on both local universities and the national government. In this sense, South African student protests are more similar to protests at other post-independence African universities, but they are still distinguished by their scope and by the intensity of violence on local soil. That must be explained, as is attempted in the final chapter of this book.

One more thing: in the US context, university presidents did, on occasion, resign under protest-related pressure (such as at the University of Missouri and Ithaca College). While this book on South Africa's university leaders was still in production, one vice-chancellor in the study was placed on special leave by the university council, two had left their jobs, and two others had announced plans to leave in the near future. The leadership costs of the crisis are mounting.

Chapter 2

The Roots of the Crisis I: Financial Exclusion

---

*Professor, as you can see, I have a beautiful face. I do not want
to use it. But I need food to eat. Money to study. A place to
live. I cannot go on like this. But if I must, what can I do?
I can make lots of money with this face.*
– Excerpt from a UFS student's email

Having spent most of my working life teaching and leading young
people, I know a blackmail note from a student when I see one. But this
particular email (see excerpt above) was not blackmail. Ntokoza (not
her real name), a young, soft-spoken woman from Umlazi township in
Durban, had travelled all the way to Bloemfontein on her own. She was
not one of the top students we had selected for full funding; her marks
were good, but not as competitive as those of other students who qualified for the limited pool of full state aid. She came to UFS anyway, made
her way into classes, squatted with some friends, and now that tuition
payment was due, she faced the real possibility of financial exclusion.

It often happens that students without a cent for their studies take
advantage of provisional registration (a partial payment arrangement) in
the faint hope that money will materialise from somewhere – a miracle,
nothing less. This provisional arrangement to access university and
attend classes is an accommodation sympathetic universities make to
give students more time to find the funds for their studies. One deadline
for payment is pushed back to another deadline and, under pressure
from student leaders, pushed back again. Suddenly, the year-end examinations loom and there are still students who do not have the funds to
pay. Unsurprisingly, students then enter the next year of studies with
debt from the previous year, and the administrative dance between

deadline enforcement and sympathetic accommodation takes place all over again.

Ntokoza had eventually run out of options as another cut-off deadline loomed, and in desperation she sent me an email, begging for assistance. 'Ask her to see me,' I instructed my secretary, and within hours the frail, downcast student appeared in my office. Rarely had I seen such deep sadness in another person, and I had to ask Ntokoza to raise her faint voice so that I could hear her from across my desk. I clicked my computer mouse and the screen showed that there really was very little money left to support students from my 'cost centres' – unless I once again dipped into my personal banking account. But if my wife found out I would be dead meat; we were already supporting too many students from the family budget. And I could not bear my secretary coming into my office and once again giving me those big eyes that said, '*Alweer*' (Not again). That would be infinitely worse than appearing before a long-suffering priest to confess that you had sinned *again*.

How does one explain the situation of this academically talented student – and many others – in a university that desperately wants to help each and every high school graduate qualifying for degree studies? Four factors converged to create this state of affairs: (1) a steady decline in the state subsidy to universities over two decades; (2) a dramatic increase in the number of poor students enrolled over the same period; (3) a growing reliance on raising tuition fees as the only way to recover institutional income; and (4) a mounting inefficiency within undergraduate institutions as the growing number of students were mainly from academically dysfunctional schools, leading to high dropout and low graduation rates. Together these four elements caused the perfect storm which, university leaders say, could be seen coming from a distance.

Declining subsidies

Without question, the primary driver of the crisis in South African universities was the declining state subsidy in successive years and its deteriorating impact on institutional budgets. The vice-chancellor of Wits summarises the situation as follows:

Adam Habib: Since 2000, we have had a political economy of the universities where the subsidy, in per capita terms, is declining. Universities have tried to compensate by increasing student fees to make up for that deficit. So if you look at the historically white universities . . . in 1994, 1993, Wits had 70 per cent of its expenses covered by the government subsidy. By 2013, 2014, it's down to 30 to 35 per cent. What the university then does is increase the fees. But there is no doubt that as we were increasing the fees by double-digit percentages – to compensate for inflation and currency exchange rates and all of that – effectively what we have done is to price higher education beyond reach. And all of these things came together to create quite an explosive mix by 2011, 2012, 2013. It's quite a threat at multiple levels. All you need is two or three sparks to ignite a crisis. And by the way, we recognise that.

So vice-chancellors were saying for many years that this is unsustainable. In fact, at the end of September 2015 I had written on behalf of the Universities South Africa [USAf] to the president [Jacob Zuma], above the minister of higher education [Blade Nzimande], arguing for a meeting with vice-chancellors in early October 2015. At that meeting all of these issues were raised. We said to him that we're heading for the eye of a storm, except we said that the storm would break in January because that's when we anticipated that the students would strike. What actually happened is it exploded ten days later in the October #FeesMustFall protest across the country. But we saw it coming.

The Wits vice-chancellor was not alone in foretelling the storm; so too did Ahmed Bawa, who until recently was the head of the Durban University of Technology (DUT) and is now the head of USAf, which represents all vice-chancellors.

Ahmed Bawa: Without question I think most vice-chancellors recognise that the system was quickly running into a kind of unaffordable situation where sooner or later there was going to be an upheaval. Some of us actually wrote about that. That a kind of perfect storm was coming at us and that we had to rapidly think about restructuring higher education. And many of us also had this analysis that you had to think of higher education as having a social justice agenda in a situation where there is an unequal society. There was the added problem that with the fees running high and with the ceiling on the amount of financial aid available, fewer and fewer students would be able to come to university.

So I think that among at least some of us there was a view that these 10 per cent increases, although they were necessary for the viability of the institutions, were sooner or later going to lead to difficulty. No amount of interaction with the Department of Higher Education and Training [DHET] resulted in any kind of conversation that would begin to look at that problem in some detail. Every single meeting we had with Minister Nzimande – and not just this minister but also previous ministers – failed to engage in any kind of serious discussion about the financial viability of the universities. So my own view at DUT was, let's just try to manage the needs of students who are most at risk, and let's just try to understand if there's capacity within the institution itself to bring some resources to the table, much to the anger of the council and so on, but at the same time just being really rigorous about trying to ensure that we don't put the university into financial crisis. But what it meant essentially is that we were spending less and less on maintenance and less and less on the kind of things necessary to build a decent research system and so on.

The vice-chancellor of the University of Johannesburg (UJ), a large multi-campus institution, foretold the same storm and unpacked its effects across the top tier of South African universities.

Ihron Rensburg: I think that all of us default to a kind of financial or economics argument to explain the crisis. And as the record shows, we've seen a long-run decline in per student state expenditure, and that decline now has the effect that the twelve leading research-productive universities now find themselves with 50 per cent or less of their income coming from the state's side. And so, over a twenty-year period we have seen significant growth in tuition fees to close that gap. In the last seven years, my estimate is that across the sector, at least among those twelve or so universities, tuition fees have doubled. And the reason why that has happened is that salaries have increased ahead of inflation as expected, and when you give inflationary increases and 60 per cent of your costs is driven by your people cost, then you're already in a big, big deficit. But of course there are other things in play as well. If we consider that in just the last three years the rand has halved in value against major global currencies, it has impacted our journal-purchasing capacity and our research infrastructure capacity, just to pick those two by way of example. And so all of these factors have basically put university inflation closer to 9 or 10 per cent on average over this last decade, and that has really been a major driver of the crisis that unfolded in 2015.

Yet even if the single most important factor in the 2015–2016 crisis was the declining government subsidy to public universities, such financial analysis means little unless one understands it in the context of the daily struggles of students on campuses. And vice-chancellors like Ahmed Bawa, who were engaged with students on the ground, could see that crisis in the eyes of the students.

Ahmed Bawa: You know, it depends on where you're sitting in the system. I spent about six years at DUT and every single year we had demonstrations. I think there was [only] one year when we avoided a major clash. And the demonstrations were always over the same issue. Every now and then the students would add other issues to the demands, such as problems in the residences, but generally speaking it was about one thing only – financial aid.

What I'll never forget is the experience I had at one of the demonstrations. I happened to be in this hall in the basement of the engineering building and there were thousands of students in there. And I thought I would take this as an opportunity to address the students. There was, as usual, a group of students toyi-toyiing, and it just so happens that I made eye contact with some students who were just behind this dancing group. And I caught sight of this group of students, boys and girls, who weren't toyi-toyiing but who were just clearly in a state of anguish. I actually saw some of the women students crying, and it suddenly dawned on me that while it is true that some students were using this issue for political ends, ultimately it was really about access to higher education; it was really about students who come from very poor backgrounds who are trying desperately to get out of poverty. And this was their one step out of poverty. Some believed in the notion that getting a university qualification would get you out of poverty. And that forced me to be much more nuanced in the way in which I thought about this, and fortunately this happened quite early on in my years as vice-chancellor.

So to be honest, I wasn't overly surprised by what eventually happened at Wits and UCT and Rhodes and UJ, and then, of course, the rest of the universities. Slowly but surely the needs of students who depended on financial aid would also reach these places.

This reference in the last paragraph to the more elite of the former white universities is an important one in that the issue of fee increases would have different meanings and impacts across the higher education sector. In fact, the student uprising revealed in dramatic ways the inequality across institutions, as UCT vice-chancellor Max Price describes in relation to arguably the most elite of South Africa's 26 public universities.

Max Price: I think that the October 2015 events actually only happened on our campus at all because of national solidarity. There were no issues for us in terms of fees and affordability; we've been fortunate to be able to manage. And by way of example, the president of the SRC – the same SRC that led the Rhodes Must Fall campaign – proposed in the council the fee increase of 10,5 per cent. The SRC was completely aligned with that high fee increase because we'd worked through it with them over a month; that was in September, a month before the unrest. And because we worked closely with the SRC in setting the fees, they understood that all of the students on financial aid were completely covered. We do not have any 'top ups' or other things that they have to pay, and therefore they face a zero per cent fee increase anyway. And secondly, because we've got a significant number of middle-class students, more than 50 per cent, who can pay the full fee, we can cross-subsidise the so-called missing-middle students,[1] which other campuses generally can't. So even the students from households with up to R550 000 in income can get the necessary loans and financial aid from us. These students do end up with debt when they've graduated, and of course the debt is bigger when the fee increase is bigger, but it's relatively manageable.

So the zero per cent fee increase campaign which started at Wits got exacerbated at the [Durban] Summit on Higher Education Transformation convened by Blade Nzimande in October 2015.[2] The minister was incredibly condescending and dismissive of the students, as was reported to me, and that created a solidarity. And of course on many of the campuses, particularly the historically white campuses, the challenge is this 'missing middle' group of students because they don't get the benefit of financial aid; they're struggling. At the Summit, our SRC initially said that our campus wouldn't be able to join this campaign, because they didn't have a problem with the fees. But once the protests took off, there was this need for national solidarity, so it affected us too.

This middle group was not a new phenomenon in universities, but now it had a name. The 'missing middle' refers to those students who do not qualify for the government's National Student Financial Aid Scheme (NSFAS), because although their parents earned above R120 000 per year, this income was insufficient to pay the overall costs of a university education, which could run on average between R80 000 to R100 000 per annum. Here is a typical student story presented during one of my daily 'open door sessions' with students; let's call her Katryn:

My mother is a teacher and my father has his own company. We did not qualify for NSFAS. The problem is there are two of us here at university, and even though to save money we decided to stay at home rather than in residence, my parents simply cannot afford to keep both of us here. My dad's company has also been going up and down. He is still waiting to get paid by a government department. One of his friends also dropped him. Can you help us?

Katryn is one of many students who are not 'the poorest of the poor', to use a familiar South African expression; they fall between the cracks. And this newly visible demographic of students who were both not poor enough and not rich enough was beginning to gain traction within the public debates and the campus protests around fee increases.[3] There was no plan for them. The poor were bailed out by government and the wealthy bailed themselves out. But the 'missing middle' were feeling the pinch of the annual tuition as they struggled to stay in the race, particularly at the historically white campuses. And it is this group, says Adam Habib, that identifies the student protests as 'not a working-class revolt; you're seeing a middle-class revolt in these universities because of the "missing middle"'.

Explosion in student numbers

If the decline in government subsidies placed pressure on institutional budgets, the rapid growth in student numbers exacerbated the situation to a crisis point. What was once an elite university system would quickly become, under the dual post-apartheid imperatives of democratisation and deracialisation, a *massified* system of higher education. The doors of culture and learning, to draw on the inspired Freedom Charter of the ANC, were now truly thrown wide open. In fact, university enrolments increased from 493 342 in 1994 to nearly 1 million (969 154) in 2014, with a targeted 1,6 million enrolments by 2030, according to a government White Paper.[4]

There were three major problems with this otherwise welcome development. First, the system had no capacity to absorb these large numbers as infrastructure crumbled under the weight of massification. Second, the majority of students now entering universities were academically weak because of a largely dysfunctional school system for the majority of learners, thereby creating massive inefficiencies in higher education. For example, cohort studies showed that of the students pursuing a three-year bachelor's degree, less than 50 per cent would attain that qualification within six years.[5] Third, the preference for university studies – a deep-seated reaction to the colonial and apartheid distaste for academic education for the 'natives' – created the so-called inverted pyramid in which the majority of post-school learners were in universities (about 1 million) and not technical and vocational education (about 700 000).

In short, there was less money but more students. With typical understatement, the Council on Higher Education (CHE), a statutory body that advises the minister of higher education, would muse that the 'growth in student enrolment was not matched by a proportionate growth in subsidy'.[6] Moreover, there were more students enrolled but fewer students graduating, creating very high inefficiency costs in an already faltering higher education system.

Ihron Rensburg: The student body shifted and is shifting at UJ. A decade ago, only 8 per cent of those in the first-year class came from Quintile 1 and 2 schools [the poorest schools]. It's 28 per cent today; and of course it's not just that grouping. It's also your Quintile 3 and 4 schools and even in Quintile 5 schools [the most privileged schools], where you've got working-class children who don't qualify for state aid. So it's a big shift and what that means is parents go out of their way to put their children in there.

Here are two critical observations: the rapid growth in the number of poor students and the demand this places on financial aid *within* one university, a confluence that would explain the ferocity of the protests at UJ and other universities with such remarkable shifts in campus demographics. That growth also impacts on the efficiency of the higher education system, as the UJ vice-chancellor explains:

Ihron Rensburg: Of course the pressure is on universities to improve success rates. As Sizwe Nxasana [the experienced banker appointed by Nzimande in August 2015 to turn around the NSFAS] argues, whether it is to finance that poorer group or the 'missing middle', he needs to mobilise close to R10 billion a year. He can only mobilise that kind of resource from the private sector, from development finance institutions such as PIC, Development Bank and so on, if there is a yield for those who put money in; they don't want to put money into a bottomless pit. There needs to be some recycling of that fund. In order for that to happen, our current on-time graduation rate of 29 per cent or so needs to improve by 10 ten per cent, he says; ideally by 20 per cent. So from 29 per cent, if you can get it closer to 35 or 36 per cent, there's an ability to turn around the situation, meaning there is money coming back into universities for such a potential scheme for the 'missing middle'. But if there is no new or improved performance of the system, that [investment] scheme is going to fall.

Lourens van Staden, the vice-chancellor of one of South Africa's most consistently turbulent universities, the Tshwane University of Technology (TUT), looks like a bunch of taut muscles rolled into one. This pugilistic-looking character is not one you would want to meet in a dark alley, for he looks like someone who would enjoy boxing your ears just for fun. This image has served him well, deployed as he has been by various ministers to bring a semblance of peace to the most difficult campuses in the country. This is an unusual role for an unusual South African: a white man of Afrikaans heritage who is fluent in an African language. True to his image, Lourens van Staden does not flinch from telling you exactly what he thinks.

Lourens van Staden: Well, I disagree with the government's National Development Plan (NDP). Where have you seen a system where there are more students in universities than in colleges and elsewhere in the post-school system? This thing should be turned around. But the current system they tried to build is useless. Sorry, I'm straight; it's useless, the so-called TVET [Technical and Vocational Education and Training] colleges. So where do the students go? Don't think they are stupid. Our kids are intelligent. They know these colleges – what would it help them to go there? Where else can they go?

Career-focused training colleges are theoretically ideal for absorbing the masses of students, but in the South African context this option is unattractive. The college cultures are decrepit, staff attitudes are negative, the work ethic is poor, competent lecturers are in short supply, and what should be a solution to the inverted pyramid problem has a serious marketing problem. And the students know it; they prefer universities. The problem, Van Staden concludes, is that there is no shortcut to acquiring competent technicians or to resolving these issues of image and reputation in a broken system of alternative 'career pathing' for high school graduates.

Declining pass rates

As student numbers have grown, pass rates have declined. In terms of subsidy income, these trends represented a mixed blessing. On the one hand, the more students enrolled, the higher the 'teaching inputs'; hence the subsidy increases. On the other hand, the fewer students who graduate, or who graduate on time, the lower the 'teaching outputs'; thus the subsidy decreases. In other words, what universities may make on the inputs, they lose again on the outputs.

So what do institutions tend to do? They exploit this formula by increasing enrolments as much as possible and put pressure on their systems (academic departments, tutorial systems, centres for teaching and learning, etc.) to enhance pass rates. The DHET, in order to demonstrate that it has fulfilled its political mandate to open up access to more and more students, sets sometimes very high targets for enrolment, which some institutions agree to but cannot meet. So to prevent exploitation, government sets 'caps' on those enrolments.

Throughput rates – a measure of the time it takes students to graduate – are more difficult to control. Unscrupulous institutions might artificially enhance the pass rates or engage in dubious practices – such as one university that allowed students to write their examinations at home and without monitoring.[7] There is just one limitation on these attempts to game the system: the overall funding pie remains constant. This means that to gain more out of the subsidy, an institution must not only do better on its own terms, but also do much better than the other 25 public universities. It is a messy business, but money is in short supply for all of them.

It is, however, very difficult to artificially raise a student's results, and most universities play by the rules in large part because of the conscience of the academic lecturers. Most pride themselves on their disciplines and the quality of their qualifications. Some disciplines, such as accountancy and medicine, are governed by external examination bodies, and there is the real threat of loss of accreditation if such scams became known. And so, with growing numbers of academically weak students from the school system enrolled at universities, more and more students struggle to master the coursework and the failure rate continues to increase.

Consider the case of Sipho (not his real name), who has visited my office at UFS many times. Sometimes he changes his name in the registry so that he will have another opportunity to plead for one more chance. It is a practice in my office that no student comes through the door unless I see his or her academic record first. This allows for students to be referred to the more appropriate office for assistance, or to prevent repeat calls to the same desk. Sipho's record indicates that he has failed nearly all his modules two or three times. A rule was created in which a student cannot fail a module more than twice. There are grounds for appeal, and most students are given a third opportunity. If they fail again, they are advised to do the outstanding module through UNISA. But no matter what Sipho is told, he refuses to accept the verdict of the various offices of appeal. He is desperate, and no amount of tutoring and special assistance and multiple opportunities can help him. But he will not take no for an answer.

I have seen hundreds of Siphos in my seven years at the helm of UFS. Every time my administrator's heart beaks. A careful reading of an academic record as a historical document will suggest one of two things: either Sipho should never have been admitted to university, given his matriculation certificate, or Sipho will never pass at a university level even if his original school certificate qualified him for tertiary studies.

Few university leaders understand that difficult transition from school to university better than Sizwe Mabizela, the vice-chancellor of Rhodes University. A kind-hearted man with boundless empathy for students, he once headed the quality assurance body that sets the standards for school-leaving certificates.

Sizwe Mabizela: What is actually happening and has been happening for a long time is that universities are receiving more and more students who are unprepared for higher education. And if you look at the performance of our public higher education system, the dropout rates are frightening. In fact, almost half of the young people who enrol at our public higher education institutions leave the system without a qualification of one kind or another. That, of course, is a colossal waste of human potential, and the reason why they're in that predicament is that there aren't any viable, attractive post-school education and training opportunities except university.

I've argued on a number of occasions that this country does not need more people with university degrees. What this country desperately needs at its level of development are more young people with artisanal skills. One can pour in money to deal with the funding of higher education. But that in and of itself will not make the significant difference, because you have young people in a public higher education system who should not have been there in the first place, who would have benefited by going to a TVET college. Unfortunately, those colleges are not institutions of choice at the moment. And so as part of resolving the challenges of higher education, we need to pay greater attention to our TVET colleges. Make them institutions of choice.

I've also made a lot of noise about the message that we send with our National Senior Certificates (NSCs): it is very problematic when you classify an NSC as a certificate, diploma, or bachelor pass. A bachelor pass sends the message that the person should go to university, and so anyone with a bachelor pass, which unfortunately does not take much to achieve, simply thinks of university. I wish we would change that classification so that some of those with a pass that is equivalent to a bachelor pass could see themselves going to a TVET college because that's what would appeal to them.

The other thing that is very important relates to the curriculum in our higher education institutions. It is one thing to facilitate physical access to a university; it is quite another to facilitate what Wally Morrow [the late South African philosopher of education] refers to as 'epistemological access'. That means access to knowledge, what knowledge is and how you construct knowledge, and all of that. We have succeeded in facilitating physical access, but I don't think we have been that successful in facilitating access to knowledge. And that, of course, is reflected in the dropout rate that I referred to earlier.

If I had my way as far as higher education is concerned, I would cap the numbers and say no more growth, and if there is growth it has to be very small and controlled, and that we must pay attention to what is happening within the universities. Improve the pass and graduation rates. Improve the throughput rate. Those are absolutely abysmal, which is one of those things fuelling #FeesMustFall. You have young people who are frustrated, who come from poor families, and they just can't make sense of what is happening at universities. They drop out in large numbers and that's a mix that leads to incredible levels of frustration.

This frustration on the part of students is real, and university principals encounter it all the time, sometimes with dangerous consequences. For example, at UFS Sibusiso (not his real name), having once again failed his course, angrily confronted his lecturer. He threatened to get physical and started to throw things around in her office. She was mortified. When she told him the results were accurate, he called her a racist. She offered to refer his plea higher up. Eventually it reached my office. After a thorough review, I told him that multiple failures after repeated opportunities and assistance meant that he would not be able to pass the course. Sibusiso then threatened the lecturer's life on social media. (An investigation revealed that he was the perpetrator, working from an off-campus site.) Personal security arrangements were made for the lecturer, and Sibusiso was expelled. Nevertheless he has found his way into the protest marches on campus. His intense frustration and anger mix in with the protest about student fees, helping to facilitate the addition of all kinds of other agendas onto the list of protestor demands – including accusations of racist lecturers and individual targeting. The real truth about Sibusiso's case melts seamlessly into the heat of the protests.

Tuition fee hikes

As subsidies have come down, tuition fees have gone up. From 2000 to 2012, the government's contribution to higher education decreased from 49 per cent to 40 per cent (and was as low as 38 per cent in 2014).[8] In the same period, students' contribution to university funding increased from 24 per cent to 31 per cent.[9] As tuition fees increased from R12,2 billion to R15,5 billion between 2010 and 2012, student debt rose from R2,6 billion to R3,4 billion.[10] In percentage terms, as a share of institutional funding tuition fees increased from 24 per cent in 2000 to 33 per cent in 2014.

The conclusion is straightforward: students could not afford the tuition hikes and the burden of debt became a reality, not only for those who graduated, but also for those who dropped out with debt and without a degree. It was a cruel calculus for the materially poor and academically disadvantaged.

Now to be clear, it is not that funded students paid the fee increases themselves, although there is little recognition of this simple fact in the protest movement. Moreover, government has substantially increased NSFAS funding in the past and present, and has promised to do so into the future. In 1991 the NSFAS funded 7 240 students to the tune of R21,4 million; by 2014 the scheme funded 409 475 students at a cost of R9 billion. Those on state funding – whether from the NSFAS, a more general fund, or the Funza Lushaka Bursary – were fully covered for most of their costs. If anything, the minister of higher education would complain from time to time that the tuition fee increases by the universities were pushing the NSFAS envelope, but the reality is that students were amply funded.

The students for whom the tuition fee increases were becoming a problem were poor students who did not qualify for NSFAS or Funza Lushaka funding, and students from middle-class families (the 'missing middle') who could not afford the escalating costs of studying at university. These are the groups among whom the pressure was building, as it was among those students for whom NSFAS had simply run out of funds. But the university protests were often led by middle-class and fully funded students presuming to lead on behalf of their poorer classmates. The vice-chancellor of the Cape Peninsula University of Technology (CPUT) makes a clear distinction between the truly poor and the better-off students:

Prins Nevhutalu: You hear all the time the discourse that informs the discussion around fee increases focused on UCT and Wits. It's all about a 'missing middle', but parading it in the name of the poor students. So my argument to Max [Price] and Adam [Habib] is, you absolutely have no need for posturing. We carry the burden of the largest numbers of poor students. You cannot argue on behalf of poor students. Argue about your own institution and say you need more money from the state, but don't hide behind the poverty of black people. The protests about fees originated on campuses that for me were not facing the harsh reality of poverty.

There is no question that the problem of inadequate NSFAS funding hits the poor the hardest, even as the burden has spread to middle-class students as well. And with every year that tuition fees increased beyond the rise in earnings of families in a stagnant economy, the predictable perfect storm came closer. In response to these pressures, frustration would push students into desperate acts. Put simply, fee increases on campuses compounded struggles with poverty in communities.

Lourens van Staden: And the way we allocate NSFAS, you give students money for certain things like tuition and often maybe for textbooks, as an example. But students also need to eat. If you are poor, where will you eat? At TUT we have a strong academic development support unit where our psychologist conducted some studies. There's a lot of prostitution, a lot of our boys are stealing in town. You find them when you drive out in the evening. Why are they doing that? Some of them are really just acting criminally because they do it to have beautiful things and so on. We did the research. But others simply do not have a meal. So for me, those who are enrolled are having a tough time experiencing equality in terms of a full stomach, or the necessary resources like textbooks or to get access to electronic resource centres, or to have a proper laptop or whatever. I mean the tools, that's imperative. And now you don't eat. It's a vicious cycle. It's not conducive for [poor students]. And then in our case, the ones that we send home by the thousands, what happens to them? And you know, often TUT is not the preferred institution among prospective students because of all the disruptions. So we might be the last resort. Still the financial issues matter to poor students here. I am not saying we should have fee-free education, because that would have disastrous implications. Just look at what happened elsewhere in Africa.

So what did universities do?

If the narrative of student protestors is to be believed, universities and their leaders are singularly unresponsive to these four intersecting crises (subsidies down, fees up; enrolments up, throughput rates down). 'Tell me,' I asked one of the student leaders in a moment of exasperation during the #FeesMustFall protests, 'what is it that you asked that we did not do?' The question was rhetorical, because at UFS we went out of our way to address every material and intellectual need of our students. My directive to my senior team was simple: do not fight with students or workers on things we can agree on. And so when the invasion of the rugby field happened (problem one) and the assault that followed (problem 2), the principal of a Cape Town university called me and said: 'Of all the universities, and all you've done, this should not have happened to UFS.' We all thought so, and we were devastated by a faction within the SRC leadership who claimed that, after decades, 'nothing had changed at UFS'. Fortunately, virtually everyone connected to the university knew better.

UFS was fortunate to have a council that took pride in its commitment to have one of the lowest fee structures in the country. This meant that even though UFS did more than most institutions in terms of academic innovation – such as the compulsory 101 core curriculum and the funded study-abroad programme for undergraduates – the institution ran a tight ship, keeping its fees low and its staff remuneration at 53 per cent of expenditure regardless of the fluctuating levels of the annual subsidy. If any university had a pro-poor fee structure, it was UFS. But you would not know that from the fierce protests of 2015–2016.

Like many other universities, Stellenbosch University (SU) used its own internal funds to add substantially to the government's loan and bursary allocations in order to meet the expanding needs of a growing student population. According to its leader, SU managed a total of R658,7 million in student bursaries, of which R155 million came from within its own funds, thereby covering 24 per cent of its total student body. With an on-average poorer student body, UFS covered 47 per cent of its student body, with R48,4 million coming out of institutional funds from a total of R427 million available for financial assistance. More than anything else, these institution-held funds directed to student funding signalled commitment to poor students, for such money could easily have been deployed in running the general operations of the university.

In addition, as indicated earlier, universities often stretch the 'payment due' dates to enable students and their families to raise the funds needed for studies. Most parents eventually find some funding to cover historical debt from previous years and current obligations in the present year of study. Invariably, this has an impact on the cash-flow status of a university and could lead to serious crises with regards to payroll. But universities go to the line to enable families to come up with funding, which serves both the student, enabling him or her to study, and the institution, enabling it to operate.

Many universities have a variety of textbook 'buy-back' schemes to help students purchase books cheaply. (This sometimes becomes a racket, with all kinds of instant entrepreneurs willing to scam desperate students.) Students share books. Publishers increasingly offer online and cheaper mass-purchase options. Students themselves organise book-return sales. Lecturers rely on book notes placed on Blackboard or other technology platforms. These schemes, with or without university facilitation, enable students to access expensive books without which they would find it hard to prepare for assignments, tests, and examinations.

Since the 1990s there is hardly a university without a centre for teaching and learning, or some centralised facility that provides additional tutorial classes; coaching in academic writing skills, study skills, and note-taking skills; sessions on reading and preparing for assignments; and countless other interventions that help bridge students from schoolwork to university studies. Academic support programmes of varying ideologies and approaches sprang up everywhere decades ago, and some universities have set up whole campuses to enable students with weak school results to do a bridging year before applying for degree studies.

Free or subsidised food schemes are often provided to cater for students in dire financial need. Some universities have gone further, providing free health services and even gym or fitness centres. In other words, universities across the country have gone to the wire to provide from within their own resources the people, resources, and facilities to meet students' emotional, nutritional, intellectual, and financial needs.

In the end, it did not matter, for what protesting students were looking for was something much more fundamental: the resolution of a *systemic* failure in the funding of higher education. All other remedies were dismissed as well-meaning but misguided, even if a massive safety net was now in place for vulnerable students. But that systemic failure went beyond universities – it was, fundamentally, a critique of post-1994 society itself and the failure of the state to live up to societal expectations of what the 'new South Africa' was *supposed* to be.

Chapter 3

The Roots of the Crisis II:
Cultural Alienation

---

*English is still the only language in which you can make
somebody feel small without uttering a word.*
– Author

If #FeesMustFall (FMF) marked a national student movement against financial exclusion from South Africa's 26 public universities, then #RhodesMustFall (RMF) captured collective concerns about cultural alienation on former white university campuses. RMF (March 2015) triggered the student movement around intellectual concerns; FMF (October 2015) followed with the sharp focus on material concerns. RMF and FMF would merge in the most powerful student movement in the country since the 1970s, with protests around financial exclusion targeting no fee increases in 2016 and, in the course of the next year, for 2017.

The FMF cause would soon dominate the new, merged agenda. Eventually President Zuma, under enormous political pressure, sidelined his minister responsible for post-school education and declared that there would be a zero per cent fee increase for 2016. It soon became clear that this decision had created a political and psychological barrier to any tuition-related increases in a university system already buckling under the effects of a long-term decline in state subsidies. Minister Nzimande (who was also the general secretary of the South African Communist Party) had earlier declared a 6 per cent fee hike. But in the extraordinary Pretoria Summit (23 October 2015) of the president, university principals, and the protestors, Nzimande received a slapdown by the president of the country and the head of the ANC. An alliance forged in struggle was coming apart on the fees issue, but the vivid imagery of the statue of Rhodes being lifted from his perch at UCT to be dumped somewhere off campus remained etched in the minds of students and the general public.

And all because of a politics student who, on 9 March 2015, carried a bucket of excrement up the hill and dumped it on the statue of Cecil John Rhodes. Barely a month after Chumani Maxwele's act of defilement, a crowd gathered around the statue, which had stood firmly since its unveiling on UCT's Upper Campus in 1934. The media reported 'a festive atmosphere'.[1] Students clambered up and down the old man's monument, which in those four weeks had been a target of scorn and was decorated in all kinds of material, including a slap of paint and a dead fish. Slowly the crane hoisted Rhodes off his perch as cellphone cameras flashed and singing and dancing marked the end of the British imperialist who had once dreamed of extending his empire along a railway line from the Cape to Cairo.

Memory, memorials, and monuments

The RMF students had with unusual focus and determination concentrated their demands on the gigantic sculpture of Rhodes. A march to UCT's Bremner Building was followed by an occupation of this nerve centre of the university's administrative operations. The protestors demanded a date for the removal of the statue. The senate of the university, representing the academic body through its professors, voted overwhelmingly for removal. The UCT council, responsible for the governance of the university, would inevitably follow the same path – but not before students, in what seemed to be a cruel and gratuitous *coup de grâce* against the establishment, broke into a meeting of the university elders and roundly insulted and humiliated the lot of them. It was a gratuitous move because the council was widely expected to make the decision for removal anyway; it was cruel because these students, born after Nelson Mandela's release from prison, vilified men and women many of whom had fought and made considerable sacrifices in the struggle against apartheid. Among them was the dignified elder statesman and chairman of council, Archbishop Emeritus Njongonkulu Ndungane, who spent ten years of his life locked up on Robben Island. For this group of protestors, it was not enough to win the decision; they had to rub the faces of their university leaders in it.

In the week prior to the removal of the Rhodes statue, the attack on colonial and apartheid symbols had begun to fan out across campuses and communities. On the Howard campus of the University of KwaZulu-Natal (UKZN), a sculpture of George V was defaced with white paint, covered in a blanket, and marked with the words 'End White Privilege'.[2] As could be expected, the shock waves of the Cape Town decision were felt at Rhodes University in Grahamstown: protestors there demanded that the name of the university be changed. In Pretoria, Afrikaner activists surrounded a statue of Paul Kruger, the nineteenth-century Boer general who became president of the South African Republic, after it too was dabbed in green paint. Then Mahatma Gandhi's statue in Johannesburg was similarly defaced, followed by the partial dismantling of a horse memorial in Port Elizabeth. It was now open season on statues, whether commemorating a British imperialist, an Afrikaner hero, an activist for non-violence, or the service of animals in distant wars.

The targeting of the Rhodes statue did not come without its contradictions. Throughout the city that surrounds UCT are ample memorials to colonial and apartheid figures. The towering statue of the country's first prime minister, Louis Botha, stands over the entrance to South Africa's democratic Parliament; a major roadway nearby was recently named after F.W. de Klerk, apartheid's last president. It was the approach of the ruling party to seek reconciliation over retaliation in the carefully orchestrated process of symbolic reparation. There was not going to be a triumphalist, Talibanesque destruction of every contested symbol and memory from the past. In this regard the approach to change was gradual and conciliatory rather than instantaneous and substitutionary. One example of the approach was the retention of the Afrikaner Voortrekker Monument in near proximity to the more inclusive memory symbolised by Freedom Park, which was established under the democratic government. An act of creativity as much as conciliation, 'Freedom Park is set up in visual and conceptual relation to the Voortrekker Monument'.[3]

That is why Rhodes still stood almost two decades into democracy, quite apart from the fact that the campus citizens simply did not care very much about the man or the memorial; the monument survived through neglect. Then RMF drew attention to the statue whose position at the lower end of the majestic Jammie steps placed him perfectly between the great Jameson Hall and Devil's Peak behind him, and the expansive flatlands of Cape Town suburbs, council estates, and townships before him. Somebody had taken some time thinking about how to position the university's founding benefactor in such a prominent place on the campus, even though this was not its original position. According to monuments expert Brenda Schmahmann, the statue was originally placed lower down the slope, over-looking the rose garden, and was moved further up in the early 1960s, after the widening of the highway below the campus.[4]

Not without reason was the statue afforded such a place of prominence. Cecil John donated this part of his Groote Schuur estate expressly for the purpose of building the University of Cape Town. Not far from this beautiful piece of real estate sits the Rhodes Memorial, also overlooking the Cape Flats and featuring striking Greek pillars, a bronze horseman, and eight bronze lions flanking a massive staircase leading up to a bust of the man himself. As a child of Cape Town clambering up those lion figures, I had no idea that such a rich and controversial history came with this stunning scenery captured by generations through the family camera.

Nor was the removal of Rhodes going to be a simple process. For months leading up to and following the demise of the statue, all kinds of public hand-wringing took place among current and former Rhodes Scholars. They found themselves in the precarious position of taking the man's money and condemning the man's deeds – and, worse, calling for his head, so to speak. And then there was that oddly named institution in the Eastern Cape: Rhodes University, where students clamoured for a name change. Interestingly, despite common belief it turns out this institution might not even have been established at the request of Cecil John.[5] Nonetheless, Rhodes University became a natural home for thousands of Rhodesians even after they became Zimbabweans. Later on it was also a place in which traumatised students from Zimbabwe would find a home after the farm evictions and 'land grabs' that devastated non-African families in that country.[6]

The truth is, very few people are keen to change the name of Rhodes University, because its meaning as a liberal bastion of excellence in higher education has long outlived the imperialist arrogance, capitalistic greed, and racial meanness of Mr Rhodes. Naturally, those fighting the proposed name change were the alumni, black (quietly) and white (loudly), who still proudly call themselves Rhodents (with an *h*). But there had to be some signal of progressive intent even without the political commitment to change anything, and so a task team was formed to explore the issue. Meanwhile, activists have coined a new, and clumsy, name for the Grahamstown institution: UCKAR – the University that is Currently Known as Rhodes.

'Professor, did you know that Rhodes had a coloured boyfriend?' asked a woman from the Cape Flats who made tea for me and other visitors to Community Chest, an influential non-governmental organisation (NGO) in Cape Town. She seemed genuinely happy to meet me, a displaced son of the area who was now leading a university in faraway Bloemfontein. The contentious Rhodes statue was all over the news, thanks to the UCT protestors. The public wondered: What should happen to the statue? Where should it go? Why take Rhodes's money but boot his remembrance off the property he yielded to establish UCT in the first place?

'Auntie, I really do not know what to do with this information,' I replied, smiling as we descended into all kinds of speculation about how a white man with a recorded disregard for black people would have to live an unseemly private life in a colonial backwater that was at once racist and homophobic. But bringing up Rhodes's alleged homosexuality, which had been whispered about for decades, into this light conversation simply illustrated a broader and continuing contention about the man and his legacy.

The protestors' responses to questions about the hypocrisy of taking Rhodes's money but condemning the man were straightforward and devoid of any complexity. It was not his land to begin with. How could he give to UCT what was not rightfully his? If anything, this was the land of the Khoisan that he had expropriated. Rhodes had the audacity to claim he was bringing 'civilisation' to the Dark Continent – how offensive is that? As a politician, he introduced racial policies to the Cape that allowed for the exploitation of black labour in his mines. And then the shift to the present: keeping Rhodes in his privileged position on campus serves as 'a constant reminder for many black students of the position in society that black people have occupied due to hundreds of years of apartheid, oppression and colonialism'.[7]

This was an articulate intellectual riposte from UCT's SRC president, but it was also a powerful emotional argument that a university which, by history, culture, and composition, is largely white would be hard-pressed to ignore. The weight of white guilt in a liberal institution susceptible to sound argument meant only one thing: a senate and council that represented the oft-observed smugness of the university's social and academic culture would inevitably support the removal of the colossal statue from campus.

Not that this was the original plan of UCT's vice-chancellor. When the RMF protests mounted, his idea was to move the famed British entrepreneur from his prominent perch to a less visible site on campus. This made sense to many scholars of memory and memorials, for the complete removal of such a significant historical figure from the campus had a political and pedagogical downside. Surely a monument is a textbook of sorts, a source of reflection and criticism. In other words, engaging in dialogue about a monument and its meaning is the kind of thing a university does. The statue can provoke discussion about things we do not like rather than eliminate them from sight and memory. In discussions about the statue's fate, all kinds of ideas came to the table, including attaching a plaque to the sculpture that explained Rhodes's role in the making of racial, class, and colonial oppression in southern Africa. But in campus climates that had become increasingly inhospitable to this kind of intellectual pondering on difficult questions, Rhodes the successful white capitalist was doomed from the start. A gaping absence now marks the space the statue once occupied, and debates moved on to other issues.

Ironically, it was none other than Zimbabwe's president Robert Mugabe, a zealous anti-British crusader ever since he fell out of favour with Queen and country, who would swat away the demand from war veterans that Rhodes's remains be dug up from his grave near Bulawayo and returned to Britain. Monuments and memorials of empire remain intact in much of postcolonial Zimbabwe, from King George's barracks in Harare to the gravesite of Rhodes, whom even a novelist of the imperialist era called 'a murky and distorted genius'.[8] Still, even in Zimbabwe various sculptures of Rhodes were removed from prominent places after independence (1980). At least one statue was attacked and defaced by protestors, while a prominent cast of the sculpture *Physical Energy* (the horseman statue seen at Cape Town's Rhodes Memorial) was moved from downtown Harare to the grounds of the National Archives.[9]

Given the global character of much of the youth protest movement, and the extraordinary bonds that still exist between countries that used to reference competing cricketing teams in the Cape as pitting 'home country versus colonial born', it is not surprising that the call for Rhodes to fall would spread to the UK – specifically to Oriel College of Rhodes's alma mater, Oxford University. A 33-year-old Oxford PhD student, Brian Kwoba, led the charge against Rhodes with rhetorical flourishes about 'stealing land', 'massacring tens of thousands of Black Africans', 'unspeakable labour exploitation' in the diamond mines, and so on.

Despite a petition with more than 2 300 signatures, the disposal of the Oxford version of RMF was swift and cutting. The chancellor of Oxford, calling up the name of the man in whose honour a new scholarship had just been created in South Africa, pronounced: 'If they aren't prepared to show the generosity of spirit which Nelson Mandela showed towards Rhodes and towards history ... then maybe they should think about being educated elsewhere.'[10] Rhodes remained standing at Oxford because of the resident power of the institution, its formidable history, its national politics, and of course its prominent alumni who warned that giving in to this crowd would be 'substituting moral vanity for fair-minded enquiry'.[11] That was the embarrassing end of any activist illusion that an African action in Cape Town would stand a chance of rocking the oldest university in the English-speaking world.

The RMF protests escalated student demands around institutional symbolism far beyond deliberations already under way at several universities. At UFS we had long engaged in a series of discussions on what to do with memory, memorials, and monuments. Some things were changed instantly when I started working there in 2009, such as the symbols carried in the university coat of arms, which represented the

Boer Republic that birthed the University of the Orange Free State. The motto of a narrowly minded Calvinist god, *In Deo Sapientiae Lux* (In God is Light of Wisdom), was changed to the more inclusive *In Veritate Sapientiae Lux* (In Truth is Light of Wisdom). Names of residences were changed; for example, the name of the racist prime minister J.B.M. Hertzog was replaced by the name of the Afrikaner struggle hero Beyers Naudé. An experimental project launched by the Australian artist Cigdem Aydemir led to the statue of the Boer Orange Free State president M.T. Steyn being sealed in pink covers to convey the plasticity of meaning associated with memory and memorials.[12] The man himself was a pre-apartheid figure; like some other late-nineteenth-century and early-twentieth-century figures, Steyn was a *volksnasionalis* (a nationalist of his people), similar to John Dube representing Africans or the early Mahatma Gandhi advocating for the rights of Indians on his visit to South Africa. Still, the giant statue would be re-presented in public space, inviting friends and foes to engage in discussion around a relatively uncontroversial figure who in fact enabled the establishment of UFS.

Then there was the statue of the more contentious Charles Robberts (C.R.) Swart, the apartheid-era state president from 1961 to 1967 and the first law school graduate of the University of the Orange Free State. Should his statue simply be taken down, in a slash-and-burn kind of statement, or was there something more creative that could be done to educate those who pass by about his contribution to the racial misery of black people? Our belief was that UFS – which must be the only university that has the word 'reconciliation' in the opening line of its mission statement – should do something more creative and educational than simply removing the monument. After all, was this not a teaching opportunity, the very business of a university?

Perhaps no one has captured better an alternative vision of what to do with offending memorials than the struggle stalwart Albie Sachs, who lost an arm and an eye to an apartheid bomb, and wrote the beautifully titled book *The Soft Vengeance of a Freedom Fighter*. His argument was that 'instead of extinguishing Rhodes, we should keep him alive on the campus and force him, even if posthumously, to witness surroundings that tell him and the world that he is now living in a constitutional democracy'.[13] Sachs then went on to illustrate by example ways in which the ANC thought creatively about what to do with memorials of colonial figures, such as Jan van Riebeeck, in South Africa House in London. Here, the mural of Van Riebeeck was covered with transparent glass panels bearing the names of slaves and indigenous people.[14]

At UFS, the C.R. Swart Building, which houses the law faculty, was due for a name change. And so a very carefully planned process of renaming got under way in which students and staff could make proposals. Feedback from students was sluggish and response from the activist element even more so, despite pleas from the law school faculty for participation. The Swart memorabilia, including a bust, were removed and stored in the basement of the building without much debate, and eventually the faculty came up with the name Equitas Building to reflect a core constitutional value. That choice made sense, but others felt a deeper sense of justice could be served by naming the building after a prominent legal scholar and activist from the anti-apartheid struggle. My own preference was to name the building after Ismail Mahomed, the ANC stalwart and activist and the first black judge to head up the Supreme Court of Appeal, lodged historically in Bloemfontein. As a lawyer representing black activists, he had to drive back and forth to Kimberley in the Northern Cape, more than 100 kilometres away, because the Free State had a particularly nasty racist law preventing Indian South Africans from staying overnight in the province. Yet the faculty remained cool to this proposal, perhaps because it was too radical, and the student leadership at the time rolled their eyes, perhaps because Mahomed was not 'African'.

Other interesting proposals were made, including placing opposite the Swart statue the likeness of another prominent law student, the activist Bram Fischer, who formed part of Mandela's legal team during the Rivonia Trial,[15] and who died some years before Mandela's release from prison. Each figure would bear a plaque explaining his respective role in the apartheid period – entrenching it through laws, in the case of Swart, and fighting it through struggle, in the case of Fischer.

This kind of thinking was very much top of mind when UFS sent its student leaders to Germany and Poland to see how Jews and Germans dealt with memory and memorials from the great tragedy of the

Holocaust. I raised more than R1 million for the trip because of the opportunity for our students not only to receive comparative education but also to bring back practical insights for what to do with various UFS memorials. But before the students could even submit their trip reports, the rugby pitch invasion and assault happened on the Bloemfontein campus. In the immediate wake of this incident, a small group of violent protestors, including off-campus rioters and the SRC president, made a run on the Swart statue. They pulled it down and dumped the statue in one of the water channels running through the campus. A transgender activist stood on the statue's head, from which position she was quoted in the media as saying 'I can't breathe', borrowing an expression from the US protest movement against police brutality shown towards black men. (During an arrest attempt, Eric Garner was choked to death by a New York City policeman while pleading 'I can't breathe'.) The events at UFS, and the protest mood in the country, had clearly moved way beyond what could be resolved through academic deliberation.

Behind the symbol

Back at UCT, it was clear from the start that what was driving the protest against institutional racism and cultural alienation had little to do with the actual statue; the Rhodes sculpture stood in for something else, and in the struggle for its removal a complex picture of a top university would emerge, a story best told in the words of its vice-chancellor.

> Max Price: Regarding the #RhodesMustFall campaign, I think one strand was primarily speaking to the sense of alienation that black students particularly, and staff to a lesser extent, had on campus. But interestingly, in the beginning the campaign had quite a substantial multiracial support; it wasn't black. I'm not quite sure what the white students were identifying with, but I think they were sympathetic, and I think that which speaks to both white and black was something I identify with from my personal experience.

Like many of the university principals who themselves were activists in the anti-apartheid period, Max Price would reflect on his own experiences in the crisis he was now required to manage.

55

Max Price: Over the years I was often challenged: why did you, Max, coming from a middle-class, comfortable background, become a radical on campus? My family was not socialist or Marxist or left-wing. I can't put my finger on it, but one of the things I had the sense of was being confronted for the first time at university with a great sense of inequality and unfairness and the degree of oppression, and feeling as a white person that I was part of that and needing to distance myself from that or needing to say 'I'm not part of that', and possibly becoming more extreme left-wing, becoming involved in workers' issues and other things, than I would otherwise have done. There still needs to be an explanation of why I reacted that way and others not, but partly it does go back, I suppose, to some deep values.

Price goes on to make a very important point about the class make-up of the UCT student body, which is very different from the student body of the historically black universities and also of those universities, such as Wits, where the student demographic had altered radically in recent years to include the black poor in larger numbers. This was also true among the 'poor white cousins' of the white university fraternity, such as UFS.

Max Price: What I think is happening in part is that black middle-class students [at UCT], often from private schools, come onto the campus and for the first time actually are significantly confronted with the fact that most blacks are poor. And they've been quite sheltered from that environment before coming here. And they're in this uncomfortable position of feeling that they're somehow privileged and they don't deserve to be privileged, and that they need to take on the battle of the broader community of black students who are poor and rural. And they become more radical than even those poorer black students and they need to demonstrate a degree of black solidarity that will say to those other black students: 'The fact that I enjoy different music, the fact that I speak with a different accent, the fact that my family is rich, that I have a car, actually doesn't mean I am different. I'm not different. I'm on your side, I'm fighting with you.' And I think that need also applies to some of the white students, but it's white students largely from my kind of background, as well as left-wing parents who were involved in the struggle. It was remarkable, the mix of people who were arrested in Parliament, outside Parliament, and there were a significant number of white students in the crowd. Among the arrested were my son and [Advocate] Wim Trengove's son.[16]

Of course, children of the black elite were also arrested in some of the broader protests:

Max Price: Brian Molefe's[17] son and Frank Chikane's[18] son [were also arrested]. Now I don't know whether the police knew these individuals and targeted them, but I don't think so. I think they were just in the crowd there. I think it's saying something about the kinds of people who are identifying with the struggle and what particular backgrounds they're coming from. So my explanation of the black–white trans-race solidarity around the original #RhodesMustFall is that black students were experiencing two things. One is that they were being confronted with other black students whom they felt they needed to take up the battle for, and the second is that they were confronted, I think probably for the first time, with an environment which does communicate that the colour of excellence is white. UCT has the trappings of the colonial, of the empire, and it valorises European culture still. It doesn't do very much to make an effort to provide other role models, or to say that there are different cultures, different histories, or to make an effort to valorise the history of these black students. So many of them say that the first time they realised they were black was when they came to UCT. And some of these people come from black townships, so it's understandable because in a black township and in school they've had hardly any contact with white people anyway. So it wouldn't be an issue. But the people who come from the Model C schools are more of a majority in many of those schools; they had a greater sense of ownership and then they come to Cape Town. Almost all of our black students come from Gauteng, KwaZulu-Natal, and the Eastern Cape, where the society is one in which four out of five people look like them. Whereas here, four out of five do not look like them. In the Western Cape, as you know, only around 25 per cent of the population are African. And so the whole environment is one which makes black students feel like, 'I'm the outsider here. I'm the minority group here, I'm not the majority.' I think those experiences come together and the Rhodes statue was the perfect symbol of all that. And it really wasn't just about the statue; it's obviously about the culture of the place. And that's a legitimate, bona fide cause, which I myself identify with and always have, and which I think needs to be changed, and it's partly our responsibility to change it. To take down the statue to address these other issues.

This acknowledgement by the UCT leader of the cultural disconnect between black African students and how they experience institutional culture is a long-standing complaint at the university and one that has been addressed in various investigations into campus problems. But what requires further questioning is the assumption of the right to be dominant, that the only accepted way to exist in various communities in South Africa is when 'black African' is dominant. What would ultimately weaken the movement, however, was not its understandable demands for cultural inclusion, but its rather unusual organisational politics.

Max Price: One of the features of #RhodesMustFall, which I think is largely a weakness, not a strength, is that it modelled itself on the global 'Occupy movements', which have very flat structures – in fact, almost no structure. There's no defined membership, people don't sign up or leave; there's no real mechanism of saying who's allowed to be part of this and who isn't; there's no election of leadership; and there's no accountability in reality. The strength [of that strategy] is that it's harder to demobilise the group or to remove the leadership, but the weakness is that it's easily hijacked by groups that come and join and form a larger number. And so the movement is continually fracturing and re-forming and fracturing and re-forming. They'll put out a statement, and they'll retract the statement because the plenary disagreed with something in the statement, and they'll put out another one. So it's not easy to say at any point in time what they stand for and who's included. But it morphed through this lack of structure to being taken over by a group that was not the original . . . that had a politics different from the original leadership or core group into something that was strongly Black Consciousness and exclusivist and essentially about race.

So, clearly race was an element – if you're talking about alienation in social culture, race is a very strong element. But the movement was explicitly non-racial to start with, and then it became explicitly racial with groups forming that excluded whites from participating. Whites then withdrew, reacting to some extent by trying to find a role. We had a group called White Privilege which tried to function, but didn't get much momentum. I think it was not a group that was interested in violence and I don't think that any of the [original] RMF group was interested in disruption to the point of stopping the university from functioning. We didn't have any lectures missed; the occupations that happened, and mostly they were without permission, were of admin facilities far away from the academic project.

Within this changing, morphing political group, the idea of women's groups and LGBT [Lesbian, Gay, Bisexual, and Transgender] groups became very powerful. The language quite quickly shifted to a so-called intersectionality, highlighting that there are lots of dimensions of power and oppression and we must attend to these and not set them off against each other. But in fact the core black RMF group is very masculinist and very chauvinist and sexist. So that's been an ongoing tension within the groups, and every now and then the women have expelled the men from the place where they meet and then there's a sort of a realignment and they'd come back. [In March 2016] there was an exhibition to mark the anniversary [of RMF] and the Trans Collective[19] painted over all the photographs and disrupted it. So those dynamics are there as well.

So RMF, the original organisation, could quickly take on other forms; there was an alignment of three or four groups and again they merged because of this loose structure. We had the Left Students Forum, we had #FeesMustFall, we had #RhodesMustFall, and they came together and ran that anti-fees campaign. And then the Left Students Forum was mainly driving the campaign for insourcing workers, which I think was a substantially different issue. Workers were not at all involved, for example, in the RMF period, whereas workers have been running a campaign for ten years now to reverse outsourcing, as have the unions, NEHAWU [National Education, Health and Allied Workers' Union] in particular. They saw the #FeesMustFall campaign as an opportunity. They aligned themselves with that, and it was very effective in making outsourcing an issue, which was almost an irresistible force. [If the movement managed to shut down the campus] the consequence for us of not writing exams on time or delaying the start of the new academic year would be completely devastating. And if we didn't have fee income this year because we had to delay new students coming in, we wouldn't be able to pay salaries to staff and workers. So I think the merger of workers with RMF really was an irresistible force.

Black awareness and alienation

Max Price makes a number of important observations about the course of the struggle against the institutional symbolism of the former white English university. The first is that RMF started as a broad, non-racial movement that drew in white as well as black students from across the campus. This kind of solidarity across racial boundaries connects with a rich tradition in the anti-apartheid struggle associated with the United Democratic Front (UDF) inside the country and the ANC in exile. The RMF movement spoke powerfully to a felt need in a divided country to organise protest and address discontent on the basis of a common inter-racial struggle. White students, as the UCT vice-chancellor indicated, were prepared not only to join the struggle against the slow pace of transformation but also to do some serious introspection, as indicated, for example, by the formation of the White Privilege discussion group. It was a movement whose public face and peaceful protest tactics largely enjoyed public sympathy.

The same kind of cross-racial solidarity was found at other South African campuses in the first half of 2015. White students were present, although in small numbers, in protests at UFS and the University of Pretoria (UP), for example.

On 23 October 2015, more than 12 000 students marched to the Union Buildings in Pretoria to protest fee increases at the very time that President Zuma was meeting with student leaders and vice-chancellors inside. As the UP vice-chancellor recalls of that event:

Cheryl de la Rey: #FeesMustFall was a broad group of students. Some, even many, were not politically affiliated or ideologically driven but were sympathetic to the issue. And I do think that affordability was a real issue for many families – not the demand for free university education, but the concern about affordability. So FMF was a broad group, and I think the group from UP assembled here with students from Wits and UJ [University of Johannesburg], after which some of them marched as a group to the Union Buildings. And when the violence broke out on the lawn of the Union Buildings, our students just came back very quickly. I actually got a note of appreciation afterwards because we opened the gates for them and we gave them bottles of water and all of that. I think they were quite shocked about what happened; they did not expect that violence at the Union Buildings. And this is a fairly broad group, across race and also across class, because it was a kind of sympathy movement.

[This moment also had] an unintended positive effect, in that many white students were totally shocked and didn't identify with [right-wing] elements on campus at all. White Afrikaans students subsequently wrote to me saying they're white, they're Afrikaans, and don't want to be associated with this kind of right-wing reaction. There were also parents who wrote saying this is not who they are, they don't want to be associated with [the right].

But was cross-racial solidarity sustainable given the weight of oppression felt by black students at institutions like UCT or UP? Was there clarity about the role of whites in an essentially black struggle? This controversy is not new to the history of struggle and protest among South African students – the most memorable comparison being the breakaway of the Black Consciousness–oriented South African Students Organisation (SASO) from the white liberal-dominated National Union of South African Students (NUSAS) in the 1960s.

In 2015–2016, student political organisations took shape, faded away, reasserted themselves, took front stage then back stage, broke old and formed new alliances. Emerging from this cauldron of competitive campus politics is a new set of actors who are more emphatically 'black conscious' in their orientation, openly violent, and boldly masculine in their approach. The numbers dwindled as moderate students, white and black, withdrew from this essentially black political arrangement and the focus of student politics gradually moved from a broad slate of issues (Rhodes and fees) to the more narrow agenda of free public education for all. The shift was especially disarming for white progressive students, who were left stranded and without a sense of how to participate in a resurgent black political moment on South African campuses.

The RMF struggle not only shed light on the class character of the movement leadership at a white liberal English university. It also pointed to the leadership's internal struggles as funded, middle-class students drove a movement on behalf of poor students. In this sense the UCT principal had put his finger on the student leaders' dilemma, as a journalist's interviews with the 2017 SRC candidates on that campus further revealed.[20] For example, Naledi, a second-year chemistry student from one of the more affluent northern suburbs of Cape Town, was asked, 'What are some of your issues in relation to the issues around fees?' Her response was enlightening:

Well, I am funded. I fall into part of this so-called missing middle. But this fight is not so much about me as to how accessible this place [UCT] is to my other family members and peers. I am one of the better-off family members and peers and I still am not able to afford this place.[21]

The reference to 'this place' as opposed to 'my university' or 'our university' is itself revealing as the student places an emotional distance between herself and UCT. It displays her sense of not owning the place, of not belonging, of speaking of this home for three or four years as being at a distance ('this place'). And as the UCT vice-chancellor indicated, such feelings may be linked to a sense of responsibility, for some born of conscience or guilt, around how that student could study in 'this place' of such obvious privilege while knowing that family and friends would struggle to do the same.

Sinawo, a sociology student from the Eastern Cape, responded to these questions with a similar degree of self-consciousness:

To distance myself from the realities of black people who are less fortunate than I am would be to assume that I am better and deserve to be in this position. For me it is not a question of I want to study [and] get my degree because I can afford it. The question for me is, why are certain people kept away from getting an education? Everywhere you go in the world there is a stigma associated with blackness. There is a certain structuralised and institutionalised approach as to how to treat black people, as to how they exist or don't exist.[22]

This reflection makes clear that for this student issues of inequality and injustice are not confined to the university to which she was admitted. 'Everywhere you go' is a statement about the broader society, and the reference to those who are 'kept away' from education is an indictment of the dysfunctional school system that fails the huge percentage (more than half) of students who start Grade 1 but do not reach Grade 12. But more than ever before, the depository for these intense feelings of anger, alienation, and rebuke is the university space. At UCT, the rage about what is wrong with society is visited with a fury on the university itself, encouraged by student leaders of relative privilege who enjoy scholarship funding. More pointedly, the charge sheet of social inequality and injustice is being delivered to the door of the vice-chancellor. When analysts like Adam Habib therefore make the standard Marxian claim about 'the revolution' on campuses headed by the middle classes, they are referring to these students at UCT, not the student leaders at the traditional black universities.

What also emerges from the RMF period at UCT and its surrounding environment, where white and coloured people represent the dominant 'demographic', is how black African students coming into this environment *discover* their blackness. As Max Price describes it, many of UCT's black students, most with middle- and working-class profiles, come to this university from environments in which they numerically and culturally dominate their living spaces and often their learning spaces. Inside the heaviness of UCT's expressly white English culture, these students come to feel that they are different and fall back on an elementary defence: their black identity. That gives them emotional and psychological security inside unfamiliar surroundings, and this largely explains the rebirth of the language of Black Consciousness on the former white campuses, while it would, of course, be somewhat out of place at the universities of Fort Hare, Venda, or Zululand.

Yet this understandable response – the aggregation of black African identities with an incipient Black Consciousness in an overwhelmingly white campus and city – is not without its problems. To begin with, some black African students hold the expectation that they must dominate the demographics in every context everywhere. This presumption links to the 'logic' of the hateful remark by former presidential adviser Jimmy Manyi that coloured people are 'over-represented' in the Western Cape.[23] Unscrupulous politicians with their eye on the Western Cape play this race card in every round of national and provincial elections. Following suit, rather than appreciating the diversity of the country and accepting that ethnic dominance is a dangerous playing field in a historically divided country, the new student politics is asserting an exclusive and aggressive language of black domination.

In other words, it is important to distinguish two things. First, there is the valid claim that the culture of whiteness, the under-representation of black professors, and the racially skewed institutional symbolism need to be urgently transformed. Second, there is a subtle, more pernicious, and indeed racist set of arguments that white domination should be replaced with black domination. Time and again I have seen black African students take such narrowly racial positions in instances where I countered decisions to appoint coloured or Indian professors simply on the basis of how apartheid classified them, or opposed the refusal to offer a position to an outstanding white professor, with excellent struggle credentials, simply because that person was white.

Then there is the added frustration of black students who attended middle-class white schools as minorities but in those circumstances could not express emotions of social, cultural, or even intellectual marginalisation. Research by one of my doctoral students on black families whose children are a minority in white-dominant schools of Roodepoort on the West Rand reveals how the new but fragile black middle class subdues and contains their grievances for the sake of not disrupting the education of their children.[24] The alternative would be dysfunctional township schools and so the trade-off becomes good-quality school education at the expense of social and cultural recognition.

Even at schools, though, there comes a breaking point, as happened first at Pretoria High School for Girls in 2016, and then at other former white schools such as Sans Souci in Cape Town, where the regulations and alleged racism concerning black hair led to sustained and intensive protests.[25] But many other black students carry a similar grudge until they reach the one place in which there is community among growing numbers of black middle-class students: the liberal and former white universities such as UCT and Rhodes. Here is Eve Fairbank's 'paradox of integration': as more and more students are included on former white campuses, they become more and more expressive about their degrees of exclusion.[26] This continuity of subjective experience from former white school to former white university is powerfully described in Malaika wa Azania's disturbing book *Memoirs of a Born Free*.[27]

Yet the feelings and experiences of this group of disaffected black youth are not the whole story. Most black students make the transition from former white integrated schools to former white integrated universities without the anger and unease of their campus counterparts. They live and learn together with other white or non-African students without excessive stress or strain. Many form intimate interracial partnerships of varying duration, and most attend the same churches, clubs, and community events. They sleep over at each other's homes and many become lifelong friends.[28]

These students are confident in their own skins and have learnt the skills of intercultural living much more easily than the alienated or angry students who attend former white universities. They also get far less media or scholarly attention than those disassociated from positive race relationships. My forthcoming book *Making Love in a War Zone* (Bookstorm, 2017) begins to explore what makes intimate interracial relationships possible within divided campuses and communities, and the reprisal costs for those who cross boundaries in conscious or unconscious ways. Yet much more research is needed on these intercultural students. Where do they come from? Who are their parents? Why are they not angry? What were their school experiences? Does class status matter to them in race relations? How do they negotiate cross-border relationships in divided communities? What attracts them to friendly or even intimate interracial relationships? At this stage we simply do not know enough about who these students are and what makes them so different from those who lead angry protests and retreat into black enclaves on former white campuses.

Nonetheless, what the UCT vice-chancellor's observations do reveal is a critical experience of black students who come from all-black schools and communities or even from racially integrated schools. They *become* black. Or better still, they become aware of their blackness for the first time. How does this actually happen? To begin with, the presence and power of whiteness overwhelms black students – and staff – coming onto a campus like UCT. They confront a full constellation of organisational arrangements, from the mostly white professoriate, to the collection of predominantly European artworks, to the names of buildings such as the prominent Jameson Hall, to the ways in which people speak English. One after another report on 'institutional culture' at UCT has examined this matter in the past.[29]

But it is also true that there are a growing number of middle-class black students experiencing cultural dislocation despite their expectation of some continuity of experience from community to campus. When students talk about 'not feeling at home', they are referring to their sense of not being part of a place, which engenders emotions such as alienation. But on a campus like UCT they are among other (albeit poorer) students who share this sense of marginalisation, and they are in a space which allows for the expression of those feelings of alienation. And when the opportunity arises, they speak in anger and do things that assert not only presence in but also ownership of 'this place' with which they enjoy such an ambivalent relationship. They are proud to be part of a world-class university, but also conscious of the need to project an emotional separateness from it. This experience stretches to all the former white campuses, although in different ways and to different degrees.

I recall a moment in 2016 when the SRC leader from UP was about to share a speaking platform with me at the invitation of a major funder of South African student bursaries. I had not met this young man before, but he came over to greet me by name, which was when I noticed that he was from UP. 'Ah,' I teased the young man, 'you are from Tukkies. I was dean there some time ago.' He responded angrily: 'I am *not* from Tukkies; I am from the University of Pretoria.' Here was a young man proudly dressed in the traditional uniform of student leaders from the century-old white university, but to him the affectionate mention of 'Tukkies' implied an emotional bond with the institution's Afrikaans values and founding history, sentiments he certainly did not embrace. I understood his reaction since that feeling was already present among non-white, non-Afrikaans students during my time as dean. 'Attending but not belonging' was a choice consciously made not only by black students but by some English-speaking white students as well.

This position of insecurity and alienation is not without its critics from black quarters. Why would black students, who are growing in number and influence, dominating the political control of student representation, and living in a democracy run by a black government, respond from what appears to be a position of weakness? Why, ask some, does this come across as a black inferiority complex? Why complain when you can simply make demands for greater inclusion, recognition, and change? Why the collapse into a kind of psychological paralysis expressed in the imitative language of American *minorities*, such as 'I can't breathe' or 'my black pain'? It is your university: simply claim it rather than pass through the place with bended back. You are free, even if you do not realise it.

In essence this is the position put forward in a widely circulated publication by former UCT SRC president Gwen Ngwenya, who takes issue with 'the dishonesty of identitarian politics' and 'fragile collective identities'. She advanced a particularly memorable line of argument when she referred to the media firestorm that resulted when a white real estate agent insulted black holidaymakers by calling them baboons for littering public beaches:

Are our identities so fragile? Does a comment by an obscure woman with no public standing put so much at stake? The sad answer to both questions is yes because what South Africa witnessed was not the surprising discovery that there are people who make insensitive analogies or who are at worst racist. We all know that. What we witnessed was the irrationality and destructive power of two fragile identities: the collective black identity that was attacked so must fight in order to save itself, and a white identity fighting defensively in order to shore goodwill with the black identity.[30]

Ngwenya argues from the position of a libertarian, one who believes strongly in the recognition of the individual rather than the compressing of all black identity into an indistinguishable collective that does not allow for the expression of ideas, beliefs, and actions outside of this majoritarian world view. Yet a Black Consciousness adherent in the 1970s might have asked the same question – are our identities so fragile? – but in response would have asserted black independence and that 'black is beautiful', rather than submit to a position of vulnerability and complaint about non-inclusion in a white minority culture.

This same theme is taken up a former vice-chancellor of UCT, the erudite Njabulo Ndebele, who queries this victim posture of the Fallists by stating: 'Against this context "black pain" in its current manifestations comes across to me more as an attribute of victimhood than of agency.'[31] From the Black Consciousness viewpoint, black well-being is not dependent on white action – even under apartheid, where 'despite the overt power of the racially oppressive system, there was something within me beyond its reach'.[32] So this black craving for white recognition is something quite strange to those who lived through the Black Consciousness movement that swept across South Africa in the 1970s. Speaking in more contemporary terms, the Wits scholar Achille Mbembe questions the self-absorption of these mainly middle-class protestors:

Why are we so invested in turning whiteness, pain and suffering into such erotogenic objects? Could it be that the concentration of our libido on whiteness, pain and suffering is after all typical of the narcissistic investments so privileged by this neoliberal age?[33]

Other critics of RMF argue that the purpose of university is not to offer students adjustment and settlement within university life but to socially and intellectually disrupt their knowledge and security of place. A university is, after all, a place of exploration and growth – hence of turmoil and dislocation – rather than a place in which to feel 'at home' and fully accommodated. Nothing a university does can, or should, make students feel 'complete' in its response to their demands, argues the Cameroonian anthropologist and UCT professor, Francis Nyamnjoh:

> Those who want to bring down the statue, like Cecil Rhode [*sic*] before them, believed that they can become complete. It is a costly illusion. Once you recognise that completeness is not possible, you can start allowing for what it means to interact as an incomplete person with incomplete others. This is not possible if the logic is that of conquest or the 'winner takes it all'. We need real conversations with humility.[34]

Nevertheless, the emotional disposition of many protesting students is one that longs for fulfilment within former white universities – the satisfaction of basic needs such as identity, security, and stimulation, as Lionel Thaver described in his sociological essay on being 'at home' in university environments.[35] Strikingly, this disposition is not at all limited to South Africa. In US universities too there has arisen a 'hurt at home'[36] posture, where 'individuals and groups display high sensitivity to slight ... and seek to cultivate an image of being victims who deserve assistance'.[37]

Language as symbol

What most analysts failed to see was the connection between the RMF protests and the language policy debates at another set of white universities, the historically Afrikaans institutions. If the statue of Rhodes symbolised racial exclusion, white privilege, and marginalisation at the English universities, the constitutional provisions and institutional statutes protecting Afrikaans as a language of instruction performed exactly the same function as far as black students were concerned at places of higher learning such as UP, UFS, and SU.

Afrikaans was a difficult symbolism, for while the Rhodes statue had few supporters in the white English universities, Afrikaans had an organised constituency of language-rights fighters both inside and outside these century-old Afrikaner institutions. Whereas Rhodes could be taken down from his perch by a mere council decision – and a wary nod from heritage organisations – removing Afrikaans as a language of instruction would inevitably become a matter settled in the highest courts of the land.

Why did Afrikaans become such a contested symbol for black students? Was this not also the language of black Afrikaans speakers, particularly those within the coloured population who, like white Afrikaans speakers, often lacked fluency in English? Was Afrikaans not the language of the poor, not just historically, but even now in the vineyards of the rural Western Cape and on the factory floors of Cape Town? Moreover, didn't the South African Constitution recognise Afrikaans as an official language, one in which people have the right to be educated? For the CPUT vice-chancellor, the clamour for the removal of Afrikaans by black activists was perpetuating an injustice against native coloured speakers of the language.

Prins Nevhutalu: Where we have not agreed with the protesting students is on the issue of Afrikaans on the CPUT Wellington campus. It is still an issue I have defended, not for the Afrikaners, but for the very large coloured majority in the Western Cape who do not speak English, who speak Afrikaans. And there's no way that we can run away from that. Mandela was very, very clear: we must guard against one group dominating another group. And so I've been a very fierce defender of Afrikaans at Wellington because we're servicing the coloured community. The majority of students there are coloured people, and obviously there are white students as well. So Afrikaans is still on the table. I have argued my position that even the ANC acknowledges that you have to accept indigenous languages, and Afrikaans, whether we like it or not, is an indigenous language. I don't like Afrikaans per se, but I cannot argue for decolonisation in the Queen's language.

There's such contradictions, people are laughing at us. I've got some guys from Nigeria whom we work with; they say, 'Hey, you South Africans surprise us. You want to decolonise the mind and yet you're using the Queen's language.' We could have had people speaking in Zulu, for example. It's not happening. So there is a lot of confusion.

But I have fiercely defended Afrikaans programmes. I took a whole day to go and talk to SASCO, tried to tell them why these programmes are important. Not for Afrikaans' sake, but for this country and for the ANC that cares about everybody, not only about black Africans. We must also care for coloured people ... Their mother tongue is Afrikaans. Will I win the war, this struggle? I don't think so.

That struggle would not be won, for Afrikaans was not simply a language of instruction; it was a symbol of exclusion.

Meanwhile, at former white Afrikaans universities, black student discontent about Afrikaans had been brewing for a long time just below the surface of the transformation debates. In one sense the concerns were very practical, if largely anecdotal. Time and again stories would emerge about the educational advantage that accrued to whites in the parallel-medium classes that some of the Afrikaans-origin universities had established. Black students would sometimes sit in both language classes and witness how the discussion of 'the scope of the examination' would give students in the Afrikaans sessions much more information about what might appear in the exams than would be given to students in the English sessions. In some cases, white students would even be given the actual questions, claimed others. Over and over again complaints were made of systematic rather than accidental advantage given to white students, such as the projection slides being in Afrikaans and the lecturer then addressing the group in broken English. The English competence of many, not all, Afrikaans lecturers was itself a bone of contention.

It was therefore no surprise that when a white lecturer at UFS handed out the two examination papers – one in English and one in Afrikaans – a firestorm broke out among some black students since the Afrikaans version of the paper seemed to contain the answer code to one of the questions. But the evidence indicated that this appeared to be a genuine error. The lecturer, conceding the mistake, pointed out that the original paper was too long and so she shortened it, but an answer code related to a deleted question appeared on the final revised paper. The lecturer had forgotten to erase the code on the Afrikaans paper, although she had done so on the English paper.

At worst, this was an instance of administrative sloppiness, as was the case a week later when a black education lecturer mistakenly attached the memorandum of answers to the English exam paper, written largely by black students, but not to the Afrikaans paper. Some Afrikaans students rushed to the local newspaper to make the point about the equivalence of mistreatment. But it did not matter; a long history of complaints about disadvantage in the English classes made evidence and argument redundant among the hard-core activist students – led, ironically, by law students – who instantly labelled the young lecturer a racist.

When the protests broke out in 2015, UFS had already prepared for the council a proposal to make English the primary language of instruction at the university. A very productive student assembly made public submissions for transformation with eloquent arguments in relation to campus discontent, which included the use of Afrikaans. As the university management, we felt the case should be taken to the council, the highest decision-making body of the university. In fact, following the Higher Education Act, the only curricular decision over which a council has any authority is the matter of institutional language policy. To the surprise of many, both the senate (representing the professors) and the council (representing all stakeholders) overwhelmingly supported the proposal for an English-medium university. But it would take months before the language policy could be implemented, in part because of the preparatory time needed on both the instructional and administrative sides, and in part because we expected the decision to be challenged in the courts by right-wing conservative actors such as the pro-Afrikaans civil rights organisation AfriForum and the trade union Solidarity.

On the other side of the country, in the scenic winelands centre of Stellenbosch, the release of *Luister*, a student-made video, raised awareness of the damaging consequences of Afrikaans-language dominance in educational institutions. The video producers asked 30 students what it meant to be black at SU and its oversight institution, Elsenburg Agricultural College. Without rage or rancour, black students and one lecturer told a deeply moving and disturbing story about how Afrikaans actually functions to humiliate and harass non-Afrikaans speakers and to ensure their failure on the campus, in the classroom, and in the dance halls, food outlets, and bars of the surrounding community. What was intended as a low-budget video documentary turned out to be an exceptional and moving narrative insight into the social and cultural encounters of black non-Afrikaans speakers in an institution that had for too long tried to shield itself from them, particularly isiXhosa speakers from the Eastern and Western Cape. In the following excerpt from the *Luister* transcript, the interviewed students relate the story in their own words:

Male student 1: We've got a huge problem with Afrikaans, bra. That is the main problem in that institution and it's killing us.

Interviewer: Is it much harder for you?

Male student 1: It's very hard. It's very hard because on the time I was doing my first year, I never understand anything that I got in Afrikaans. I was just sitting in the class and look to the lecturer while he's speaking this language. Talk, talk until the end of the class. I bust on that institution because I was just studying my books only.

Female student 1: You get into your lecture hall and the lecturer will then say that the lecture today will be mostly in whatever language and the language that you don't understand, those people usually go and get the translation devices. So, you hand in your student card and you get your translation device and then as the lecturer goes on explaining you have this translator whispering in your ear.

Female student 2: So you listening to the lecturer and at the same time you also listening to the translators and you can't hear because the translator has to whisper because they can't speak to you loudly because we are in a lecture. So they whisper, whisper and you can't exactly hear and I think the lecturer's voice overrides the translator's voice. Also, with the translation devices, they very delayed and sometimes they use words, like, that aren't supposed to be . . . like, they don't have the correct jargon because they're not engineers. They've never studied engineering, they studied language. They learn on the job the engineering jargon so they don't know everything. Sometimes they'll just repeat the Afrikaans word that the lecturer said and then it's, like, but I'm here for English, you know. If you ask a question in English then he answers in Afrikaans or no, the best thing ever is when he forgets to speak Afrikaans and then he's speaking in English and everyone's fine with it. No one complains and then he's, like, oh guys, you need to remind me when to speak in Afrikaans. Like, it doesn't make sense. Like, no one complains.

Male student 2: And the question is why do we have to go the direction of translation in the first place? Why must I get second-hand information? Everybody knows what, we gonna have to wait now in class and when people switch, then I'm automatically, then I must go and run to the translation facilities.

Female student 1: So we stood up and we said that enough is enough. We need to say . . . we need to get rid of this policy and we need to have a more inclusive language policy.

Female student 3: And then we went to the Head and then he said he will instruct the lecturers to be in English. Then after that the Afrikaans students thought we were going against the race, of which we were not. We just wanted to hear the concept of the lecturing because at the end of the day we have to go back to our rooms, you have to study through everything so that you can understand.

Male student 3: I cannot after twenty-three years of freedom . . . be in a space where I'm fighting to simply, simply go to classes that I pay for like any other student. To go to class and understand what is being said in class and not have some whispering voice behind me that I can't even see, that, you know, even at times you get little snippets and you understand exactly what the lecturer has said and you know that the interpreter is wrong, that you know that if I raise my hand and say no, but what you said is wrong then you disrupt the entire class on its own.

Female student 3: So now they feel that we are attacking their Afrikaans, of which we are not. They can ask questions in Afrikaans, they can get notes in Afrikaans, as long as the lecturer will proceed and be in English so that everyone has the same understanding.

Male student 2: Conversation . . . this . . . Afrikaans just for conversation is something else. I like it by the way, I love Af . . . I've found that, really, when I go back home I brag with my Afrikaans. I don't have a problem. And I can socialise with ladies and whoever with the Afrikaans. But when you . . . I have to go to class and then I sit with a lecturer that speaks academic Afrikaans, I can't get that. I don't get it. I don't understand it. And those same lecturers, when we go outside and they can even say hey, but your Afrikaans is alright. When we are outside and just talking casually. But outside class and in class that's just . . . it doesn't work. I can't get a thing.

Female student 4: We compromise a lot because I for one at home don't speak English. I have to come back from school then back to isiXhosa all the time. And when I get to Elsenburg, I have to speak English then . . . it's Xhosa there with my friends.

Female student 5: Because we're not English speakers, we Xhosa, they're Afrikaans. They must also compromise so that we can understand each other in one language.

Female student 4: So I think compromising will make everyone happy.

Female lecturer: People feel excluded on the grounds of language and language, as we know, is never neutral.

Male student 3: It has been hard pressed, it has been enforced on us as black students especially that you just have to be docile. You're fortunate to be here and I absolutely hate that. My mother cannot be making the sacrifices that she's making for me to be treated as if, to be treated as though, you know, you should be thankful that you even here.

Male student 5: Well, there's this idea, right, when they talk about transformation in Stellenbosch. They're, like, *ja*, we actually have been working very hard, you know. Like we have translation devices to accommodate non-Afrikaans speaking students but, like, that's bullshit. Who gave you the power to accommodate me? To accommodate me you must have the power, right? You must own the thing that I come into, that, I mean, I am not supposed not to be there. So they say we're accommodating them into an Afrikaans university. That's nonsense. There's no such thing as an Afrikaans university. They claim we must be accommodated by the Constitution so that we can have our language and culture but at the same time they are so powerful that they even accommodating the majority. You can't . . . have it both ways but it happens every day here. And the worst part is even black people, like, accept that thing that no, actually they're accommodating us. I'm, like, but you shouldn't even be using that term. You can't be accommodated. Not here. Sure, if you are in France, but not here.

Male student 6: Every time I wake up, I feel like I'm an outsider. I don't belong here. I once went to the toilet . . . to pee and came out of the toilet and this guy was gonna use the same toilet, there are two toilets on our floors, he switched. He went to another toilet just because I came there. And I feel sad that there's ... my friend is not there. I feel sad because he's the one who really face it. He was called names, he was called a kaffer last year.

Whereas UFS used the parallel-medium model separating English and Afrikaans classes, SU used a dual-medium policy in which both languages were taught in the same classroom using a mixture of techniques. These included *fluistertaal* (whispering), where other students translated into the ears of those attending the lecture, and alternating between English lectures, Afrikaans slide projections, and subject notes. The whispering technique, enthusiastically championed by a former vice-chancellor at the institution once called Potchefstroom University for Christian Higher Education, was pedagogically flawed and courted political disaster. Yet *fluistertaal* remained popular in white conservative circles because, as *Luister* showed, it perpetuated the dominance of Afrikaans in the education of students.

More importantly, *Luister* demonstrated how intertwined Afrikaans was not only with instructional modalities in the lecture halls but also with everyday social discourse and cultural interactions. It remains deeply associated with the casual violence, racism, and contempt against black people in a part of the country – the rather isolated Stellenbosch area – where black African students, unlike many (not all) coloured students from the area, are not Afrikaans *magtig* (competent). And this is the main reason why, sadly enough for many, Afrikaans will not endure as a language of instruction in any South African public university. Its powerful political symbolism through association with the apartheid past weighs far too heavily in the inherited memories of black students. But for now, its prominent position in some universities casts a long shadow over the daily lives of non-Afrikaans campus citizens.

Like the statue of Cecil John Rhodes.

Chapter 4

The Unfulfilled Promise

---

*Our parents were made promises in 1994. We're
just here for the refund.*
– Text from a student protestor's poster

Strini Moodley was one of the heroes of my youth. A co-founder of the
Black Consciousness Movement, alongside the legendary activist and
intellectual Steve Biko, Moodley captured the mood of my generation
when we were channelled as so-called coloured students towards our
very own ethnic institution, the University of the Western Cape
(UWC). Moodley was confined to a university for Indians, while the
various 'tribal groups', who became 'ethnic groups', were handed their
own institutional destinies – the University of Zululand for the Zulus,
the University of the Transkei for the Xhosas, and so on. Moodley and
Biko saw right through these divide-and-rule tactics of the apartheid
regime. They coined the terms 'Black', to refer to all the oppressed
(Indian, African, coloured), and 'Black Consciousness', inspired by similar movements in North America, to express both unity and an assertive
pride in black identity.

And so the invitation from the Umtapo Centre to deliver the tenth
Strini Moodley Annual Memorial Lecture in May 2016 at the
University of KwaZulu-Natal was a tremendous honour for me. I spoke
about the late Moodley's contribution to political thought and his
unique experience of having pursued learning on two islands, Salisbury
Island[1] and Robben Island, where he played the pondering game of
chess with Nelson Mandela. And I spent some time talking about the
various kinds of violence enveloping South African campuses at the time
and the long-term consequences for the future of the post-apartheid
university.

From what I could tell, the lecture was well received – until the question period started. First up was Andile Mngxitama, the ex-Economic Freedom Fighters (EFF) activist and now leader of Black First Land First (BFLF), in what appeared to be an orchestrated move with about four other black activists. He began by delivering a personal insult (reported by the media), then dismissed the lecture out of hand, making it clear that he was not going to respond directly to the speaker. In response to my thesis on violence, all Mngxitama wanted to say was that 'we are going to burn down all the university buildings in this country ... as [Frantz] Fanon said'. There were gasps of shock from the audience, and then the other men in his team made similar statements of dismissal and revolutionary intent. When this protest performance was over, the rest of the questions returned to the lecture content and I enjoyed an interesting exchange with the audience. By the end of the session, the audience itself had smacked down the BFLF leader and his angry accomplices, making it clear that his views were dangerous and that he did not represent the politics of Strini Moodley. That part the media did not report.

The rediscovery of Fanon

It is easy as a youthful activist to find inspiration in the poetic words of the Martinician psychiatrist and freedom fighter Frantz Omar Fanon (1925–1961). Which idealistic activist would not be moved by his inspiring challenge that 'every generation must, out of relative obscurity, discover its mission, fulfil it, or betray it'?[2] And in a South African student protest movement bereft of signature literature or heroes in the present, it mattered little that such fighting words from an anti-colonial struggle were being transposed to the letter into the context of a constitutional democracy – even when it came to the uses of violence.

South African Fanonists scrambled to explain that the author of *Black Skin, White Masks* and *The Wretched of the Earth* was in fact not a proponent of violence, that Fanon was being 'misread', and that 'it is his commitment to reason ... and not violence that lies at the heart of his thought'.[3] But it was too late; his words were taken as read. Excerpts from his work were ripped from context and used to justify violent protest action: for example, 'The colonised man finds his freedom in and through violence' and 'Decolonisation is always a violent phenomenon'.

And then this: 'At the individual level, violence is a cleansing force. It rids the colonized of their inferiority complex, of their passive and despairing attitude. It emboldens them, and restores their self-confidence.'[4]

Shortly after Mngxitama delivered his threat at the lecture hall, one building after another started to burn on campuses from Cape Town to Johannesburg and from Mafikeng to Durban and Pietermaritzburg. And nothing prepared the vice-chancellors for these flames of fury as the costs of damage crept upwards towards R1 billion. Televised images of burning offices, classrooms, libraries, and residences were played over and over again as leaping flames signalled a completely new phase in the protest movement – one that was intentionally destructive and violent.

The protest experience from the vice-chancellors' viewpoint

It is not in the vice-chancellor's job description, but one of the routine tasks of a university principal in South Africa is to receive 'memoranda of demands' from protestors. The process starts with a small group of students meeting in a designated area. The students start to sing, in part to give themselves confidence, in part to attract a crowd, and in part to intimidate those who are the targets of the memorandum. The songs are nearly always sung in an African language. They may be rich and inspiring struggle songs from the past. Sometimes they are newly created or adapted for the purpose of insulting an unwitting enemy – whether a mining boss or a politician or a vice-chancellor – in a language the target might not understand.

Gathering around the growing number of protestors are the onlookers and the hangers-on, happy to join in the march out of a combination of boredom and curiosity. In the case of a well-organised march, the media would have been pre-alerted, although in the age of cellphones and instant-messaging systems this is not strictly necessary. Images of the protest are taken, posted on social media, and rushed off to media houses. The crowd moves from some central gathering place and then approaches the administration building, where the senior leadership team of the university does its work. If the initial crowd is too small, as is often the case, other students are cajoled to join in, sometimes by being threatened or physically pulled out of classes.

Vice-chancellors used to be alerted about protests in advance, as there are legal protocols requiring official permission to march so that adequate security can be in place to protect the protestors as much as the non-protesting students and staff. Now students simply march when they wish to and show up at the admin building's main entrance to deliver the memorandum of demands. After some more singing and toyi-toyiing on the spot, including the shouting of derisive comments at management, a speech is made by one of the protest leaders. Then the memorandum is handed over to the senior manager, who is asked to respond briefly and to sign the memo to indicate that it has been delivered. The most important thing you learn as a university leader in such a spot is that however deeply you are insulted, and whatever lies the speech maker delivers (and there are likely to be many), you do not respond. Things could turn ugly very quickly.

The manager accepts his copy of the memo and retreats back into the administration building, with the crowd singing in celebration for having delivered an ultimatum for management's response. Then the group disperses. From a vice-chancellor's perspective, that is how a 'good march' proceeds. But that kind of peaceful proceeding is rare these days on a South African university campus. More often than before, protest actions turn violent, as was certainly the case by the start of the second year of protests in 2016. In that sort of scenario, vice-chancellors and their teams scramble.

Student struggle and the national narrative

Why did the relatively peaceful protest movement of 2015 turn so violent by 2016? The vice-chancellors have much to offer on this question.

Lourens van Staden: This whole situation is very deep-rooted in the sense that there's a lot of dissatisfaction since 1994. There was a lot of excitement [then] and now a lot of anger. When I mix with students here, and also when I was administrator at Walter Sisulu University, there's a deep dissatisfaction and people are angry, if I can put it in those terms.

During the 2015 protests, which also took place at this university [TUT], I saw that the protests at the traditional universities such as UP,

UCT, and Rhodes were more intense than here. So it is deep-rooted in my view, going back to the expectations created after 1994. Before [the first democratic] elections there were all these promises, empty promises.

Inside the Union Buildings with President Zuma in October 2015, the students indicated to him the problem of wasteful expenditure in the country. Look at South African Airways, SABC, Denel, and the money wasted [on these state-owned enterprises], which could have been used for education. In these conversations with the president, the students made a lot of sense to me, and that is actually the day that I really started to understand where it comes from. I'm not a psychologist, but the psyche of this dissatisfaction is underestimated from government's side.

Adam Habib: I think that firstly the protests would never have happened had we not reached in the society a level of polarisation. I think that there is a political polarisation in the society largely born out of two things: the growth of inequality in the society and the polarisation that that engenders, and then, of course, the anger that flows out of corruption, the failures of the state to deliver, all of those kinds of things. And in a sense, some of that [anger is] seeping across institutional boundaries to create a fairly unhappy middle class, sometimes student based.

We now have a group of students, largely post-1994 youth, coming into historically white institutions in large numbers. At one level, they were given the promise of freedom. At another level, in existential terms, that promise is denied to them in who's teaching them, in what they're seeing in the cultural symbols that they are located in, and all of those kinds of things. And in a sense they think 1994 did not deliver on that promise in existential terms.

Tyrone Pretorius: I pick up that a significant part of that [protest] grouping is students who are so disgruntled with what's happening in our country as a whole, and obviously these are youngsters who are not steeped in the traditions of the ANC. So they in a sense are expressing anger about what's happening in our country.

Ihron Rensburg: There are two issues perhaps worth noting or considering: the promise of the new democracy, and the ideals expressed in the Constitution. That Constitution holds out not only political democracy but also economic democracy or socio-economic rights as a precondition for the consolidation and transformation of the new nation.

It seems to me that there is a gap between the promise and the reality, and I think that nowhere is the gap more significant than in public school education, with our inability as a nation-state to make leaps forward in terms of quality.

So in a decade we've made considerable progress, but it's really on the quality front that we're struggling and that I think is where we're simply failing our nation. And [students experience] this gap between the promise and the reality, such as in their horrible experience of schooling, which includes many dropping out.

It seems to me that this negative experience of schooling is a major contributor to pushing young people out of the school system. While we are able to retain as many as 80 per cent up to Grade 9, we lose the next 30 per cent of children between Grade 10 and Grade 12. What happens is we have annual cycles of outflows of young people who leave school with less than a high-school-leaving certificate or one that enables them to get into a degree or diploma programme. Between the ages of 16 and 19, we see this massive dropout, and annually we add to that number of young people who have left, who are not in school, not in college, not in university, not in any form of training, and are unemployed. When you have that number of drop-outs, somewhere between 3 and 3,5 million young people, you sit with really a catastrophic outlook. So there is this mismatch, then, between the promise of democracy and the experience of democracy, and this annual escalation in the numbers of those who have little hope and for whom social and economic opportunity is simply not there.

Sizwe Mabizela: Some of them [students at university] had very difficult experiences at school in terms of racial interaction. Remember, these are young people who have grown up with the Constitution promising them that they would be treated in certain ways. And they have endured some form of discrimination at school level. Then they come to university as 17- and 18-year-olds, and they find they can now assert themselves. They can express themselves, and there is this frustration they experience between what the Constitution promises them and the way that they experience the university, particularly white universities. We still have remnants of discrimination and racism and the like, and so the gap between what is promised by the Constitution and what is actually experienced creates frustration.

What is happening in our higher education system reflects what is happening in our society more broadly. There is a sense of disenchantment, a sense of discontent with what is happening. People are frustrated. They say that 22 years after the advent of democracy there has really been very little change, there is corruption, and people are frustrated. It does not help that the governing party itself is in a state of chaos. So the protests reflect what is happening in this country.

Ahmed Bawa: There is now a very deep-seated kind of anger, which means that we were not simply responding to some ordinary student [protest] action. There was something else going on, something which was extremely deep-seated. And I began to wonder what it is that can galvanise a group of five or ten students to say, 'Well, actually, you know what? Let's attack the buses.'

I've thought quite hard about it. I don't agree with the simple explanation that this is student mobilisation to win a struggle; I don't think it's that simple. I think there's a deep, deep resentment about what's happened in the ANC. Well, actually I should say in the ruling elites, and this was really seen as an opportunity to strike at the heart of the ANC. I think the universities largely got caught in the crossfire.

The university principals make the critical observation that the roots of the campus crises lie outside the university, and that this was expressed in a general feeling among students that the government had failed to deliver on the promises of the liberation struggle and on the values of the Constitution. The students did not *feel* the benefits of democracy, equality, and dignity in their daily lives. Further, they endured continuous experiences of struggle from home to school and community to campus, and it affected them deeply. Their lives were a constant struggle just to survive economically, to be recognised culturally, and to be respected racially. They had had enough, and they were now very, very angry.

But this anger is not irrational. It is lodged in a narrative, widely held among protesting students, in which the very terms of the transition from apartheid and the creators of the new nation were mercilessly attacked.

> **Max Price:** UCT's RMF students were linking up with the national narrative which says that the settlement, the negotiation at CODESA [Convention for a Democratic South Africa] was a sell-out. Mandela sold us out; the TRC [Truth and Reconciliation Commission] was a whitewash; whites have never paid for what they did; the economy is in the hands of white capital. And all of that is because the only real way that you can get change is through a violent revolution, according to Fanon, and we haven't had our violent revolution yet and so actually what we need is that. And any vehicle that can be used for achieving the revolution is useful.

Protest violence and the issue of security

To understand how the 'rainbow narrative' – encapsulating South Africa's multiculturalism and peaceful coming together to form the new democracy – could be rejected and replaced by such a violent narative, it is important to understand that for the more radical student protestors at the heart of this new insurgency, the counter-narrative has a much deeper set of causes which the university, as part of the system, seeks to suppress. The UJ vice-chancellor puts it this way:

> **Ihron Rensburg:** And this is where the narrative comes from which says that the university is part of the reproduction of capitalism in South Africa – and in particular, brutal apartheid capitalism. And because you [university management] are using violence through your protection services, you are using violence combined with state violence to keep that reproduction going. So the public order policing and the tactical response team are organs of violence used by you to

protect your project, which is the reproduction of capital, and therefore it is our [the students'] duty and our responsibility to use our own violence.

This counter-narrative thus sets the tone for the justification of violence – namely, a rational retaliatory response to the provocation of *institutional violence* as it operates to protect the role of the university in the reproduction of capitalism and capitalist relations. And this counter-violence would, at times, make a distinction between its targets.

> Tyrone Pretorius: Here at UWC our violence somehow was driven by – and they [the protestors] kept on saying this to me – the argument that 'it's just buildings; that's our violence'. And they would often say to me, 'You can replace buildings. Why are you calling the police to beat us up? You can't replace human beings but you can replace buildings.'
>
> And so right from the beginning we brought in security only after we could not manage the situation with our own campus security, and the protestors claim that that is the reason for the violence. And after their meeting in the student centre they attacked those buildings so viciously. I don't know if you came up through the ground floor, they basically destroyed that, all of that, that whole section. We've got them on video and they claim they were provoked by security. But we said, 'Where's the security?' It was a Friday afternoon. There's not a security person in sight on the video cameras. So it was senseless in a way, but it was also making the statement that 'it's just buildings, burn it down, you can replace it'.

The protestors' argument thus turned against security not only as part of a violent system but because, they claimed, the very behaviour of the security personnel provoked students into violence. But what the university leaders saw left them exasperated with the students' line of reasoning. The account from the vice-chancellors' perspective runs like this: the students would march; the march would turn violent, with attacks on property, threats to staff, and disruptions of classes; the management would then bring on additional security or call in the police to

86

protect lives and property; and the students would then claim that it was the security and police that caused the violence in the first place. This claim was illogical and untrue, but it was the narrative reported on every campus to the outside world.

> **Max Price:** There are still groups that answer that 'it's the violence of the system' or 'it's the violence of exclusion' and that 'there are different kinds of violence and therefore management has no grounds to defend the use of private security'. I can't make the argument on their behalf because it's just so illogical to me that I can't see it, but they still think that we shouldn't have private security. And they sort of default to other sorts of things: that the security staff are ex-militias, that these are apartheid policemen who now have a new life, or that the security guards are male and that they catcall women. And all sorts of things.
>
> These are guys who get their adrenalin from beating people up, so I have no illusions about these private security people being master mediators or negotiators. They're not that, and it's unpleasant that we have to use them and they're intimidating and they make you feel scared. But no one gives me any decent answer to the question, 'If someone's safety is at risk, what must we do?'
>
> The main answer to that question is that we must call the police, so there's been a shift from arguing against the police to arguing against private security. I have argued in favour of private security because I've made the case that we have control over the private security but we don't have control over the police. The argument in favour of the police – and this is made by one of our students, he's written a *Daily Maverick* article on this[5] – is that having private security confuses where this line of conflict is between us and the state, and it should be clear that our fight is with the state and the state funding of higher education, and the police represent that. And that's why we should not have private security.

The question of whether there should be security on campuses is a point of great contention among academic staff, especially at the English liberal universities. Some staff made the argument not about 'security as part of the system' but about the ideals of an open university, which are threatened by the very notion of a securitised campus. Such a line of argument resonated with the uncertainty of the vice-chancellors of these universities; they too felt, at an existential level, a sense of ambivalence about how to act in the face of imminent threats to life and limb, and to public property.

Max Price: We did not have violence initially, but what we did have was barricades and disruption. So we had a situation where people could not work because they were prevented from going into classes or to their offices. And we brought in the police [19–20 October 2015]; we got interdicts the first day that happened and brought on the police to implement the interdict. And I do not know if we could have done that differently – but the staff and the students reacted horribly to that in ways that we completely underestimated. We just got it completely wrong.

I've reflected on that a lot, and on our campus I think the police presence was a complete shock to staff. We've not had any police on campus for 25 years, since about 1991. And police are so strongly associated with the apartheid period and being against protestors that it was almost an article of faith that police would never be allowed on campus. For management to call the police onto campus was therefore a betrayal of the values of the university. We had staff marching down to Bremner [Building] and we had petitions saying, in effect, how could you do this?

I still do not know if we could have done it differently. We had to call the police to clear an occupation, to remove barricades, and to protect the right of people to attend classes. There was actually an exam for 350 accountancy students who were meant to write. They were prevented from getting into the exam hall. I thought that was completely outrageous. We called the police, but they would not come onto campus unless I got an interdict. We did not have private security then, so we got an interdict to stop people from preventing others from writing exams, then called the police to clear the barricades and to allow people to come back, because we had already postponed the exam for a day.

That triggered this massive reaction, and what's clear to me is that there was a relatively small group of people who were willing to support the fees protest. It was the first day of the protest, it was a Monday, no one even knew about the protest before the Monday, but on the Monday there were barricades on campus, people couldn't get in. I think it was a small group, I think most people were outraged by the barricades, but the police coming onto campus changed that and we all of a sudden had massive support for the student protest and opposition to the management. So I have to say in retrospect that was a bad call, and what we should have done I'm not sure, but our action resulted in that escalation. And having done that, we ended up with a shutdown because no one was willing to support the fact that we had police on campus.[6]

This ambivalence towards the presence of security and police in the liberal mind goes to the heart of what an open university is in the historically liberal Cape,[7] and is not felt with the same levels of anxiety at the historically black or the traditional Afrikaans institutions, where openness in the culture of these campuses was never ingrained in their founding missions or operating ideologies. Instead they were, more than the liberal universities, direct offspring of the apartheid state with security built into their institutional DNA as a defence against perilous ideas from the outside such as the *rooi gevaar* (the communist threat), *swart gevaar* (the black threat), and the *Roomse gevaar* (the Catholic threat).[8] Securing the campuses at these institutions would therefore not provoke the kind of existential angst felt at UCT.

Cheryl de la Rey, the UP vice-chancellor, had spent several years as a student and a senior leader inside the 'open university' culture of UCT, and would regard this capitulation to security management as a compromise on principle.

Cheryl de la Rey: We now have security we didn't have previously, and I deeply regret that because I think universities by definition should be open spaces. But we found ourselves in a situation – or at least I found myself in a situation where, having seen what had happened at other campuses, I had no choice. I had to protect people and property. And I was particularly disturbed by the burning of artwork [at UCT].

Where is the rule of law?

In the main, however, the vice-chancellors saw these cries by the students to do away with security as nothing more than an attempt to declare open season on the facilities of their fragile institutions and perhaps even burn them to the ground. They viewed the arguments about the pain of symbolic violence and the necessity for retaliatory violence as opportunistic mind games. What the more militant students wanted was for the barriers in the way of an assault on public property to fall. In this sense, the rules of the game had changed, as the vice-chancellor of Nelson Mandela Metropolitan University (NMMU) explains.

Derrick Swartz: I think what we faced was a breakdown of the conventions through which we used to contest politics in higher education until now. The culture of dissent and contestation. We were shaken. I mean all of us, for up until then we had made assumptions about the rules of engagement. And we all had boycotts and strikes.

I started in 1999 and I had quite tough struggles at the University of Fort Hare in the early days. And although it was trying, and it sapped you for a long period, generally all the contestants sort of stuck within the rules of the game and the institutional order that the university's statute [rules and regulations] had created. The rules were clear until now: council was independent of senate; the integrity of faculty to make decisions on academic accreditation and examinations was not questioned; whatever judgements academics typically make within their zones of autonomy were accepted; and all of this implied the buy-in of students into that social contract. Our understanding of student governance through the SRC was reasonably stable and the order was accepted – at least in terms of its anatomical features, its make-up, so to speak. I didn't hear many voices questioning the very fundamental make-up of that system.

But from October [2015] the consensus around that system's make-up, its *raison d'être*, as well as the culture of dissent and the rules of engagement was profoundly shaken in a manner that I had not seen before. And it made me think of that point in history where you reach a kind of a pre-revolutionary moment, where everything is questioned. Not just the inner workings of something, but the entire order in which that is wrapped. It did not result in a revolutionary over-turning of that order, but I thought of 1968 in Western Europe, with the Paris [student] uprisings. I was thinking about the movement before 1994 that had collapsed the apartheid system, and I was wondering at the time whether we are not seeing a second revolution.

With accepted conventions of protest being overturned, and the author-ity of governance and management being disrespected, even despised, vice-chancellors were in the invidious position of not knowing how to reinstate order, control, and predictability in the running of their uni-versities. Such tests of governance stretched beyond campus into society itself, such as the challenge to legal authority by a UJ student who styled himself as 'the real Che Guevara', not the supposedly more pragmatic, reasonable Argentine revolutionary who fought for justice.

Ihron Rensburg: So [Che] appears in court charged with violent con-duct. One of the strange things for me is to see young student leaders with no tolerance among them. The attitude seems to be: 'So if you don't agree with me, I'm going to go and get my baseball bat and smash you up. If I don't get my way, I'm going to deal with you.' This is now the real Che Guevara.

So this student goes to court and he's asked how he's going to plead and his response to the magistrate is, 'First of all, I don't recog-nise the laws of this land. I don't recognise this court. I don't recognise the Constitution of this Republic. And as a consequence I have no alternative but to use violence to advance my work and my project and that of my comrades.' And the magistrate says to him, 'So what do you expect me to do now?' At which point he just sits down and shuts his mouth and the proceedings continue.

Something similar happened on the other side of the country, in Pietermaritzburg. A group of violent protestors were arrested and duly appeared in court. According to a journalist, 'Accused number one, who along with his fellow students cannot be named, muttered that he too would not "stand for colonial laws" before begrudgingly rising to his feet.[9]

University leaders would soon discover that whether it was their own disciplinary committees or the courts of the land, students would not accept sanction from either quarter. Another round of massive university disruptions in September 2016 started with UCT students demanding that those disciplined by the university and interdicted by the courts be allowed to return to campus. When Max Price delivered his submission to the so-called Fees Commission at the Centre for the Book in Cape Town, he was temporarily held hostage by a group of students demanding that he withdraw the interdict and drop the charges against expelled students, who should be allowed to continue their studies.[10] On campus a movement was brewing called #BringBackOurCadres. Soon classrooms would be disrupted, professors intimidated, and students allegedly whipped or threatened with whipping by stick-wielding protestors for continuing classes.[11]

Then, with Blade Nzimande's long-delayed announcement on 19 September 2016 that he would allow universities to set a fee increase of up to 8 per cent for the 2017 academic year, a trickle of protest in the Cape evolved into a national shutdown of most campuses. But what energised this latest round of protests was the non-acceptance by UCT students of court decisions applying interdicts against violent 'cadres', barring them from campus.

Where did this sudden disregard for the Constitution and the rule of law come from? What enabled this dismissive attitude against institutional authority, whether it was the disciplinary committee of a university or the courts of the land? Why were the authorities of these established and once-accepted structures not only ignored but held in contempt? To understand these attitudes among students, one needs to understand the contempt for the courts in the broader political arena under the presidency of Jacob Zuma.

In a developing country, political leadership often sets the tone for public behaviour.[12] In South Africa, the president had over a long period of time undermined not only the legitimacy of the courts but the credibility of the presidency itself. No other event illustrated this more clearly than Zuma's refusal to abide by the decision of the Public Protector that he pay back 'a reasonable percentage of the cost' of renovating his home in Nkandla, KwaZulu-Natal, for which taxpayers laid out R246 million. Instead of respecting this Chapter Nine authority from the Constitution, the president decided that the Public Protector's rulings were mere recommendations and not court orders. What followed over a period of seven years was an unsavoury spectacle which had its high point in the South African Parliament, where the Economic Freedom Fighters (EFF), a breakaway group of the ANC, used every opportunity to demand – and chant – that the president 'pay back the money'. Zuma refused, and the parliamentary sessions became the setting for a prolonged, confrontational, and public display of impunity against the laws and the governing authorities of the country – until the Constitutional Court made a damning finding that the president had defied the Constitution and not upheld the rule of law. In the words of the Chief Justice, 'The Constitution, rule of law and accountability is the sharp and mighty sword ready to chop off the ugly head of impunity.'[13]

It was not only the Nkandla scandal that created this culture of impunity in the broader society. It was the president's being relieved of charges of rape and corruption. It was his appointment of openly corrupt persons in senior positions in government and parastatals. It was the one scandal after another about corruption in the civil service and in the large state-owned companies, and the very serious charges of 'state capture' by the Guptas, a wealthy and influential Indian family. It was the president's family members who found themselves enriched and promoted without a blush of embarrassment. The two contexts – state actors and student actors – were connected in the sense of creating a poisonous culture of contempt for the rule of law in national government and campus governance. If the country's president showed contempt for the law, why should communities respect it?

Ihron Rensburg: There's one other dimension to be added here and that is the declining commitment to the rule of law from Union Buildings to Hammanskraal [where there was violent resistance from communities to eviction from municipal land]. I'm just picking on Hammanskraal because it was in the news this week [of 26 May

2016].[14] That decline in commitment to the rule of law means that those in political power will struggle to establish authority or to establish direction. And they know it because they know that they are unable to address those in Hammanskraal for whom the idea of rule of law simply is not applicable. What does rule of law in Hammanskraal actually mean? What is my reference point for the idea of rule of law? When I look at the newspapers, when I look at television, the images and narratives that come to me are of, to put it mildly or pragmatically, a lack of commitment or a declining commitment to the rule of law. I think the evidence is piling up that there is a declining commitment to the rule of law in the Union Buildings. We're talking about South Africa, not in an exceptionalist sense but in the expectation that we have of ourselves.

So that idea of a declining commitment to the rule of law and the loss of legitimacy in the Union Buildings creates something close to a toxic political and social culture in our nation-state. And it seems to me it is that culture of impunity, from the top down, which provides the ideal playground for anarchy and anarchists.

This same contempt for due process and the rules of natural justice was evident at Rhodes University during the student protests against sexual violence. Once again, the highly sensitive concerns about rape and the outrage of sexual assault in general would dismiss any regard for due process and the rule of law, as the vice-chancellor recalls.

Sizwe Mabizela: The recent protests that we had in April [2016] around the issue of sexual violence also came out of nowhere. What actually happened was that a small group of students calling themselves Rhodes University Chapter 2.12 [the section of the Constitution declaring 'the right to bodily and psychological integrity'] started to raise awareness about sexual violence. It was a Monday when they put posters around campus condemning sexual violence. I issued a circular to say that as the university leadership we were firmly behind this group, and that we needed to address issues of sexual violence in our society and in our university. So that seemed to go smoothly until a list was posted on the SRC Facebook page containing the names of about eleven male students. And before long there was a view that this was a list of rapists, and so students gathered together and went from residence to residence hunting down these young men and holding them hostage overnight.

Of course, I argued with them that that was unconstitutional, that it was wrong to do things the way they were doing them, and that we needed to have people properly charged and then taken to the police station. But that did not work. In the event, they took the law into their own hands. I disagreed with the manner in which they went about highlighting the issues of sexual violence in our society, but I supported the cause itself because gender-based violence in our society is just so endemic.

But vice-chancellors did not have the luxury of thinking and theorising about how to deal with this growing lawlessness on their campuses. They had a solemn responsibility to their councils and their communities to contain this assault on institutional rules and legal authority. Otherwise the universities would simply collapse under these threats to people and property. Their experience in trying to fulfil these managerial obligations made one thing clear: it was almost impossible to predict, control and manage these volatile environments.

My colleagues at UFS referred to this dilemma as 'the unmanageability of the crisis.'[15] In addition to managing social media (see Chapter 9), there was the difficulty of managing multiple security authorities, a frustration I experienced during the Shimla Park incident in which rugby supporters clashed violently with protesting students and workers in February 2016. The campus security was completely outnumbered and outmanoeuvred by the protesting students and workers. When I tried to reach the head of security, his cellphone battery was dead; in any case, he was immersed in the to-and-fro with the student–worker group as they moved towards the rugby stadium. When I tried to reach the colonel in charge of the public order policing unit, he did not answer his phone – in part, I suspect, because one or two of his men had been injured in a pitched battle with students. Yet, on a previous occasion the police chiefs had made it very clear that they did not take orders from the university management; they had their own line of command. And then there was the difficulty of managing the added security brought onto campus from a Johannesburg company. For these personnel, the university authorities were an unknown entity, and their command structures operated according to their own routines. Getting the local police, the public order police, the campus security, and the Johannesburg security firm co-ordinated around the same tasks was time-consuming and nearly impossible to achieve.

Managing a university in a post-truth world

Beyond social media and security management, perhaps the most difficult aspect of managing the crisis related to the emergence of what could only be called *a political economy of lies*. These lies were not random, sporadic, or the result of error; rather, they were bogus claims and outright falsehoods put forward by protestors as part of a systematic campaign to advance their cause and their myriad complaints against the university and its leadership. The pervasiveness of lies nearly paralysed some of the vice-chancellors, in part because to be accused in public of something that was so patently untrue impacted on their personal dignity. Moreover, the tactic of spreading such falsehoods undermined their sense of the essence of a university's purpose – the pursuit of truth. Ahmed Bawa noted that in his meetings with stakeholders to discuss issues around the protest, he 'discovered ... just how dishonest some students are and that you had to be very aware of that'. But he was not alone.

> **Tyrone Pretorius:** In the beginning, at a national level, we were all sympathetic to the idea of access and affordability because that's what UWC has always been about. While we were sympathetic to that, what was happening at UWC was not even remotely aligned to those concerns. It was about destruction, it was about violence, it was about lying. You know the Vusi Mahlangu affair [the student-worker activist who falsely claimed he was kidnapped and assaulted and when 'found' was charged with perjury and defeating the ends of justice][16] happens over and over here on this campus. Some of the students would claim that they had been assaulted by security, that they had been harassed, and the women students would claim they too were abused by the security. And so we have that constant

creation of incidents and episodes in order to mobilise students. It happens on a daily basis.

They once tried to run riot on campus because allegedly one of the cleaning ladies was shot by security with a rubber bullet. They posted pictures of paintball pellets on their Facebook site. We took the lady to the campus doctor and he examined her from head to toe. The doctor could find no bruises, nothing to indicate that she had been shot.

This is an elderly lady, and something may have hit her but not something that leaves a bruise, because the doctor could not find anything, and our security was under strict instructions: no firearms of any kind. So we investigated the students' allegation and found there's nothing to it.

There's that constant creating of a narrative where they are the defenders of everything that's right and noble and all we [management] do, according to them, is lie and be dishonest. The reason that we're not outsourcing, for example, according to their Facebook page, is because we are all getting kickbacks from the vendors and we're in the pockets of vendors, and 'reliable sources' tell them that this kind of corruption is happening. So I don't think I have much sympathy for the group on campus.

We had an incident here on campus where a group of them, at two o'clock in the morning, attacked the security at the entrance with knives and then went around the campus at that time of the morning posting lots of graffiti all over. But they miscalculated, because they tried to repeat the anti-white sentiment that happens at UCT and at Wits and the 'F*** white people' slogan. But because this institution is nowhere similar to UCT and Wits, and because of the kind of reaction that they got, they quickly stepped away from that campaign around anti-whiteness.

The creation of lies would form part of what has been called *catastrophising*, which turns 'commonplace negative events into nightmarish monsters', leading to the belief 'that what has happened or will happen [is] so awful and unbearable that you won't be able to stand it'.[17] Nothing demonstrated this phenomenon more clearly than the 'wiper water' incident at UFS.

One Friday evening in 2016 a group of male students drove their car past a group of female students walking on a sidewalk of the Bloemfontein campus on their way back from a church service. A traditional campus prank that stretches back over the decades – to when the university was all white – was about to become a major management catastrophe. As the car passed the female students, the driver activated the windscreen wipers in wash mode, thus sprinkling water on the pedestrians. The women laid a complaint with security, and a search to find the students in the car began immediately. The women students, by all accounts, simply wanted the university to determine who the disrespectful male students were and act on this personal affront. If the students inside and outside the car were either all black or all white, the incident would probably have ended right there.

Then the catastrophising kicked in. A group of students led by the SRC president took to social media expressing complete and utter outrage over the incident. This event demonstrated, once again, the disrespect of racist whites for black victims of their tyrannical rule as white supremacists on campus. And then the *coup de grâce* – the claim that 'the liquid was urine'! If university management denied this, the students charged, they were once again aiding and abetting the racists who operate freely on the campus. From that moment on, those of us in management were playing defence as news spread about the 'throwing' of urine onto the bodies of innocent black students.

The SRC president – a law student, no less – had already positioned himself as judge, jury, and executioner in the case. The liquid was urine. The male students were racist. The management was in denial. No amount of appeal for calm, or a plea to allow the investigation to proceed in order to determine the facts of the case, would pacify the students, especially with some in the student leadership catastrophising every single incident on campus into a racial event.

The campus security worked through the night. They eventually identified the car and the students involved, and had them make statements as part of the investigation. The offending car itself was investigated. The clothes of the women students were collected and subjected to laboratory tests at the university, with an instruction to the scientists to act as speedily as possible. Until the results came in, we in management held our collective breath for one compelling reason: urine has a special place in the politics of UFS. Back in 2007/08, a notorious student-made video capturing the act of urinating, or, more likely, pretending to urinate, on the food of five black workers by four white students constituted the most serious human rights violation on a university campus in the post-apartheid period. The so-called Reitz incident, named after the residence where this atrocity happened, remains seared on the institutional conscience and led to my appointment the following year to help deal with racial integration on campus. Thus the mere mention of 'urine' in any campus event is likely to create emotional upheaval and unleash political rage across campus. The SRC president knew this, and milked the event to his political advantage.

The lab results indicated that the liquid on the clothes was water, most likely sprayed from the car by the windshield wipers. The SRC leader then questioned the white head of the laboratory – although all the tests were conducted by black scientists in the lab – and suggested a cover-up. But by this point the harm had already been done. Nothing could reel in the lies or contain the emotions that had been whipped into a frenzy by dishonest, unscrupulous student leaders in the midst of a broader protest movement that was barely manageable in the first place. In the meantime, the affected students resolved the matter among themselves with an apology from those in the car and the gracious acceptance thereof by those sprayed with water.

But the lies could become very personal and exasperate a university leader, as shown in this excerpt from a September 2016 interview with the Wits vice-chancellor by a journalist from *GroundUp*:

Interviewer: The SRC has called you an intellectual thug on Twitter, adding that you don't quite understand the struggle that pushes them to demand free education. Do you have a response to that?

Adam Habib: People say all kinds of irresponsible things, and I wonder whether sometimes the people who make these statements just blurt the first thing that pops up into their heads. Because some of these things are so utterly outrageous, they are not even sensible in any normal world. So I don't know what the accusation is. I don't know why I am targeted. Actually, I think the fact that I haven't acted suggests that I have been very, very patient.

For much of last week, I wasn't even in the country and this incident was being managed by my colleagues. I don't know what they mean by 'thief'. Can they put some accusation on the table? *Ja*, I've heard people make accusations of corruption. You know what? I'm very, very open to be audited. Let somebody declare their name and make the accusation, and if the accusation is found to be true I'll be forced out. But, if the accusation is found not to be true, they must agree to be fired or effectively expelled for making unwarranted statements against individuals. I'm happy to be investigated. I don't have anything to hide. Everything I have is in the public domain. My public life is very, very transparent. My politics has always been public. My circumstances have been public and there is nothing I have that I am particularly ashamed to have in the public domain.

So, I am very, very willing to be investigated. But, whoever wants to make the accusations . . . have the courage to stand up and put your name out and . . . if it's found that it's a false accusation, that you are prepared to pay the consequence of putting up false information and fundamentally trying to erode the stability of the university. Have the courage to put your money where your mouth is.

Yet few vice-chancellors have had the experience of having their name so scandalised in the public domain as Prins Nevhutalu, principal of the multi-campus CPUT, one of the institutions at the centre of the on-going violence sweeping campuses across the country. His crime? Challenging a corrupt tendering process at his university.

Prins Nevhutalu: As early as 2014, I had taken the position that no student should be involved in the tender process. No union representative should be involved in the tender process. I noticed, however, that the transport tender in particular attracted a lot of interest from unions and from students, with the result that from the beginning, as the process started, there was a big attempt to make sure that it did not go ahead. We started in 2014 and up to today we have not concluded it.

A scoping exercise, led by a consultant, told us that we could provide an expanded transport service for our students for R18–22 million. But we were now paying R50–60 million. Something was going on, and so I said, 'Let's decide', and that led to the violent protests. Council simply could not make a decision. Even up to today they have not made a decision. As a consequence, we had to extend the current transport tender, and we're paying about R40 million instead of R18–20 million. And when I decided that we're going to get an external person to run with the process, that's when allegations of corruption were made against me. It was intended to stop me.

The lie was that this company which had made a submission for the much cheaper R18 million transport tender bought me a ticket to go and contest the vice-chancellor's position at UKZN and that they gave me R1 million. Absolutely untrue of course and without any evidence, but this was the retaliation for trying to push for a much more cost-effective transportation tender.

At stake here was an issue seldom attended to in the many commentaries on the student protest movement: the extent to which the movement was compromised in particular institutions by long-embedded cultures of corruption, especially in the tender processes of universities – as in the different levels of government. 'I discovered,' said Ahmed Bawa, as he tried to dig for explanations for the ongoing turbulence at his university, 'that very often there were issues of money in the background ... the kinds of issues around [the] kind of deals being made with providers of some kind or the other, coming to grips with that.'

In the context of tendering, the university was fragile because it has a major concentration of resources available for plundering by unscrupulous people on and outside the campus. All kinds of entrepreneurs were panting at the opportunity to lay their hands on institutional resources through tendering for contracts ranging from catering services to travel agencies, cleaning companies, new building construction, and even auditing services. In South Africa tenders were fair game for the corrupt, even at some universities. And at these institutions, student protests to gain a grip on university resources were nicely camouflaged under the more noble cause of 'fees must fall'. The run on institutional resources was particularly evident on the rural campuses of disadvantaged universities, as explained by the vice-chancellor of North-West University (NWU).

Dan Kgwadi: Universities are a microcosm of the society [around them]. There was a village 40 kilometres away from Mafikeng that demanded a tar road; the village torched all the schools, and then they even threatened the crèches. I mean, if you are going to do that with a crèche, you really have got a different agenda.

And if we get students from communities that react like this, that's the same approach that they bring to campus because they say, 'If you are angry, this is how you react'. And I actually engaged with a very senior politician at some point, wanting to know how come this is the culture we have. His response was very interesting to me because he said people told him, 'No, if this property goes down, then there's a tender on the way to come and build that up.' So it's the business relations that are also linked to the destruction of property.

I was therefore not really surprised when, after the torching of the buildings on our Mafikeng campus, as the buildings were burning, I was getting SMS text messages from people offering me office spaces. People saying, 'We actually can give you temporary offices for this or we can help you with that.' And so, even as you are still trying to douse the flames in a crisis, there are already some business solutions coming. That tells us we should not be very simplistic in looking at the crisis in universities and analysing it separately from the business interests that benefit from this turmoil.

So now I'm suddenly sitting with quite a number of people saying, 'Your tender processes, how are you going to run it? How does it work? That building, to do the reconstruction, are you going to go on a tender, open tenders?' I said, 'No, we have the tender processes that are clear in terms of how we will deal with these problems.' Business interests seem to destabilise our environment. When I go to funerals these days, literally as I am coming back from the funeral I am approached for university business. That is why I never go back to the family house after a funeral because I will hear, 'Chief, I've sent you a proposal' or 'I wanted to talk to you, I've got this proposal'. And it's all business-related, and you can imagine that if you start to take proposals at funerals and other social events, what will happen to you in terms of really running the university.

That is why now you hear the challenges or the calls for attacking the autonomy of universities. Because from a business point of view, it is seen as if this autonomy is locking people out who have some business interests in how the university is run, and that's where the whole concern about autonomy comes in. It's not really because people are interested in terms of what you are teaching or research- ing; no, it has nothing to do with the core business. It has everything to do with the tender processes and the tender side of things. I have heard quite a number of the political structures also resonating with this challenge on the autonomy of universities, starting to challenge the councils, to say 'councils must fall'. And you see it, by the way, fol- lowing this whole Fees Must Fall, there was also now this Councils Must Fall, and also vice-chancellors and if necessary SRCs – any structure that stands in the way of unscrupulous people laying their hands on the resources of a rural university.

It should be evident at this point how ingrained violence has become in the logic of student protests and in the organisation of a university's defences. But that violence, as has been shown, is not simply pathologi- cal in its character nor pure and noble in its intent. Violence runs seamlessly between community and campuses, creating continuities with the past and resonances with the present. We also learn from the university leadership that when a country is corrupt and poorly man- aged, those stressors show up in the campus population, often with destructive consequences for fragile institutions that struggle with man- aging the new normal – a violent, unstable, unpredictable, and increasingly lawless campus climate. And those conducting the violence, as the next chapter shows, are as diverse as the purposes of student activ- ism in contemporary South Africa.

Chapter 5

A Leaderless Revolution

The problem with leaderless uprisings taking over is that you do not always know what you get at the other end.
– Chinua Achebe[1]

Only one historically black university in South Africa has defied the apartheid odds. Black institutions of higher learning were originally created as sites of inferior education. They were located in isolated, mostly rural areas – hence the adopted name 'bush colleges' for the collective of ethnic universities birthed by the apartheid state through the ironically named Extention of University Education Act of 1959. Like the other bush colleges, the University of the Western Cape (UWC) was designed to fail. It was heavily staffed by second-rate Afrikaner academics who could not make the grade at the well-funded establishment universities, such as nearby Stellenbosch. UWC was deliberately denied high-status disciplines such as medicine and engineering. Its original facilities were barely comparable to those of a white high school in the leafy suburbs. There were no spacious sporting grounds with high-quality athletics tracks and state-of-the-art gym facilities. The library holdings were elementary, and luscious lawns and gardens that adorn the marketing brochures of more ambitious universities simply did not exist.

The modest set of founding buildings was surrounded by wind-blown sand dunes and bush, with an infrequent train service running behind the campus and even less frequent bus service operating between Cape Town's northern and southern suburbs. For those who had the misfortune of being classified 'coloured', and could enrol nowhere else without a special permit to attend institutions like UCT, it would take hours and three or more modes of transport to get from the southern suburbs to these outer reaches of the northern suburbs. Many students had to hope and pray that their rudimentary Afrikaans would carry them through. That was my fate, and I came to hate my undergraduate years with a passion. Yet today's graduates of UWC look proudly on their alma mater for what it was able to achieve despite the intentions of apartheid's ideologues. While most of the historically black universities succumbed under the weight of financial pressures and chronic protest cultures, UWC would find its place among the top third of South Africa's universities.

UWC built a formidable research track record, with research chairs and centres of excellence dotting the campus. It hired some of the best scholars in the humanities and the sciences. It secured funding for arguably the most impressive building for the biological sciences ever seen on the African continent. It expanded its infrastructure to create one of the more attractive campuses in South Africa. It opened its doors to students from across the country and the continent, thereby altering its ethnic birthmark that apartheid's founders had stamped on it. It developed within its institutional culture and ethos what an earlier vice-chancellor posited as a leftist critique of society. And it invested heavily in the upgrading of qualifications and competence among its academic staff. Thus UWC proved beyond doubt that high-quality education and groundbreaking research could coexist alongside an institutional mission that prioritised the education of the poor and the working classes of the region and beyond.

What UWC had achieved was impressive by world standards, given where it had started and with what official intentions. But its academic standing and financial status would always be vulnerable as subsidy returns went into decline and tuition fees came under threat. The promising transformation of a 'bush college' was about to face its toughest test yet – a test it would likely lose because of a pernicious student culture that was beginning to entrench itself at UWC and in South African universities more broadly. To understand how this happened, one first has to get a grip on the social identities and ideological markers of student political organisations in present-day South Africa.

Who are 'the students'?

One of the most misleading aspects of campus-unrest reporting in the media is the near-universal convention of referring to the protestors as 'the students' – as if the protestors are one large amorphous mass of discontented students roaming across and disrupting university campuses. Part of the difficulty of resolving the chronic crises on campuses since 2015 lies in the failure to discern the many and shifting variations in political, ideological, and strategic orientations of the most crowded field of student organisations that South African campuses and communities have ever encountered. In essence, there are three broad classes of student organisations and activists.

Traditional student organisations

The first class of student organisations represents the traditional student bodies, which by and large represent mother bodies from outside campus and, in most cases, in the South African Parliament. The ANC is represented by the South African Students Congress (SASCO), which in most cases takes its cue from the ruling party in government in terms of a broad commitment to non-racialism and to opening up access to education for the poor. The ANC's primary political orientation is to keep campuses open even while broadly supporting non-violent and non-disruptive protests. While SASCO, like the ANC, used to be dominant on most campuses, this has not been the case in recent years, which partly explains the hotly contested student politics in university environments.

The Pan Africanist Student Movement of Azania (PASMA) is the student body of the Pan Africanist Congress (PAC), which, like the ANC, was exiled in the 1960s and unbanned in the 1990s. Its primary political mandate is the restoration of black land ownership and support for a more radical black representation in the content and character of education. PASMA is suspected to be a key player in the more violent protests, refusing any resolution of the campus shutdowns towards the end of 2016.

The Economic Freedom Fighters (EFF) is the student body representing the senior organisation of the same name, a movement that split from the ANC after the charismatic leader of the ANC Youth League, Julius Malema, was disciplined by and expelled from the party. The EFF has a radical and populist economic programme that includes taking back land from white and foreign ownership. In its parliamentary operations, it plays the role of hounding Jacob Zuma, current president of South Africa and the ANC, by holding him accountable for corruption and, memorably, for paying back taxpayer money used to upgrade his Nkandla homestead in KwaZulu-Natal. The EFF is widely suspected of being involved in the more radical and violent protests on South African campuses.

The Black First Land First (BFLF) organisation, whose leaders broke away from the EFF, is not represented as a registered body of university students, but its members often appear among and sometimes within the leadership of student protests to press for a more destructive agenda – the burning and looting of campus facilities without any compulsion to speak to, let alone negotiate with, the university management.

The Democratic Alliance Students Organisation (DASO), allied to the Democratic Alliance (DA), is a liberal student organisation whose role is similar to that of more traditional student bodies – to represent the needs of ordinary students to the management of universities. It is non-violent and non-confrontational in its politics but effective in carrying forward the needs of individual students as they arise on campuses. DASO would make history by winning SRC elections on traditional black campuses, such as the University of Fort Hare.

AfriForum Jeug (AfriForum Youth) is a conservative Afrikaans organisation operating on the former white, Afrikaans university campuses to defend and protect the cultural assets of their people. The group is therefore all white in composition. Its members have often appeared in confrontational roles with black student organisations when the protest agenda has to do with the removal or downgrading of Afrikaans as a language of instruction, or any other matter in which white Afrikaans students are seen as being targeted for discipline or attack. AfriForum students are typically linked to a broader white civic organisation by the same name, and to allied groups such as the trade union Solidariteit (Solidarity). They find ample and undisguised support for their cause in the white Afrikaans media.

The Black Consciousness (BC) group is less a formal organisation than a reawakening of the political philosophy behind the movement founded by the activist-intellectual Steve Biko, who was brutally murdered by apartheid's security policemen. The influence of Black

Consciousness is most directly felt in the intellectual agendas shaping the student protests around culture, curriculum, and community.

Hashtag groups

In the second class of student organisations are the new hashtag groups. ('Hashtag' refers to the use of Twitter hashtags for Internet activism.) The first of these was the #RhodesMustFall group, which, in its origins at UCT in March 2015, was broad-based, leaderless, racially open, and focused on the cultural alienation and symbolic exclusion of black students (and staff) on the campuses of former white universities. This group started off as non-violent, 'occupied' university buildings, and disrupted various administrative activities, including a meeting of council, on UCT's campus. Out of this group emerged a sharp interest in the intellectual transformation of universities, centred on the decolonisation of culture and curriculum.

Months later, in September 2015, #RhodesMustFall (RMF) at UCT was eclipsed by #FeesMustFall (FMF) at Wits, with its demand for a zero per cent fee increase for the next academic year. Initially FMF was a broad coalition of various student groupings – including some traditional organisations. But it gradually became more violent, thereby losing sympathetic black and white students who supported the initial non-violent push for financial inclusion. The growing violence that stretched from the end of 2015 into and throughout 2016 is a direct consequence of FMF. As RMF ran out of steam, it would merge with FMF, the latter primarily focused on the transformation of the material conditions of students. All the hashtag groups that have sprung up since RMF and FMF are simply campus-specific versions, such as #UPrising or #OpenStellies, of the originals.

On the left, a number of students formed more radical organisations aligned with outsourced workers on campuses. These were more sophisticated groups who went by names like the Workers and Students Forums (at UFS) and the Left Students Forum (at UCT), and whose activism was deeply invested in leftist ideology, the class struggle, and the rights of workers excluded from regular employment and material benefits. Their primary agenda was the insourcing of campus workers, and they received support in varying degrees on different campuses from the traditional unions. The alliance that would develop between students and workers was the result of these worker organisations on campuses.

Cross-cutting groups

The third class of student organisations could be called cross-cutting groups, as their demands are drawn from both traditional and new forms of student protest. Their focus is represented by a new word in campus vocabulary: 'intersectionality', or the overlapping of social identities and related systems of oppression and discrimination. These cross-cutting groups take the view that existing organised activism ignores key issues such as gender inequality, sexual assault, and transgender oppression. Instead, the dominant agendas in activism continue to project patriarchy, masculinity, and heterosexual identity as the norm. Worse, the experiences of these cross-cutting activists in existing student politics are 'exhausting and draining [treatment], macroaggressions, intimidation, exclusion, lack of support, invisibility, antagonism, dismissal'.[2] They demand the recognition of gender-diverse people, including womxn, queer, and trans people.[3] Similar to UCT's Trans Collective in its concerns about women, the Rhodes University Chapter 2.12 was formed to protest against the alleged silence of university management in the face of rape and sexual assault on campus, and led to the #RUReferenceList, which outed alleged rapists in the student body on social media.

Who's in charge here?

In the classical science fiction story, the alien alighting from the spaceship that has just landed on planet Earth makes a reasonable and understandable request: 'Take me to your leader.' The fictional visitor from outer space would be mightily confused if it landed among students on a South African university campus in 2015–2016. University leaders experienced just that sort of confusion too.

Styled on the 'Occupy movements' in the US and elsewhere, both RMF and FMF prided themselves on the fact that there was no single leader responsible for the movement. The collective was the leadership, and more than one voice would give expression to the struggle through the media. What happened in the process was that established structures representing student voices, particularly the SRC, would quickly be overridden as the voice of the movement, causing consternation not only among elected student leaders but also among university principals.[4] Who exactly do you speak to in order to hear complaints and resolve issues?

Some SRCs landed on their feet and integrated themselves into this instantaneous and broad-based movement without too much disruption to their continued leadership role, but they had to be nimble and inclusive of the new platform. At other universities the SRC was effectively displaced, if not disbanded, with the emergence of the new hashtag actors. In some cases there was outright confrontation between the factions, but the SRCs always came out the weaker party from such a conflict. And one of the reasons the SRCs were often vulnerable to displacement was that on several campuses they were frequently in conflict among themselves, especially around election times. Nowhere was this more evident than at UWC, where long before the Fallist movement started there was a very different kind of contestation going on – around the SRC elections. The vice-chancellor tells the story.

Tyrone Pretorius: What happened at UWC does not conform to the national narrative, and that narrative is certainly not how I and my colleagues experienced the crisis. At UWC, when the Wits students started their campaign around the fee increases, we had just completed a SRC election which three groupings – the EFF, PASMA and the DA [DASO] – claimed was fraudulent, as they normally do when losing. The election was stolen, they said, and they demanded an investigation. And then the #FeesMustFall happened nationally, and what happened at UWC was that PASMA and the EFF immediately latched on to and mobilised around #FeesMustFall. But we remain convinced that the unrest here had its origins in the contested SRC elections.

Most of the student demands at UWC were different from what was happening elsewhere in the country. I mean, we had demands that were very specific to UWC. You know, it was the bus service; it was the security at the railway station. It was the normal demands from our SRC that come every year. Those demands then gained momentum around the writing off of historical debt, which is about R270 million, and we could not agree to that. The SRC then became quite marginalised by the group making these demands.

What was new, however, was the level of hostility. You know, even when I was a student and we had student demands, there was never that level of hostility against the university and staff. There was an amazing amount of hostility. The disrespect, the postings on Twitter and on Facebook.

I must say it is worrying when commentators and analysts say that this is a social movement. We should be worried because anyone can stand up and claim, 'I'm speaking on behalf of #FeesMustFall.' They march into my office and they say, 'There's no space in residence for this student. #FeesMustFall demands [that] . . .'

And I say, 'Who are you? What are you in #FeesMustFall?' They reply, 'No, I'm a member of #FeesMustFall.' So, because of the nebulous nature of this situation, anyone can demand anything in the name of #FeesMustFall. You can't ask them, 'Where's your leadership?' They would say, 'No, we're a movement, we don't have leaders.'

Part of the difficulty is that we need to recognise the fact that there is no true #FeesMustFall movement. We need to recognise that there is probably a small grouping of activists that genuinely, I mean ideologically and theoretically, are motivated by things related to decolonisation and transformation. I believe there's a small grouping like that. But I also think it has attracted so many different groupings that use the power of this moment for their own ends. We do know that the EFF, PASMA, and the political party agenda play a role there. We do know at UWC in particular that a small group of students disgruntled about their experiences under the previous vice-chancellor hijacked this movement for their own. We also know that at UWC the SRC election was a huge bone of contention. And then obviously there are those activists that would join any campaign because it's just part of their make-up. I think if we recognise the many aspects of the student activism, we understand the chaos.

Then there are people for whom this is about regime change, and there's just two ways you have regime change in any society: the one is at the ballot box and the other one is through anarchy. And I pick up that a significant part of that grouping is extremely disgruntled with what's happening in our country as a whole, and obviously these are youngsters who are not steeped in the traditions of the ANC. In a sense they are expressing anger about what's happening in our country. So it's a mix of all of those feelings, hurts, and anger in very different protesting groups.

Yet it was not simply the confrontations around the institution-specific protests of UWC that happened prior to and despite the growing FMF movement in the country. It was also the fact that as the SRC-specific protests merged with the national protests, it became clear that the student leadership and its followers were intermingling with students from other campuses, and with some unsavoury characters from the community.

Tyrone Pretorius: In some instances of that intermingling our students were clearly there, but in that time it was extremely difficult for us to manage access to the campus. You know that CPUT is just across the road from UWC. We monitor the trains coming in; we do know that UCT and CPUT students often joined up, either to give Max Price some headaches or to give Prins Nevhutalu some headaches or to give me some headaches. So yes, there were external people as well. I remember the Friday that I addressed protestors in the student centre. I could see some people that no way could be students. And there were local gangsters from the surrounding areas also in the crowd.

Inter-campus mobility allowed students from various institutions to shore up the numbers on any one campus. This became one of the tactics of the student movement, and sometimes protest leaders considered mobilising high school students and those from the technical and vocational colleges. There was strength in numbers, and it made the management of student protests even more difficult.

Prins Nevhutalu: Because of their proximity the CPUT students would cross the road and reinforce UWC [protests]. And we had to find a way of breaking that and I think we were very successful because we now have intelligence. If we know something is brewing at UWC, we shut our gates and do not allow anybody to come in, so we have a way of controlling the situation to some extent.

At one moment UCT would be flooded by students from other Cape universities (CPUT, UWC, and to a lesser extent Stellenbosch) as well as youth activists from non-student organisations such as BFLF. A small group of UCT activists would therefore quickly be dominated by militant youth from elsewhere who would act violently, since for them the risks were low and the chances of being held accountable were virtually zero. Similarly, at UP students could descend on its Lynnwood Road campus from UNISA and TUT, and also from Wits and UJ, once the call was made for reinforcements. This was an effective tactic in undermining local management of the protests. There were also activists who changed registration from one campus to the next to instigate protests around the country.

Prins Nevhutalu: Max [Price] realised that one of his instigators at UCT was one of my 2015 ex-students. And [this ex-student] also appeared at Wits on TV . . . he was there. So this one is a hired mercenary because he is allowed to go almost everywhere.

As student protests escalated, a new word entered the managerial arsenal of the vice-chancellors: 'intelligence'. There were too many surprises, too many unexpected and calamitous revolts by students. The unprepared-ness of management for a protest here or a crisis there meant that senior teams were always in reaction mode. Appeals were made directly to the cluster of government ministers concerned with national security to assist in providing intelligence that could prevent the incineration of university property under the relentless waves of protest. Several universities made their own arrangements with private firms or individuals to enable planning for the safety of students, staff, and security. As petrol bombs started to make their way onto campuses, university leaders were seeing levels of violence not present, much less tolerated, during the anti-apartheid struggle. Things were becoming deadly serious, especially after a worker at Wits became the first casualty of the campus wars. An asthma suffer, she succumbed from breathing the fumes after students released a fire extinguisher in a residence called Jubilee Hall. Intelligence had now become a matter of life and death.

Politicised campuses

Whatever gains might have been made by 'intelligence' were constantly undercut by the degree to which the campus environments had become politicised. Campuses have always been political environments, places where students learn the habits of democracy, such as winning and losing in elections, and how to lead. But this was different, as the NWU vice-chancellor explains.

> **Dan Kgwadi:** It was really now a heavily politicised environment in which the academics found themselves. You know, I've never had to think and operate in a more politically conscious environment than I've had to in this period. One was not necessarily to look at students as students. You had to think of what is the force behind their actions. So for me it was more political and you really have to think in a very informed political way. You would see that when you address the students you would not address them as a vice-chancellor; you had to operate more like a Speaker in Parliament.
>
> And the threats that were coming now to vice-chancellors – it was now more personal. I come from the Mafikeng campus, where issues of the poor are not really new. We've dealt with these over the years, and the solutions that we implemented were quite acceptable and managed. We could work out something; we were very innovative and very progressive in dealing with these issues. But all of sudden the method did not seem to be working. There was no intention to accept anything as a solution, because the problem had to be escalated from time to time. That is exactly what made me get the feeling that there's a bigger story behind the story.

This transformation of many university campuses into heavily politicised environments had been a long time in the making on black majority campuses, where most of the students were poor. But in 2015–

2016 the contestation was not about contrasting ideas or intellectual positions on, say, the purposes of the university or the content of the curriculum. It was now a simple contest about political power and access to resources as part of the everyday life of students. As Lourens van Staden of TUT curtly put it: 'Their sport or activity is politics. There's nothing to do. There's *boggerol* [nothing] on that campus in Nelson Mandela Drive. What is there? So their excitement is politics.'

Within such politicised environments, the traditional student organisations were certainly not acting alone. They were established with the assistance of the parliamentary parties and even funded, in many cases, for their political campaigns ahead of an SRC election. This external influence on campus politics frustrated some of the vice-chancellors:

Dan Kgwadi: An election year always pollutes the campus environments, and for Mafikeng specifically, I was not surprised because the political environment there is always like that when it is SRC elections. I am only partly joking when I tell students that 'the only person that has not yet come to the campus to help and canvass and campaign for students is Ban Ki-moon, the secretary general of the UN'. You see, all political leaders come here canvassing and helping students for their own party politics, for the SRC elections. And there is also, as I learnt, a lot of funding from political parties that goes with that process. And therefore that already sets up an institution, a campus, like an incubator [for national politics]. So it is no surprise that the damage that we saw in the university sector was the highest on the Mafikeng campus.

Since the campuses often become the staging ground for national politics, the places where future leaders are prepared for their respective parties, it should come as no surprise that student activists took their cue from what was happening in Parliament, in terms of both organisation and behaviour.

Dan Kgwadi: You start to see people trying to mimic what is happening in Parliament. I think the state of Parliament as an institution is not really serving as a good role model for our students, because the environment there is so toxic. I sometimes even get worried enough to say we shouldn't be publicising [parliamentary sessions] anymore because it sets a tone that is not very good. Students now always want to be seen to be obstructive, instead of debating and moving forward. When you sit with them in the boardrooms, you can see how they quickly want to turn the meeting into a parliamentary session. You hear the language: it's exactly the same language that you pick up in Parliament, and that becomes a challenge as well. So that institution really needs to get its house in order for the rest of the country to be back in order as well.

For Sizwe Mabizela at Rhodes, there is no question that the reasons for 'the ease with which we resort to destruction and the attitude of dismantling things and destruction' lie outside of campus. 'Go to Parliament,' he argues, for that is where 'this attitude of disruption' can be found 'and that is very problematic'. It was perhaps inevitable that in a short period of time the university campuses became sites for playing out the broader politics of the country. In a telling summary of the status quo, Derrick Swartz of NMMU observes that 'universities [have] become the theatres for solving what is essentially a societal contradiction'. The interconnectedness of these spheres of conflict is detailed by the UJ vice-chancellor.

Ihron Rensburg: The extreme polarisation in politics itself between the ruling party on the one hand and the opposition parties, in particular in relationship to the Economic Freedom Fighters, is toxic or adds to this toxicity in our environment. What you then find is that you have open conflict and everything is fair game. So whether it is the local ward or councillor, or whether it is the local mayor, or whether it is the local school or college or university, it is fair game. It's power for the cause, so to speak. And these [become] theatres of war, if I can call it that, or theatres of conflict. I think we should expect that factory floors and mines will also see a deep escalation of such conflict as we see the emergence of the new contesting union federation. We should see conflict and contestation expanding into other spheres as well.

And this is where campus politics tears apart, as internal rivalries escalate because the stakes on the outside are so high. But it is not only the contestations in Parliament, such as between the ANC and the EFF, that are reflected on campus. It is also the strife *within* the ruling party. After the announcement of the zero per cent fee increase, when one group of ANC-aligned SASCO students fell in line with the presidential recommendation that students should go back to class, on other campuses this message was largely ignored. When Blade Nzimande announced what is effectively free education for the poor and the 'missing middle,' the president of the ANC Youth League lashed out against his cabinet colleague for not going far enough. Even on one campus the various factions within SASCO held different views on whether to continue the protests or return to class. The rival groups are merely reflecting factional divisions in the senior ranks of the ruling party.

Whatever cross-party and non-sectarian solidarity had been built up around RMF and FMF by October 2015, a major split would take place between those largely under ANC influence who returned to classes and those bent on demonstrating their independence of power in relation to the strikes. The EFF and other radical groups had a field day on campuses as they gradually ratcheted up the assaults on buildings and property. What were largely shouting matches and insults inside Parliament, with the occasional punch-up between the EFF and ANC-instructed security, had taken a much more violent turn on university campuses.

This left the ANC with a problem: how could the ruling party, eager to maintain its public posture as the revolutionary organisation of liberation, regain its dominant influence on campuses where contending political parties had assumed the mantle of radical protests? The ANC could either fight the EFF and other 'opportunists' on campuses, or join them and claim that the protests were their idea to begin with. This dilemma explains the rather embarrassing spectacle of the president and his minister advising students to go back to class only to find other senior ANC officials aligning themselves with the protestors. It was clear that students too were aligned to party factions on the outside, and this was reflected in the chaotic and often unmanageable politics of the university. The varying fortunes of the ANC on the different campuses could also be explained. Where the ANC was firmly in control through its student surrogates, campuses were relatively calm; where the ANC-aligned SASCO was divided internally as well as in contention with rival parties, there was chaos. And this volatile cocktail of student politics would change from one election cycle to the next on campuses where the dominant party changed hands more often than was the case in national and even provincial politics. From the viewpoint of the vice-chancellors, 'Take me to your leader' was therefore a futile request.

Prins Nevhutalu: We went to a workshop or a meeting with the students and agreed that we can *defer* the debt of students but that you do not *extinguish* the debt because it's still there. It's still on our books, it becomes part of the balance sheet. We agreed with the students and we said, 'If you can prove that you cannot pay it upfront, we're prepared to reduce it, but you still have to pay.' So while we were having this meeting with the students, a new group came in and said the first group of students were no longer representing the student leadership. The new group came in and filled up the place, and they sat in there until four o'clock and forced everyone out.

Tyrone Pretorius: There was a time when I started getting fed up with this leaderless group because you meet on a Monday with fifteen of them, you agree on an agenda for discussion, and on Tuesday the fifteen have been removed by the mob and there's a new fifteen. Then you'd have to start all over again. I remember signing an agreement on a Tuesday at three o'clock in the morning. We had been sitting with this group from probably nine o'clock in the morning until three o'clock the next morning. We signed, they signed. We came out of that, they posted victory on their website, and the next morning I wrote to the campus community. I wrote that I think we've dealt with the issues, that students understand where we're coming from and we understand where they're coming from.

I had just pressed 'send' when there were students demonstrating and protesting again outside. And I went down only to see there was a new group that said, 'No, the group of last night had no mandate to sign an agreement. This is not an agreement, this is a record of a meeting held; we are here to negotiate as a new group.' So I got fed up with that and I said, 'No, there's no more talking.'

On the traditional black campuses, as indicated earlier, the protests were routine and cyclical, revolving around bread-and-butter concerns such as tuition fees, transport, and accommodation. On the former white campuses, the agenda stretched to broader concerns about symbolic violence, cultural alienation, gender oppression, and curriculum dissonance with the black experience – concerns which would later merge with and become submerged under the #FeesMustFall agenda. But on the multi-campuses of the same university, an interesting phenomenon was observed. The TUT vice-chancellor points out the media's tendency to name a part as the whole.

Lourens van Staden: After the president announced a zero per cent fee increase [in October 2015] . . . only Soshanguve's [one of the TUT campuses] 14 000 students did not write exams. The other 40 000 wrote on all campuses. No journalist is willing to say that Ga-Rankuwa, Pretoria, and Emalahleni wrote exams. They paint all our campuses with the same brush. The long and the short of it is that the political influence or interference or penetration, whatever you would like to call it, is different from one campus of TUT to the next.

So despite the zero per cent increase, the students from the other campuses were okay. But Soshanguve became very violent and dissatisfied because the EFF was in charge of student politics there. During this time, Julius came to the Pretoria campus to address our students. And it was very interesting: in Pretoria they chased him away, but he went on to Soshanguve, where they started to disrupt the campus there. This shows the interference of a political party.

As far as the ANC is concerned, our chancellor is Dr Gwen Ramokgopa, the aunt of the [then] executive mayor of Tshwane; they assisted to solve the unrest situation. So the political interference in university education to me is huge. It is huge. We should take it out. How, I can't tell you now.

If you look at the so-called township campuses after the merger [of universities], the playing field has not been levelled. You can see that from the facilities you see there, the residences. You could say the analogy is that there's a 'five star' residence here [Pretoria] but it is 'two stars' there [Soshanguve]. One of the students came to me and said, 'You know what, Prof? Standard Bank is not Standard Bank.' I said, 'What do you mean? What is a Standard Bank?' He said, 'When you go to Standard Bank, be it in Soweto or in Johannesburg, it is the same colour, it is the same furniture. Everything is more or less the same.' Then he says, 'At TUT, Standard Bank is not standard.' I tell him, 'Thank you, my son; I understand where you are going.' So you listen to the students, and some call the merger here 'the murder' in terms of how things developed.

Differing politics explain why, for example, the UFS Qwaqwa campus could be completely at peace during the protracted fees protests while the Bloemfontein campus, some 300 kilometres away, was in disarray. 'Why should we close just because they have problems?' the Qwaqwa students would complain. There are few white students on this rural campus, and if there is any inter-group conflict it is related to the grow-ing and now dominant numbers of Zulu students from northern KwaZulu-Natal, and their affiliation with the Inkatha Freedom Party (IFP) student wing, the South African Democratic Students Movement (SADESMO). The traditional clients of the campus, Sesotho speakers in this former homeland, have become a demographic minority. Each of the 'merged' campuses would demonstrate variations on this theme of a very different student politics depending on which site of the university you studied.

Campus microclimates

If student behaviour could be different for different campuses of the same university, this study also found that even within a single campus there could be very different experiences of the institution, its dominant culture, and its politics. These differences could be attributed to *micro-climates*, for which a slim literature exists to describe the intense spaces occupied by members of a subgroup within an organisation. Borrowed from the field of ecology, a microclimate in the scientific context refers to 'atmospheric conditions' affecting a group of organisms, such conditions being different from the larger climate (macroclimate) experienced by the rest of the species in that ecosystem.

Applied to organisations, and to universities in particular, microclimate studies are rare and have been conducted to describe the limiting experiences of lesbian, gay, bisexual and transgender (LGBT) students and staff in one university,[5] and those of women and 'minority'[6] academics in departments of another university.[7] For purposes of this study I wish to define microclimates in universities as the emotional, psychological, and political canopies under which students (and staff) organise themselves, share among themselves, and together make sense of the negative experiences of the broader campus environment. This conception of microclimates makes three important shifts: it casts microclimates as the dependent variable, the outcome of what activists do rather than simply what is negatively done to them; it restores agency to campus communities, meaning they act on their sense of being marginalised, ignored, or oppressed; and it allows for an expressly political agenda on the part of the subgroup rather than simply casting its activism as 'standards, behaviours and attitudes' in response to negative conditions.[8]

And so when students collect themselves in UCT's administration facility, changing its name from Bremner Building to Azania House, or when students at Wits choose as their organised site for assembly the floor of Senate House, renamed Solomon Mahlangu House, they create over days, weeks, and months very powerful 'emotional, psychological, and political canopies' shared by this group of activists. During the 2016 protests, one of the most intense microclimates developed when a group of Rhodes University students occupied a building in order to express themselves on the alleged inattentiveness of the administration to the problem of rape on campus. To appreciate this development, one needs to understand the larger organisational setting within which such a microclimate emerges.

Rhodes University is a peculiar kind of institution compared with the 25 other public universities. Also a centurion (116 years old) among universities, Rhodes is a small, single-campus liberal arts college surrounded by the small city of Grahamstown in the Eastern Cape. Rhodes is a residential campus, with a very high ratio of students (about half) accommodated in 52 residences. More than most, this university consists of a tightly knit community where, legend goes, everybody takes lunch at the same time and the vice-chancellor goes home to eat and relax during lunch hour. When a protest breaks at Rhodes, it becomes all-engulfing. Yet even within the campus smaller communities of affiliation are quickly formed – such as when the women students rose to start a campaign against rape and sexual assault on their campus.

Sizwe Mabizela: Early last year with the #RhodesMustFall campaign, a group of our students occupied our Council Chambers. They were there for about three weeks or so. And I decided that for as long as they did not interfere with the running of the institution, we would just leave them there. So from time to time, I would go up there, and in a fatherly manner just check out how they were doing, just to hear them out. What frightened me was the manner in which they had created a world of their own, and that again, here, you realise the power of the mind to create a world. It's a world which those people inhabited and no one else could inhabit it until they bought into it. And at times when I engaged them, they would just go into hysteria. One would start crying and then all of them would cry. I was just puzzled: what was going on? But again, it's one of those things that are difficult . . . And I saw it again with the rape protests. A small group of students who in a way creates a particular world, a particular solar system, where, as I indicated earlier, what may be logical and rational for you, occupying one planetary system, might not be such for them, because they have created this different world. And I think some of our students do need psychological attention, and this is a point which was also emphasised by a group of social workers and psychologists who came earlier this year. They very confidentially said they were observing some of the behaviours of some of these young people, and they were saying they might need some counselling and some might need psychiatric assistance and some of them displayed personality difficulties. And so we do have these students in our universities, but we must embrace them and we must create a safe, secure, loving, caring, and empathetic space for all of them because each one of them is someone's daughter or someone's son, and they're all important.

I am certainly not passing judgement on the authenticity or otherwise of this vivid and moving example of how a microclimate functions within a university. But this episode does help explain why it is so difficult for outsiders to grasp the levels of anger and anxiety that often lie behind a protest on the campus or in the streets. For those actions were preceded by such intense 'canopy encounters' by subgroups of students long before they become marchers or protestors in the public eye. Such circumscribed environments also explain how the macroclimate can often function in a perfectly 'normal' way without being affected by the intensity of the microclimate, as the UCT vice-chancellor illustrates.

> **Max Price:** Ultimately what matters is that the institution should survive and should remain strong and that we should deliver the academic project and that people should be able to get to class. And if that's the measure of success, we had a very successful 2015 academic year. We had more PhDs than ever before, more research output ... and for most people who weren't involved in the actual conflict here around the administration, the university had an almost normal year from an academic point of view. And I think that if we had got tied up in disciplinary cases and in punishment and in not engaging, I think we would have had a very disrupted year and they would have been able to mobilise large numbers of people in ways that would have been much more intrusive into the academic environment. By being willing to talk and engage and compromise and keep the discussions going, even though there were principles that were being compromised ... in retrospect I still think we did the right thing. I don't think I would have handled it differently a year later. But there were many times when one compromised on principles.

But that capacity to continue moving the academic project forward would gradually be undermined towards the middle of 2016, when microclimates would infringe on, even dictate, the terms of the larger campus environment as one university after another shut down in the wake of violent protests across campuses. Increasingly vice-chancellors were wondering, how does this end?

Understanding the protests: some concluding remarks

For the ruling ANC, an escalation in protests was not the expected outcome of Minister Nzimande's late September 2016 announcement that university fee increases for 2017 were 'not to exceed 8 per cent'. Nzimande had initially promised to announce a fee increase. Then he backpedalled, saying, rightly, that the authority to set fee increases belonged to each university council. (This was not something that was heeded in the previous year when the president announced the zero per cent fee increase.) Thereafter, the minister delayed any further announcement, citing the need for more consultation. As the year-end loomed and university principals became jittery about how to plan their 2017 budgets, Nzimande eventually broke his silence by offering an institutional guideline: no university should increase its fees above an 8 per cent cap. He might as well have set the cap at 1 per cent because anxious students, already starting to burn campuses in places like Pietermaritzburg in anticipation of something less than free education for all, now set upon the facilities of multi-campus universities with a vengeance.

At first the politicians in the ruling party appeared stunned, but before long they trotted out a familiar explanation: namely, that there was a 'third force' behind the surge in protest violence. 'Third force' is the intellectually lazy explanation politicians fall upon when they run out of ideas or wish to evade the truth. It could not possibly be that the policy was wrong-headed or that the subjects of the ANC's kingdom were disobedient. So politicians grabbed an explanation from the 1990s – when a third force, other than government and the liberation movements, was instigating violence either to ensure that negotiations failed or to strengthen the hand of the apartheid state in its talks with the ANC and others. But this time there was no evidence of a sinister, manipulative, and pernicious set of actors working behind the scenes to ensure the downfall of government. Those leading the violent campaigns against universities were well known to the politicians through their intelligence networks and ample media footage.

A much more reasonable and nuanced explanation is that a protest movement that started out with a simple, coherent, and forceful social justice message was 'hijacked' by radical militant and anarchistic elements among the students who genuinely believed that they could achieve their immediate and strategic goal of free education for all through the targeted assault on university property and management. For the more left-leaning students and opportunistic outside elements, this shift towards violence was not even about free education. It was about collapsing government and ushering in fundamental changes to the social and economic system that governs South Africa.

For the radicals in this latter group, the target was therefore not the size of the fee increase (zero per cent announced in 2015 was a temporary reprieve at best) but the oppressive capitalist system whose economic and social logics entrenched the inequalities that continue to plague the post-1994 era. The big prize for some in this group was some form of socialist government that would usurp the authority of the captured and corrupt nationalist government led by the ANC. Yet for others in this militant group, the goal was a decolonised state in which the nationalist project was handed to a new set of owners with their sights set on the reappropriation of 'white monopoly capital' and the redistribution of stolen land to the African masses. These different threads, and others, ran through the violent strategies of this marauding band of militant students and their political principals off campus. The radicals who sought regime change were nonetheless accompanied by students for whom the more practical objective of the struggle might simply have been to gain access to higher education without present or future financial burden.

And there was no better playground for pursuing these revolutionary ideas of a militant minority than the most vulnerable of institutions in democratic South Africa – the public university. As the final chapter will show, it would be a misguided political plot that could leave in its wake a terrible cost: the irrevocable slide into oblivion of the continent's most prestigious universities, tracking almost perfectly the fate of the postcolonial African universities to the north.

Chapter 6

The Personal Costs
of Crisis Leadership

'Daddy, are they really going to kill you?'
– From an interview with the Rhodes vice-chancellor

What was about to happen was inconceivable even during the darkest days of the apartheid state's assault on universities or in the responses of student protestors to those academic leaders then regarded as stooges of the white government. In a twisted sort of way, apartheid's rulers had regard for education largely because of their historical experience that schools were critical to the alleviation of poverty, the creation of group identity, and the promotion of social mobility for Afrikaners through the twentieth century.[1] More than privileged resources were needed to build the strongest academic schools in the country; also required was a foundational culture, a set of grounded beliefs about education as *opheffing* (upliftment) in the wake of the defeat by the British in the South African War (1899–1902).[2] With this logic the Afrikaner nationalists did not deny black people schools and universities; from 1948 onwards they actually built more education institutions for them. Their crime was to provide education *differentially* – to the great advantage of white youth and the serious detriment of black youth, a legacy that remains as visible scars on South Africa's social and education landscape.

Yet even in those dark decades there was one constant that bound together all South African education institutions, whether urban or rural, black or white, rich or poor, established or new. The educator, the leader, was respected, looked up to, and held in high regard by communities and by those whom they taught and led.[3] That changed, of course, after the heroic student struggles against apartheid education in 1976, which left in their wake a complete disregard for education authority that was never really regained, either in schools or universities. Even so, the event that took place on 9 March 2016 at the University of Stellenbosch represented a new low in student contempt of, and disrespect for, university principals.

The season of unreason

Vice-chancellors Max Price of UCT and Wim de Villiers of Stellenbosch University were seated on the stage of the Woordfees literary festival discussing the state of universities in South Africa. The chairman of this event, Henry Jeffreys, was the respected journalist and first black editor of *Die Burger*, once the enthusiastic voice of the Afrikaner National Party in the Cape. In the midst of the proceedings, a group of black protestors suddenly arrived. At first they sat quietly on the stage, where the discussion was already under way. Then chaos erupted, as the protestors started to argue with members of the audience, who wanted the event to continue. The Afrikaans language of the audience was a convenient target for the protestors: 'What language do you speak? I do not accept your language!' Efforts by the Woordfees organisers, the chairman, and the vice-chancellors to engage the protestors, even to bring them into the discussion, failed completely. Once again, another public event, like many others on university campuses, was disbanded because of disruption by a small group of angry protestors.

It was an undignified spectacle to see two senior leaders of major universities being heckled and humiliated as they left the venue. Max Price was confronted near his car by the angry youth and forced to return to the venue. Wim de Villiers also returned to the venue as a safety precaution. Price told the students they had disappointed Nelson Mandela. The students shouted back: 'Did we fail Mandela? No! Mandela failed us!'[4] The two university leaders appealed for reason, but to no avail. The protest movement had now entered a season of unreason.

What does 'unreason' mean in this context? It can be defined as the refusal to engage in or allow for reason or rational exchange as a means of resolving a dispute. In what would become the modus operandi of disruptive protestors, reason is displaced by chaos, the lack of order, and disruption. Only one voice is allowed to speak, and that is the loud, angry, and collective voice of the hostile disruptor bringing a grievance into a public space; any attempt at reasoned or rational exchange in the name of 'what a university is about' would be shouted down. Crucially, the disruption is *performance* in that it requires participants to dramatise their grievance typically through the interjection of fiery statements, song, dance, and, on occasion, physical confrontation with a targeted person or resistant member of the audience. However, it is not only performance; it is *recorded* performance for instant distribution on social media. The purpose is both to celebrate disruption and to inspire similar action on campuses elsewhere. Through the Woordfees event and others, a pattern was being set.

It was not only the university vice-chancellors who would be subjected to this display of unreason. Even academic figures known to the protestors for their radical credentials and sympathy with the movement would find themselves confronted by the performance of unreason. This was the case when UCT professor Xolela Mangcu was silenced at a panel discussion of the Centre for Humanities Research at UWC. The discussion included some prominent scholars of student movements and focused on the capture of universities by capitalist interests – the sort of topic you would imagine radical students might wish to learn about. But Mangcu, who had staunchly defended student protests for more than a year, was dismissed as having sold out to white interests, and when he complained about getting his 'comeuppance', he was dismissed by the disruptors as self-indulgent.[5]

In a similar vein, Christi van der Westhuizen, a critic of Afrikaner nationalist politics and institutions, was shaken on receiving a hostile reception from a small group of UFS students after giving an invited talk on white privilege. She expressed concern about this 'anti-democratic stance' within the student movement and was genuinely perturbed by what had just happened:

> I was attacked by a small group of students for daring to speak. My effort to analyse the changing positions of whiteness since the 1980s offended these detractors. It interfered with their essentialised versions of whiteness and blackness. They insisted that white people should be silent.[6]

The mistake that Mangcu and Van der Westhuizen made was to assume that they could engage these disruptors in a season of unreason. Their retorts meant nothing to the students, for Mangcu was a sell-out and Van der Westhuizen was a settler. The dismissals were, of course, wrong, irrational, and downright insulting. The disregard for the two activist-intellectuals made no sense, but that is the point of unreason. It does not need a logic for its disruption; indeed, it was the *unreason* governing these spectacles that gave them any meaning at all.

I can give a personal example of my experience of unreason, which took place during that horrific week of the disruption of a rugby match and the intense violence that followed on the UFS main campus. One evening I received word that the women students in one residence were afraid of moving outside to purchase food, so I went to a local Domino's and loaded up my van with pizzas. Returning home via a back route through the campus, I noticed a young man with a hammer and chisel chipping away at an outdoor sculpture, one of our newer and more progressive artworks on campus. Against all common sense, since this was a particularly dangerous week on campus and there was no security in sight, I stopped the car and approached the man. I could see that this was one of our former students, who had been excluded from the campus for his very poor academic results. Slowly I moved towards him while he continued his attempts to collapse the legs of the impressive sculpture *Bull Rider*. The artist, Willie Bester, was known in the 1970s and 1980s for protest and resistance art, often sourcing his materials from scrap-metal waste. This sculpture depicts a life-size bull being ridden by a man, with another man walking alongside and guiding the bull. Calmly I asked the young man, 'What are you doing?'

He did not move but offered the reply, 'I am bringing down white supremacy.' Stunned, I gave him a brief lesson on the meaning of the sculpture, the work of a struggle artist offering a satirical view of a power struggle. In response came the voice of unreason: 'I do not have to give you a reason for what I am doing.' I took one more step towards him and he fled into the darkness.

University leaders were the main targets of this politics of unreason. Some might argue that it all started on 16 March 2015, when, in the wake of the initial defiling of the Rhodes statue, UCT management convened a seminar on the subject of heritage, signage, and symbolism at the institution. A panel consisting of academics and cultural heritage specialists would speak first, followed by a response from the SRC chairperson. As Professor Crain Soudien, then deputy vice-chancellor, began to set the scene for the seminar, hands and placards started to go up among students in the lecture theatre, and they stayed up. This seemed to irritate Soudien as the chairman of the event; he acknowledged the hands for later, and at one stage he asked a student to put down his hand. But the hands stayed up, and instead of handing over to the panel, Soudien kept speaking, perhaps sensing the possibility of disruption, on the one hand, and attempting to secure an intellectual climate for the discussion, on the other hand. His appeal was to pure reason:

> It is important for me to emphasise how we manage a meeting such as this, noting all these hands that are going up . . . I'd like us to leave this meeting with absolute confidence in a sense of what a university is all about, to . . . give each of us an opportunity to express ourselves and to hear the point of view of the other . . . [to achieve] a deep sense, a deep sense of a university operating at its absolute best as a space which is fundamentally about position, counter-position; argument, counter-argument.[7]

Reason, in other words.

The students were now restless and Soudien was forced to take the hands. One student asked for the SRC chairperson to speak first. After some back and forth, the deputy vice-chancellor had no choice but to make the illogical decision of having the student president, Ramabina Mahapa, speak ahead of those to whom he was supposed to respond. The student leader got up and sang a protest song, made an eleven-minute speech about the lack of transformation at UCT, then informed the meeting he had no interest in listening to the others – and left the building, taking with him half the audience. Scenes like this would take place repeatedly across university campuses: forced disruption, exclusive student-disruptor speeches, and the termination of a planned meeting without any need for dialogue or the recognition of 'what a university is all about'.

This shutting down of the right to speak did not emerge in a vacuum. In 2010 Samantha Vice, a Rhodes University philosopher, had argued in a widely publicised paper titled 'How Do I Live in This Strange Place?'[8] that white South Africans should withdraw from the political space – such as in criticism of government – and exercise humility in the light of their unearned privilege for which they, as whites, should 'cultivate' guilt and shame. Whatever the nuances in Samantha Vice's advocacy of white political silence, it was read on the streets and on campuses as whites having to shut up in the face of black presence and black authority. Vice was roundly criticised even by sympathetic reviewers for this ill-considered attempt to pronounce on the rights of citizens to speak in a democracy.[9] But what was *not* said was that, once again, the white academic voice assigns to itself not only the right to speak but also the right not to speak; that level of self-awareness passed her by.

Nonetheless, Vice contributed to a climate in which angry black voices on campuses would take that charge seriously in a thinly veiled racism that silenced not only whites but anyone of any colour who did not share the protestors' views. At Vice's own university this intolerance would express itself on more than one occasion, as the Rhodes vice-chancellor recalled.

Sizwe Mabizela: One dimension that has troubled me immensely about the recent student activity is the essentialisation of race and the view that by virtue of the pigmentation of your skin, you are white. You therefore can't say anything about black people and the experience of black people. You must be silent, keep quiet. You know nothing about it. And I think this is so antithetical to what it means to be a university.

One of our outstanding professors, who happens to be a white woman, an excellent academic, has been so frustrated because in political science, three black students were simply saying to her, 'Shut up! You don't know what it means to be black.' The same thing happened to another of our white academics, a South African, who wrote a book on ubuntu, and he was taken to task: 'What do you know about ubuntu?'

Yet this serial silencing and the non-violent disruptions of early 2015 were mild in comparison to what would happen in subsequent months as mere disruptions escalated into violence and even threats to the lives of vice-chancellors. What the public did not know was that the activism of a once noble and just student movement had transmogrified into a deadly vigilantism affecting university principals, their spouses and children, and the staff around them.

Leadership projection and personal reality

Textbooks on leadership insist that in a crisis leaders must look composed, project calm, express certainty, and act empathetically as they absorb the fear and pain of others.[10] It makes sense, of course, that a leader does not spark panic among followers in the heat of crisis. In a deep institutional crisis, leaders are expected to project strength even as the media cameras hound them at every turn, when thousands of followers in the university assembly scan their faces for any signs of weakness, and while enemies search for the slightest hint of buckling under the pressure. What this kind of normative posture masks, however, is the managerial uncertainty, emotional turmoil, and personal distress that afflict leaders when they retreat behind their office doors, seek treatment from their physicians, or return home at night physically and emotionally exhausted.

In more than one study of university leaders under pressure in other countries, researchers would reveal something like this: 'I did not anticipate the depth of personal anguish virtually every respondent expressed in dealing with crisis scenarios [even decades after a catastrophic event].'[11] 'Without exception,' found Randy Wayde Mills in his landmark research on university presidents and their leadership, 'the participants in this study responded that the experiences they had in dealing with crisis changed them forever.'[12]

South Africa's vice-chancellors would also be changed forever as a result of institutional crisis. Here are their stories.

Max Price (UCT)

As indicated earlier, Max Price was a student activist in the apartheid era. He had experienced stress before, but the tension and pressure he experienced during 2015–2016 was different – intense, unrelenting, and personal. As a public health expert and medical doctor, Price not only felt the stress in his mind and body; he also knew what it meant. And what distressed him more than the student protests was the seeming loss of support from some of his academic staff – those who complained bitterly about bringing police onto the UCT campus.

The first time I had the sense that the faculty and the university were not behind me on that issue [police on campus] was very disturbing. And we backtracked; we apologised for bringing the police on and we said we would work through it, develop a protocol, and that's what I did. And now I think I've got overwhelming support and so I feel that staff are behind us again.

But that was the first period that I became really distressed. On the one hand, the sense of not being in control of the situation, where actually my job was to try to keep the ship afloat but not being able to control this external environment, this tsunami that was going on. And secondly, this question of distance or antagonism or hostility; the lack of confidence from the academic community in me, in this particular setting, of how I had handled that situation.

And then the uncertainty, and the sense of these sorts of high-stakes decisions. How to handle a particular situation has affected me, it's certainly affected me. I feel stressed and I wake up early and I can't go back to sleep because I'm turning these things over in my head. Sort of physiological manifestations of stress, which I certainly experience.

So I'm not bravado about it. I think it has certainly affected me; it has a huge impact on your family, particularly my wife. My kids don't live at home so they're independent, they're less affected by it. But my wife, she certainly gets drawn into the minute-by-minute issues, and in her case I feel bad on her behalf. It affects her in a slightly different way as well because she's an academic in the university but can't really function anymore as an independent academic, an independent voice regarded as having her own views, because the assumption is that people can't say anything in front of her if they want to say something about me. So that changes her relationships with people.

That is an additional stressor that I feel responsible for. But I seem to have been born with a thick skin and an ability just to not see the things that I don't like to see, in a way. So I don't feel the personal attacks; I'm able to say, 'Well, it's because I'm in a particular position; if it was someone else it would be an attack on them.' And on the whole I think I'm able to maintain my calm in these hot situations where students are shouting or trying to provoke me.

Sometimes I wonder whether that [calmness] maybe makes it worse. That [students are] trying to provoke me, and if I'm un-provoked or if I'm not getting upset, maybe that results in them going further. I'm not sure. But most of the feedback I get from my col-leagues is that not being provoked sort of maintains the calm, and just listening and being able to just absorb the punches is the more effective way, and I think I do that pretty well . . .

Probably other people would have to say whether [the stressors have] affected how I'm relating to other people outside of my family. Whether I've become sort of short with them or other things. I think that I'm containing it within my own internal, domestic support system. But it's stressful.

I've enjoyed my job; I've been here nearly eight years. I never had any doubts that I was really enjoying my job and loving it, and I thrived on that adrenalin as well, on being in some tough situations – and we've had lots of them.

The period of the protests and from the twentieth of October 2015 until after the exams was a horrible period. And it's been completely consuming. We have a crisis team and we spend eight hours of the day managing a crisis, not doing any real work or anything else.

Price reorganised his senior team so that he could depend on one of his deputy vice-chancellors to handle the crisis negotiations.

What that means is that I'm able to look after the campus and make sure the rest of the university keeps going. And that's certainly taken a lot of the stress off – meaning the immediate stress, the daily unpleasantness of being in a meeting where someone's confronting you or trying to humiliate you.

As I listened to Max Price, a colleague and friend, I was torn inside as I could sense him struggling to contain his emotions. Here was a good man, with struggle credentials and a sincere commitment to increasing access to high-quality education for disadvantaged communities, and to transforming this top university. In the new climate, however, whatever the vice-chancellor and his team did was not enough. In his remarks there was a sense of self-reflection, acknowledgement of his limitations, and even a hint of resignation in the face of overwhelming events on his campus. As Price opened up about the most intimate of issues – personal health, close family, relationships, and leadership regrets – he shifted between confidence and vulnerability. Yet what surprised me was that he swayed towards confidence when I inquired about the incident in which a petrol bomb had been lobbed into his office – a potentially life-threatening event. How did that event affect him?

Actually, not at all, surprisingly. It's odd in that it's affected the people around me in a way, but because it didn't really affect me I didn't appreciate how the people around me were being affected, and I ignored that at my cost because it seems to them like I don't really care about them. They feel like the administration building is their space, it could have been one of their offices, it's a kind of home away from home.

It happened at about midnight and there was no one here. The truth is that the damage is not huge. Unfortunately, that pile of papers I still have to read is still there – they've been cleaned of the soot but they weren't destroyed. The carpets and the ceiling were destroyed. Again, I didn't take it personally at all. And I don't know who did it, and RMF sort of denied involvement, distancing themselves from it, but I'm sure it must have been one of their associates. I haven't really figured out why it hasn't affected me; I mean, it was just an office and somehow I didn't feel it personally . . .

Also, I recognise that it was an attack on the institution, not an attack on me. I also regard it as the act of a fringe group. I don't think there's a lot of people involved, I don't even think there's a few people. I think of it almost as a sort of rogue element in the movement that did this, perhaps out of desperation, rather than something that is symbolic or representative of a trend, a big problem or a widespread feeling.

Shortly after the petrol bombing of the vice-chancellor's office, Sisonke Msimang, an activist academic and a darling of the militant protestors, wrote an opinion piece from which this excerpt is taken:

> So I looked at the pictures [from the UCT art collection] and felt sick at the fact of them, and I felt sick at their being burned. Then I learnt that the vice-chancellor's office had been petrol-bombed and I felt very sick indeed. What if there had been in there a black woman cleaning. What would we then say about collateral damage?[13]

Ihron Rensburg (UJ)

Ihron Rensburg had experienced the sharp edge of apartheid's brutality. A pharmacy graduate from Rhodes University, he was a prominent anti-apartheid activist in the Eastern Cape who was brutally tortured by the security police. Committed to the liberation ideals of the ANC, Rensburg would be called on to provide senior leadership in the first Department of Education under the new government of President Nelson Mandela. But in the student politics of today, that history means nothing. Instead Rensburg and his comrades were, like Mandela, seen as sell-outs to the transition to democracy.

> Look, it's been extremely taxing. I remember when things really started here at UJ. In fact, the day of the march to the Union Buildings [23 October 2015], that's the day when there was really desperation from the 'independents' [non-party-affiliated student activists] but also from more anarchist elements in SASCO to stir things and they couldn't stir it [by themselves]. And their Wits comrades joined them to come and stir and our response was to initially hold back. Then, when the risk was increasing as we were heading for exams, we drew the line. And it was one evening during [exams] that we see this group of 200 storming to the campus residence that my family occupies; that was probably 28 October.

And for the next five, six weeks, as we were managing exams, we had to move out of the house. Our own house is rented out until we're back there in another two years' time, if all goes according to plan, so we could not go back there.

We then had to move from one B&B [bed and breakfast] to the next. Every three nights, move. And it took its toll, but the thing that I think helped me was to have a partner who was thinking on her feet with me. So it was not a case of collapsing into depression mode. Yes, anxiety and stress escalated dramatically during that period, but one draws on one's peers, on one's partner. You pick up the phone. They ask, 'How's it going? What's happening? How can I help you?' So I can ask, 'Is there any way you can you help me with this or that type of thing?' Having that kind of network is important.

I should also add that one of the things I've been doing with my wife for the last thirteen, fourteen years or so is transcendental meditation [TM], for what it's worth. Doing that twice a day for twenty, twenty-five minutes does amazing things in terms of bringing balance, whether it's to one's health or one's emotive state or one's cognitive state. I'm relying also on my religious connections and membership of the church and being a leader in the church, drawing strength from that spiritual side. It is very important.

But ultimately, you have to lead. If you sink in, if you collapse, it's not an option. And so you have to gather yourself. In my instance, even as we were moving from B&B to B&B across Johannesburg – we moved constantly because it was important not to be noticed and not to be settling at a particular space because you don't want to transfer risk, security risk, to these establishments – even amidst that, doing the TM, and being able to draw courage and support from my spouse and from my colleagues, allowed me to be able to step up to the plate, so to speak. Without that, I certainly would have battled.

Dan Kgwadi (NWU)

Unlike other vice-chancellors, Dan Kgwadi experienced threats on his life from two very different quarters: from racist whites who could not bear the thought of their alma mater, the Potchefstroom component of the newly merged North-West University (NWU), being managed by a black man who, in addition to his race, appeared to be less enthusiastic about their self-apportioned cultural asset, Afrikaans; and from angry black students who wanted to destroy the other component of the university, the historically black Mafikeng campus, which had formed the second component of the NWU merger.

A physics and chemistry major (BSc), Dan Kgwadi started his undergraduate studies at one university in the merger, the then homeland University of Bophuthatswana in Mafikeng (later named the University of the North-West, before the NWU merger). He then received a PhD (in physics education) from the Potchefstroom University for Christian National Education. Put bluntly, he studied on a black campus and then a white campus – only to lead both of them, and a third component (the relatively small Vaal Triangle campus in Vanderbijlpark), as the first black vice-chancellor of the merged NWU campuses.

The threats that were coming to vice-chancellors were now more personal. You could get the idea that this is no longer about us running the institutions; it was like you were personally held liable for decisions which were implemented . . .

When it comes to issues of safety, this is something that worried me a bit because I started to worry about the safety of my colleagues and, of course, about how I was portrayed and personally attacked. And people were trying to muddy me politically, you know, trying to put me in a political box to suggest how I must be viewed. When I learned that there were investigations about me, as to which political party I belonged to, it got me worried. This was no longer simply university management issues that we were dealing with; these were serious political matters.

So the minute you start worrying about your safety, you start to think about tightening up your security. For example, as vice-chancellor I used to have late-night meetings, even meetings with the students in the residences, but I cannot do that anymore. It is not a very safe environment to have an evening meeting with the students. There are cases where students were found with guns and pistols on campus, and this was a further indication of an environment which was not very safe.

While vice-chancellors find themselves being muddied politically, the unfortunate thing is we don't have the blue lights and official security of the politicians. Nor do we necessarily want to be found in that space, because then the academic freedom that we stand for is compromised.

I was invited to Wits not long ago for a seminar, and you could tell that the freedom of space where academics can express their views is no longer valued, because people always tend to think or express themselves in a political way. If people reach stagnation in terms of their arguments, then they just resort to labelling people as sell-outs. You are a sell-out because the activist is not able to logically challenge your point of view, or he feels he has lost the argument, and that is when [the activists] resort to naming and labelling.

After the Mafikeng campus was reopened following the arson attacks of 24 February 2016, I tried to resuscitate student life, to bring back an academic environment. We now have a plan that every Friday there is a debate scheduled. Students must get into a debate because one must try and mentor them into accepting views that are not the same as theirs. We try to develop the understanding that a university is a free space, a place where you can express opinions, differing opinions. This is difficult because you start to see people trying to mimic what is happening in Parliament.

My family? It is something that I'm not very vocal about. My daughter is now a first-year student, and you know where she is going now? I took her to Monash University, because I thought there is no way she can go to NWU. It would be quite a risk. I would not want her to be exposed to that. She will not be just another student, because of her name. For some people, she would even as a student have to account for my sins, for the decisions that I took . . .

If you go on Facebook, you won't believe it – I mean, some of the issues directed at us as a family. So the family has had to accept and understand this at all times. You always want to make them calm by saying, 'No, don't worry, don't worry about what they say.' It is a security matter, as I said, for the family. It's always a security matter. As the rector[14] of the Mafikeng campus, I had to go and order security for my own family's house.

It was so bad that I actually had to come home quite often from the university in Potchefstroom to Pretoria. Whenever I found the time, I would drive that long distance to come and sleep at home so that my family experiences a normal environment, so that they do not panic and say, 'You're not here, so what could be going on?'

I am now finally in the vice-chancellor's house in Potchefstroom; I just moved into it last week, after two years. For security reasons I could not move into that house. Now, for me it's almost worse because you get the left-wing and the right-wing always going for you. Some feel that there's no transformation or it's too slow and they've lost patience with you. But others feel like, 'No, this is not transformation, it's a revolution.' So you get it from all sides. One group, radical blacks, calls you a sell-out and labels you as counter-revolutionary for not speeding up change. Another group, right-wing whites, believes that you are actually deployed by the ruling party to come and deal with them. You can't win.

In a toxic environment such as this, you cannot take your family to live where you work. When I was on the Mafikeng campus, they had to deploy a police Casspir [armoured truck] in front of the rector's residence. Now imagine you wake up in the morning and there's a Casspir right outside your house. How do you explain that to the family? The young ones, how will they grow within an environment like that? . . .

[Although I'm now living at Potchefstroom, I still] always have to be careful. When I'm at the university campus, I must check the times I must be in and out. And as I said, with Mafikeng it's even more worrisome because you find guns there. During the strikes, a student was shot. There was live ammunition which was allegedly used by the security. But the results from the ballistics showed it was not from the security guards. They also found 25 other cartridges on campus.

This is a Bosnia, it's a battlefield, and therefore you cannot be reckless when you are here. The other day I went with the family to go buy a tent. We went to this military place where they sell tents. There were a number of other things they had there, including a bulletproof vest. A family member said to me, 'Hey, you need this thing. Don't you think you need to buy yourself one?' Now can you imagine if people start to think like that? Since when does a vice-chancellor need to think of wearing a bulletproof vest? The situation on campuses has gotten worse than one would really have expected.

Tyrone Pretorius (UWC)

Tyrone Pretorius is a quiet and reserved man, an accomplished research psychologist who returned to his undergraduate alma mater (UWC) as a professor and then vice-chancellor of the institution. He is a career academic, having progressed through the academy from lecturer to dean to deputy vice-chancellor at UWC before serving for a short spell as the president of the South African campus of Australia's Monash University in Midrand. Ironically, two of his specialisations as a psychologist were coping and stress. As the leader of the one historically black university that defied its apartheid past, he would need those insights to guide him through the turbulent protest period.

Even people who have been around since the days that this campus was, you know, out there during the 1970s and '80s were quite rattled by last year [2015]. And in a sense it has brought differences between staff to the fore because there's a group of staff that called themselves 'concerned academics', and the rest of the academics were upset because does that mean they are 'unconcerned'? But the 'concerned academics' have aligned themselves very clearly with the #FeesMustFall students and they constantly criticise all of the decisions that we take as management.

So last year brought these differences between the different groups of academics quite sharply into focus. What also happened is that students had begun to distrust the academics because there were those students not participating in the protest and they still had to receive instruction from the 'concerned' lecturers. The non-protesting students therefore feel they will be victimised by these academics who have declared that their sympathies lie with the protesting group.

This has created quite a bad dynamic in all directions. The SRC is quite vocal about the matter because they say, 'How can we go to class and pretend that this lecturer that's teaching us is unbiased, has our best interest at heart?' As I say, even people who come from the struggles of the 1980s have been quite rattled by the situation. But then obviously UWC has changed over the years, so we have a lot of new people who have never experienced this sort of unrest and they were quite anxious.

They wrote to me on a daily basis asking, 'Can you guarantee our safety?' and I had to say, 'No, I'm a vice-chancellor, that's all that I am. I take decisions that I hope will secure your safety but I can't guarantee anything.' And then there's the constant uncertainty, because you start your day normally, you have your first lecture, you're busy with your second lecture, and here the mob comes running in and screaming. I'm quite worried. Last year there was a very, very real sense of anxiety and people were basically traumatised.

The vice-chancellor relayed a story that revealed how close to serious injury or death staff members at UWC would come.

I don't know if you know Lois Dippenaar. Lois is one of our directors in planning. She sits in the office just below [where we were sitting] on the second floor. On that Friday afternoon when protestors attacked the admin building, her desk is at the window, and a brick flew past just in front of her face. You know, just flew past. Of course people are deeply traumatised by events like that.

This year [2016] there's a sense of anxiety. What's going to happen next? When is it going to happen? But what worries me is that there's almost a sense of normality about the situation. There would be students protesting here in the square but classes would be going on with other students walking past the protestors, and staff walking past them, and there is almost an acceptance that this is the new normal. That we should expect that [the protestors] will congregate, they will sing and dance, and then they will go on a rampage through the campus. That worries me. Yet I think in general the resilience of the staff has been remarkable. They've handled it, but it has been quite traumatic and stressful.

Sizwe Mabizela (Rhodes University)

If there is one vice-chancellor with a genuine heart for students, it is the genial and soft-spoken leader of Rhodes University. Sizwe Mabizela is a mathematics graduate from the University of Fort Hare, the famed alma mater of 'the greatest generation'[15] – Nelson Mandela, Govan Mbeki and others. Mabizela cut his teeth as a mathematics professor at UCT and Rhodes. He is now vice-chancellor at Rhodes, where his PhD in parametric approximation from Pennsylvania State University must sometimes seem light years removed from the task at hand.

Yet Mabizela has remained remarkably grounded in his role despite the attacks on his person from protesting students. As he puts it: 'My own position is that all my students are important and I have to do everything possible to protect each and every one of them.' On this commitment he remains undeterred, despite the family taking a battering from the protestors.

Gosh, it has been very difficult. It has been incredibly difficult. Fortunately my daughters are in a boarding school, but they have had to go through counselling because, being at school in Grahamstown, they read much of the negative things written in the media and the social media and it does affect them.

There was one posting which was saying that I needed to be killed and they really struggled with that. They asked me, 'Daddy, are they really going to kill you?' So they had to go through counselling. It has taken a toll.

I have had two death threats and the police have investigated those. It does take a toll on one because you really don't know what tomorrow will be like. And even in terms of student demands: they make one set of demands, and if you try to respond to them, they don't really care about those demands since something else is now on the table. So this uncertainty is not healthy, it does take a toll.

I jog every morning, which really helps relieve a lot of stress. I do have spiritual support. I'm Catholic and my priests are there all the time to support me. I pray my rosary almost every day and that is something that has really sustained me. But on the whole, things move along.

My wife lives in Pretoria, but she has coped. She has coped well. Look, there has been stress, and right now not knowing what will happen with higher education going forward is putting a lot of stress on the family, but we'll just have to take it one day at a time.

Prins Nevhutalu (CPUT)

Unlike his vice-chancellor peers, Prins Nevhutalu achieved seniority within South Africa's science councils as a leader in what would become the National Research Foundation, the premier authority for the funding of social and scientific research in the public universities. His undergraduate studies in the biological sciences at Turfloop (or the University of the North, now the University of Limpopo) would no doubt have sensitised him to the struggle and politics of black students. But even those experiences decades ago were far removed from what he now faced as vice-chancellor of CPUT.

During this time of crisis I felt hopeless. I mean, I was threatened; [the protestors] used to email pictures of a gun, of Boko Haram. Then there was a week when they threatened to come to my house, they wanted to bomb my house . . .

I told my wife about this. Then the university decided to post security people at my house and alerted the police to patrol the place. We did not normally have security; we live like ordinary citizens. So my wife became very worried. On one of the days after the police had just gone – I think two days after the security had gone – there was singing coming from the church next door. But the singing sounded like the same song the protesting students would sing. It sounded as if there were students coming. My wife stood up and said, 'They're coming for us.' She was terrified. I also felt they were coming for us. I went out and listened. I expected to see a crowd coming from far off, but it was only people singing in the church.

That was the extent of our fear. I used to go home and try to get tired. I'd stare at the ceiling until three o'clock in the morning. When protestors burned a building, the guy who used to patrol here phoned me at about three o'clock to say, 'Student Financial Aid is burning.' I was awake even before the phone rang.

I was concluding the interview after diverting to a different topic when Prins Nevhutalu suddenly added a disturbing and sad closing line, something that must have weighed heavily on his mind:

> She [his wife] was terrified. She really was terrified. She could not believe that they were coming for us and we're the only two in the house and my bedroom is on the second floor. We were starting to look at how we would jump.

As for Tyrone Pretorius, Nevhutalu's distress as a leader extended beyond his family to the senior administrative staff around him, as shown in this equally disturbing vignette that he shared:

> There's a young woman here, Maresce Geduld-Jeftha, she was the acting director of finance. As a rival group of students forced themselves into a meeting, she was insulted [by a protestor]. I could take it, I don't care, but I stood up and said, 'You don't do that to her, to my staff members.' The council members were all quiet. My chairman did not speak out or say a thing, until he expressed agreement with the students.

It was clearly not only the immediate family of the university leaders who came under fire from the student protest movement, but also those who worked closely with them in the senior administration. And in defending those close to them, vice-chancellors could not always rely on academics or even council members in their institutions.

Derrick Swartz (NMMU)

A veteran of the youth struggles against apartheid, Derrick Swartz would sharpen his activist teeth at UWC, where he obtained all his degrees. Regularly drawn into post-apartheid duty, he would serve on boards and commissions of government until he took on the difficult task of turning around the financial fortunes of the University of Fort Hare. More than most university leaders, he understood student struggles experientially, and his studies in sociology and the politics of development would give academic substance to his activist commitments. But as he would discover after he took the job of vice-chancellor at NMMU in 2008, he was now living in a very different era. On a personal level, his reaction to the campus crisis was one of deep disappointment but also gratitude that he escaped the worst of the abuse.

Mercifully, [personal attacks] didn't happen to me, but I've been profoundly shocked by a segment, arguably a very small segment, as part of a revolutionary doctrine, thinking nothing about breaking and burning down the system. And I heard this guy Andile Mngxitama [of Black First Land First] saying something along the same lines.

That is not a progressive ideal for me. That's a completely reactionary and crypto-fascist reaction. So it did shake me, as it did a number of higher education beacons. And I was going to leave NMMU next year [2017] anyway, but it just made me feel profoundly disillusioned with the fact that the promise of higher education, the way we set it up in 1994/1995, had become shrivelled up into an aberration, so to speak.

How have I coped with it? Look, I'm tough, you know. I don't like fighting, but I'm not going to allow someone to walk over me either. I have a way of expressing my own views and interacting with my students and so on, and it became very clear that the way in which we vice-chancellors had been set up and projected as 'the other', that is not who we are.

It has helped to start engaging and to give ourselves, the students and the management, a chance to understand each other's positions. There has been a sense of rapprochement between a significant sector of those students and ourselves, at least at a kind of an interpersonal level of engagement. The underlying issues are still very much there, and the new situation will push us to a point where we have to test the quality of the relationship that has been nurtured up until now. But I'm actually not sure how that's going to work out.

Students are in a difficult situation. They know that there is more than that which they projected us to be. At the same time, they see us as representatives of a social order with which they have profound difficulties. And so you're a manager or a leader representing a system and also, at the same time, someone that they can see understands their issues as well.

So I've not been traumatised. I have to say I'm tougher than that. I've faced much worse during an era long gone by. And none of the students threatened me or my family or any of that. Mercifully, that didn't happen. But I think just from looking at that period, I was profoundly shaken by that experience. I know a lot of my fellow vice-chancellors suffered exceedingly more. So I really didn't suffer, I have to say. I've been blessed – just lucky, I mean.

But when I see Max [Price], the humiliation of students throwing water at him, holding his senior colleagues hostage – that never happened here. Students tried to get me to sit down on my knees. I said, 'You must be joking.' No person will ever do that to me, ever. That was done to me during the [apartheid] period. I've come through fire and brimstone, so make no mistake: I'm a lovely guy, but there are some things I'm just not going to do in front of all of them. And I went to the amphitheatre and they calmed down. I said, 'If I want to sit down here, it will be when I feel like doing so and on my terms as well, not because you say so.'

But I saw the personal abuse. Death threats against people like Tyrone [Pretorius], for example. Ihron [Rensburg] himself, who literally fled from his house. I mean, that's terrorism, that's rough stuff. So I really felt for my colleagues during that period and I was worried that something will happen on our campuses. We were just lucky since October [2015] to now [early 2016] that a life has not been lost by a student shooting another student or a staff member attacking students.

People are scared that the protestors will pull out a gun and shoot. So I almost got the sense at some stage that there was this sectarian group looking for *die lont* (the spark), looking for this trigger event that will become a kind of a 1976, and taunting the cops to shoot and so on. And it may still happen.

Cheryl de la Rey (UP)

In the end each vice-chancellor found ways of coping with the enormous pressure of their job. Cheryl de la Rey, the principal of the large, multi-campus University of Pretoria and a psychologist, acknowledged that the stress is real: 'Anyone who says otherwise is not being truthful.'[16] She says that she contains the daily stress of leading the university by keeping to regular working times, staying out of the media as far as possible, and acknowledging the limits of her control.

Lourens van Staden (TUT)

In the case of Lourens van Staden, the bouncy leader of TUT who takes on the job of university management with the attitude of a pugilist, the personal scars are evident throughout my conversation with him. Qualified to teach and lead in technical colleges, the former technikons, as well as universities, Van Staden has come to be known as 'the fixer' in higher education. A government minister appointed him as administrator at the chronically troubled Walter Sisulu University in the Eastern Cape. Later he was invited to act as vice-chancellor at the volatile and unstable TUT, a large multi-campus institution in Pretoria. By throwing himself into the fray, Lourens van Staden has, with considerable political savvy and managerial intelligence, kept these difficult institutions functioning despite his white skin – although aided, no doubt, by his fluency in an African language. But there were high personal costs to pay.

> How do I cope with this? By not having a hidden agenda. I'm not an angel. I'm a chess player myself. From a very young age, I studied that game. So in a way, I play chess with them [the protestors], but the outcome of the game must be in the best interest of the university. When I go to bed I might not sleep. I don't sleep well, but I don't have a hidden agenda, for that would work to the detriment of the academic project of the university.
>
> This job makes you tired, you are bruised by the way they [the protestors] deal with you. I've been taken hostage by students in Soshanguve. And you know what? The bottom line is they wanted to talk about the problem, the challenge at hand. So I cope by trying to be honest. I use some people as a sounding board, to check whether

I'm still connected, because I do not know everything. I get emotional. But I love education and that takes me through, sleep or no sleep. I have to make this thing work.

I cope by engaging. It might sound silly to you, but my lifeline is to talk. If we speak to labour here, say about insourcing, this is how I worked: After I collected the memo of demand [related to insourcing], I formed a task team to look at insourcing of outsourced services. I then sent a messenger saying, 'There are four types of services. Give me two representatives each and they can join.' This is how I am. They are not in the employ of the university, but I told them to come and see us. They get ripped off by the outsourced companies and they do not have decent living conditions.

Before long, the worker representatives started to insult us, swearing, breaking our furniture, and then they walked out. And despite that, now our labour, these guys, they are fighting, ready to fight. They did not show up for the scheduled meeting. Later they jumped the fences and they were violent there in the Sunnyside guesthouse we had arranged for the meeting. They toyi-toyied here outside the gates for a week. Eventually they came. They're with us now and I'm going to insource some of them.

So you need to keep on pursuing to have a conversation with somebody. When things are really terrible, then I try not to go to bed if I think there's a possibility of moving forward . . . This is what I do here. It helps to be proactive. When the politics is very hot, you must still be cool-headed, and I push for solutions as long as possible. And then when I feel that I've done my level best, I sleep, but I'm still mulling over things. This is how I stay sober.

But for now my main drive here is only one thing, and that is passion. That is all. I want this place to work because of the immense potential here.

There cannot be a sharper contrast with the pugilistic persistence of Lourens van Staden than the approach of Ahmed Bawa at another seasonally unstable institution, the Durban University of Technology (DUT).

Ahmed Bawa (DUT)

In a First World country, Ahmed Bawa would be the academics' vice-chancellor. A theoretical physicist who thrives on thinking about his science, Bawa is an intellectual in the best sense of the word. His thinking stretches effortlessly from the physical sciences to thoughtful engagements with broader human questions. It is therefore not surprising that when serial crises confronted him at DUT, this vice-chancellor would immerse himself in student conversations to determine what was really going on. Yet such habits of thinking and engaging would not assuage the personal stress he experienced.

I'm not totally sure whether my approach to understanding student activism was partly to help me to cope with what was going on or whether it came from a deep set of reflections. I suspect it's a mixture of both. But when I caught on to this notion that actually these demonstrations at the beginning of every semester may not be such a bad thing – because it provides the students with the opportunity of learning – that helped me to navigate.

However, by the time I got to my sixth year as vice-chancellor, I was really tired. I mean, I got to the point where I was hating the job. It was no longer an opportunity for creative engagement. I was just saying, 'My God, this again.' Notwithstanding the fact that I understood that there was a need for us to try to get as many students into the university as possible – within limits, of course.

On the family side, perhaps it's fortunate that my wife and I lived in different cities, so it was only when I came home on the weekends that she got a sense of the turmoil and so on. During the week, she was pretty insulated from it because I was there and she was here. So that helped to some extent.

But I don't think she was insulated from it completely. After all, she works at UJ and she experiences it on a daily basis too. What really perturbed me, I have to say, were instances where staff members would, for their own political ends, simply side with the students on issues which they knew full well were unachievable and would then lead union action. For some reason that really turned me off, much more than the student actions. There was one occasion when staff

150

members gathered outside Milena Court [the building housing the senior management team] and began to chant, 'Get the Indian out of the castle', which really drove me crazy.

This racist chant caught me off guard in the interview. I had to ask, 'Are you serious?'

Absolutely. And you know, I looked and I smiled at it, and then I actually went downstairs and said, 'You know, I think you've got it wrong because there are no Indians in the castle here.' But for some reason I was much less accommodating with staff than I was with students. But generally speaking, I think my personality allowed me to deal with this in a kind of rational way at most times. Except when I felt that students were lying to me and where I thought they were trying to manipulate me. I don't mean politically manipulate, but where they would tell me different stories which were untrue. Then I would freak out.

I asked Bawa about his decision to move on: 'So as you get ready to leave, what's going through your mind?'

I once met Clark Kerr [former president of the University of California]. He was about 85 years old then and I just wanted to say hello to him. I was so taken by his books [on universities]. I had this long conversation with him and he was telling me about his experiences. As I was leaving, he tapped me on the shoulder and said, 'My dear boy, I hope you understand that when you leave the university, nobody will ever remember that you were there.' So I have to say that I think all I have left are reflections about what I tried to put in place and which I hope will continue in some form or the other.

Six years on the job. And you know, many people said to me, 'You really need another four years to see these things through', and I think that's true. But I just couldn't bear the thought of it. Not because I wasn't managing everything, but because I'd just felt that I reached the point where I wasn't enjoying it anymore.

151

Ahmed Bawa left DUT in April 2016 to head up Universities South Africa (USAf) in Pretoria, a body representing the vice-chancellors of the country's public universities.

Chapter 7

Sense and Non-sense in the Decolonisation of Curriculum

Hell was let loose.
– Ngũgĩ wa Thiong'o[1]

The year is 1968, five years after Kenya won independence from Great Britain. The setting is the University of Nairobi, and what was about to happen there would become known as a landmark event in the politics of curriculum. The head of the Department of English, in the process of making proposals to the board of the Faculty of Arts, introduced a set of uncontroversial initiatives but with a contentious phrase that would spark 'the great Nairobi literature debate'.

> The English department has had a long history at this college and has built up a strong syllabus which *by its study of the historic conti-nuity of a single culture throughout the period of emergence of the modern west* makes it an important companion to History and to Philosophy and Religious Studies. However, it is bound to become less British, more open to other writing in English (American, Caribbean, African, Commonwealth) and also to continental writing, for comparative purposes.[2]

The italicised phrase sparked objections by three lecturers, including Ngũgĩ wa Thiong'o, one of Africa's foremost writers and critics. Together these lecturers not only called for the closing down of the English department, but laid out a platform for a new curriculum with this provocative query:

> Here then, is our main question: if there is a need for a 'study of the historic continuity of a single culture', why can't this be

African? Why can't African literature be at the centre so that we can view other cultures in relationship to it?[3]

This rejection of the notion that Africa is merely an extension of the West was an intellectual turning point in the postcolonial scene. What followed is encapsulated in this crisp observation by Ngũgĩ when he argued the case for curriculum change in his short but remarkable book *Decolonising the Mind*: 'Hell was let loose.' Indeed, calls for radical change to a university curriculum will always summon forth the forces of Hades, for curriculum transformation strikes at the very identity of a higher education institution by asking troubling questions about how a university sees itself in relation to the nation and the world.

Thinking about the decolonised curriculum

During my time at UFS, a prominent student leader, who was intellectually one of the best young university minds I had the privilege of engaging, regularly visited my office. He enjoyed stopping by simply to talk about what I called 'knowledge and society' questions. I relished the intellectual sparring with this talented student. 'The problem,' he told me on one occasion, 'is that we [students] seldom read beyond the first chapter of Fanon's books.' I offered to give him three classic works in exchange for a longer debate on seminal ideas in the anti- and postcolonial movements: Frantz Fanon's *The Wretched of the Earth*, Albert Memmi's *The Colonizer and the Colonized*, and Aimé Césaire's *Discourse on Colonialism*. For any student wanting to get a grip on the foundational ideas of the critics of colonialism, these were indispensable readings. None of these writers spoke at any length about curriculum, however. Theirs was a broader anti-colonial struggle against the occupation by colonisers of African and Afro-Caribbean countries. What contemporary scholars do is to infer from their work possible implications for the decolonisation of the curriculum.

Nonetheless, if there was one arena within the broader student protest movement of 2015–2016 in which there was very little deep thinking going on, it was in the sudden, though certainly not unexpected, flag raising on behalf of an old culprit, the university curriculum. There is a reason why the curriculum always emerges as a rallying point in student protest movements: it carries symbolic value that far out-weighs its instrumental functions such as the choice of subject content, teaching methods, and the acquisition of learning. The curriculum stands for something else. It represents a set of values, commitments, and ideals, and in its very constitution offers the most tangible evidence of what curriculum theorist Michael Apple calls the selective tradition. Put simply, those in power consciously *select* what is worth teaching and knowing and, in the process, assign value to what goes in and what is left out of the curriculum. That choice is a political act.[4]

Despite the predictable attention received by curriculum in social transitions or student protests, it is precisely because of its symbolic value that very little if anything in the curriculum changes once the shouting is over. The fact is, very few activists have the time, inclination, expertise, or support to 'make curriculum' differently *within* institu-tions. This is as true for the People's Education struggles in the 1980s[5] as it was with the attempted radicalisation of the state curriculum in newly independent Zimbabwe,[6] and as it will be with the most recent flag-raising moment: the call for the decolonisation of the curriculum on the part of South African student protestors. Little will happen because cur-riculum change is not really the point of the decolonisation rallying cry in today's campus struggles; rather, the purpose is to mount a hill, raise the flag of discontent, and then descend back into the realm of the 'set-tled' curriculum.[7]

By way of illustration, consider a recent YouTube recording that went viral. A UCT student protestor speaking on a panel is captured on video railing against Western science as a project of modernity and concluding that 'science as a whole should be scrapped off, especially in Africa'. Local belief was ignored, she said, as in the case of a community in KwaZulu-Natal whose members believe they can use witchcraft to summon lightning to strike somebody. Then the student asks, 'Can you explain that scientifically? Because it's something that happens.' She goes on to point out that Newton saw an apple fall and created an equation, and only then was the concept of gravity established, regardless of what might have been observed earlier in parts of Africa. #ScienceMustFall became the new hashtag for the latest target of decolonisation. Mockery, memes, and mirth ('How can a Fallist be opposed to gravity?') took off around the world even as some rushed to offer a qualified defence.[8] It is true that science, like all knowledge, is a product of society and therefore partial and incomplete. But claims that science is 'colonial' and needs to be scrapped 'as a whole', or that someone being struck with lightning is a victim of an African's wish, are, of course, ridiculous. But the facts do not matter to this non-science student and her supporters. In fact, her rant is not about science; it is about signalling one's opposition to enemy knowledge in the same way that marching armies raise a flag as they advance to battle. Science will not 'fall' for another reason, and that is because scientific knowledge functions within powerful institutions.

Whether it was the push for Outcomes-Based Education advanced by South Africa's powerful trade union movement in alliance with the government's Department of Education,[9] or the drive by the energetic minister of education, the late Kader Asmal, to overturn the religious prescripts of the school curriculum,[10] or the efforts of the respected academic Mahmood Mamdani to Africanise the UCT curriculum[11] – all these events demonstrate the deep complexity of dislodging what I have elsewhere called *the institutional curriculum*.[12]

This does not mean that there will not be a flurry of low-level activity, or some knowledge adjustments here and there, that appear to respond to the students' rallying call for decolonisation. In fact, most of the elite universities, in response to student pressures, have hurriedly assembled curriculum review committees, and alert academics have hastily cobbled together multimillion-rand research proposals in an effort to capitalise on the rare opportunity presented by the 'decolonial turn'. But this political moment will be short-lived and little different from routine curriculum review as student protestors graduate and the activist agendas shift their focus – until the next call for radical changes to what and how and whom we teach.

What is this thing called decolonisation?

On and off campuses, this is the question I get most often: what is decolonisation? As with any social science construct, there is no singular or fixed meaning of the term, and the best one can do is to try to make sense of decolonisation within the contexts in which the word is used. More than one source acknowledges that 'decolonization has multiple meanings, and the desires and investments that animate it are diverse, contested, and, at times, at odds with one another'.[13]

To begin with, the call for decolonisation – and for the decolonisation of curriculum in particular – has a long history, and not only on the African continent. Strictly speaking, decolonisation means 'the end of colony' and therefore refers to the period preceding the collapse of colonial rule in Africa and elsewhere. That in fact was the original usage of decolonisation and it made logical sense. Get rid of the colonial power as an object of anti-colonial struggles and in the quest for independence from the European colonisers.

But following independence a movement arose, along with a persuasive literature, which argued that you can remove the colonial power as it retreats to France or England or Portugal, but its legacies – from how capitalist economies are reproduced, to how authoritarian politics are conducted, to how cultural preferences are exercised – live on in the now free territory. Furthermore, the colonial authority and the postcolonial state remain in an intimate relationship, tied together with social, economic, and cultural bonds that continue to express the power of the former coloniser ('the metropole', some postcolonial writers call it) and ensure the dependence of the colonised.

In other words, the coloniser might have left, but colonial influences still determine how the new African rulers, in this case, exploit the people they govern and suppress anti-colonial ideas. In the realm of culture, African foods, hairstyles, music, and artistic works still show preferences for European rather than African traditions, styles, and values. The postcolonial critics therefore argue that the continuing strong connection between the colonised country and the newly independent country makes relevant the renewed call for decolonisation long after the retreat of empire. Unfortunately, the postcolonial critique of society is often so embedded in unnecessarily obscure and impenetrable language that most students and the public are left outside of this important debate on who we are and how we behave after our political freedom is achieved.

There is an additional problem with this kind of critique in the South African context, as opposed to those African states where, in the words of social anthropologist Francis Nyamnjoh, 'colonialism was non-resident'.[14]

The implication is that colonialism remained *resident* in South Africa, a conundrum once expressed in some political quarters as 'colonialism of a special type'. White South Africans are not colonial subjects, nor has South Africa been under the yoke of Great Britain since 1910. Following centuries of white presence in South Africa, 'settlers' became 'natives', as Mahmood Mamdani might have called our fellow citizens. It is not only hurtful to whole communities of citizens, but also historically incorrect and politically divisive to insist on this kind of settler-versus-native language as it relates to white South Africans. After many generations of co-existence at the southern tip of Africa, all South Africans, of any colour, are governed by the same Constitution and subject to the same rights and responsibilities.

Yet it is exactly this kind of pernicious language that has been re-asserted in the current student protest movement. The blatantly racist confrontations between black students and white students or staff often invoke the settler language as it relates to a primary claim of more radical movements, such as the Economic Freedom Fighters (EFF) and the PAC, for the re-appropriation of stolen land.

So what does it mean to decolonise the curriculum in the wake of colonial rule or apartheid? There are at least six different conceptions of 'decolonisation' when it comes to the subject of knowledge as embedded in the school or university curriculum. But as these conceptions are introduced, it is important not to read them along ridges of sharp distinction, for there are proponents whose thinking stretches across more than one category. Ngũgĩ, for example, advocates decentring the European curriculum in his general argument but emphasises African languages in place of English as a commitment to Africanisation. The distinctions lie in the emphases of meaning in various works by recent curriculum scholars.[15]

Decolonisation as the decentring of European knowledge

In this view of decolonisation, the problem is that educational institutions organise curriculum content around the knowledge, values, and ideals of Europe, the site of both colonial and postcolonial authority. Under apartheid, for example, South African students were likely to learn more about the European wars against fascism than about African wars against colonialism. Even for the war fought exclusively on home soil, the conflict was presented as the Anglo-Boer War, a battle between warring whites, rather than as the South African War, in which blacks were active on both sides of the conflict. But even after apartheid, the argument goes, the ideas and inventions of European and American philosophers, psychologists, sociologists, chemists, mathematicians, and architects still sit at the centre of the curriculum in the social sciences as well as the natural sciences.

In a more generous conception of decolonisation, the decentring critics argue that in Africa, for example, we need to replace Europe with Africa at the centre of the curriculum. This does not mean that Europe is deleted from the curriculum, but that European content – values, ideals, orientations, achievements, and so on – is secondary to, and an outflow from, a new knowledge system that places Africa at the centre, rather than the other way round. Put differently, for the advocates of toppling Europe from the centre of curriculum, this *recentring* approach[16] restores the place of the African and African knowledge at the heart of how we come to know ourselves, our history, our society, our achievements, our ambitions, and our future.

In a sense, recentring can be seen as a 'soft version' of Africanisation in that what changes is the relational position of an African-centred curriculum to the rest of the world, and the West in particular.

Decolonisation as the Africanisation of knowledge

Whereas the decentring position wants to exchange Europe for Africa (or Asia or Latin America) at the centre of the curriculum, the 'hard version' of Africanisation is about the displacement of colonial or Western knowledge and its associated ideals and achievements as the standard against which to measure human progress. For the pan-Africanist, the call for Africanisation in the curriculum is a nationalist imperative that asserts African identity and rejects the imitation of Europe in the quest for African knowledge, culture, and aspirations in the substance of what we teach and learn. For students, this means reading books by African authors, learning about artworks by African artists, rediscovering African greatness through scientific achievements by Africans, studying African cinematic works, and so on. Crudely put, the curriculum is and should be about Africa, not about Africa in relation to Europe and the distant West.[17]

Ngũgĩ wa Thiong'o came closest to addressing the decolonisation of curriculum specifically on the African continent. From his home in Kenya, Ngũgĩ made the striking observation that the curriculum sailed calmly from the colonial era into the postcolonial period as if nothing had changed: 'African children who encountered literature in colonial schools and universities were thus experiencing the world as defined and reflected in the European experience of history.'[18] Moreover, 'the structures of the literary studies evolved in the colonial schools and universities had continued well into the independence era completely unaffected by the winds of cultural change'.[19]

For Ngũgĩ, curriculum decolonisation in postcolonial Kenya meant teaching and learning through the African languages rather than through the colonial language, English. At one stage Ngũgĩ famously announced that he would henceforth not publish in English as part of his commitment to the Africanisation of Kenyan languages, and to challenge what his Nigerian friend and fellow writer Chinua Achebe called the 'fatalistic logic of the unassailable position of English in our literature'.[20] The colonial 'language was the means of spiritual subjugation'[21] from which Ngũgĩ would now escape as 'I would reconnect myself not to the Afro-European novel of my previous practice but to the African novel of my new commitment'.[22]

Decolonisation as additive-inclusive knowledge

This 'soft version' of decolonisation recognises the value of existing canons of knowledge but asks for recognition of new knowledge and its addition to established curricula.[23] While Harry Garuba, a professor of African studies at UCT, questions whether simply adding new items to the curriculum in place might be 'rather like adding raffia chairs to the master's living room', he nonetheless offers some practical advice to proponents: 'In your own discipline, you may, first, want to adopt a content-driven additive approach and expand the curriculum already in place.'[24]

The problem is that the addition of content is necessary but not sufficient for full decolonisation of the curriculum. For Suren Pillay, a professor in humanities research at UWC, what is 'left out' might have to be 'added in' through 'the justice of now including Africa in the university, naming things and building new statues, and adding a new course to the degree and adding a book to the syllabus'. And yet, he asks:

> Should we now settle for a supplemental concept of history, where we now add African Studies onto the existing curriculum with the danger of once more ghettoizing it from other mainstream disciplines? Or do we have to reconfigure the entire curriculum in ways that allow us to think the world, now equipped with the intellectual heritages that we have been taught to ignore from across the previously colonized world?[25]

This was certainly the approach of subordinated groups in places like the US, where in the 1970s courses in African studies and gender studies were added to the curriculum following civil rights and campus protests about exclusion. These knowledge groups, if you will, were often endowed with their own centres with facilities and staff to boot, but without disturbing the dominant canons of the institutions. In the same way, multiculturalism as it developed in the West, and as it reared its head at various points in South African schools, was intended to accommodate and include those left out, often through the celebration of the traditions, cultures, and beliefs of marginalised groups. Needless to say, the additive curriculum remained marginal to the establishment curriculum.

Decolonisation as critical engagement with settled knowledge

This conception of decolonisation is less concerned with either repositioning or replacing the existing curriculum than with empowering students to engage that knowledge by asking critical questions such as: Where did this knowledge come from? In whose interests does this knowledge persist? What does it include and leave out? What are its authoritative claims? What are the underlying assumptions and silences that govern such knowledge?

There is a fascinating corollary here to debates about what to do with the Rhodes statue and other controversial South African memorials.

Simply removing these colonial and apartheid symbols, or placing them out of sight, eliminates the opportunity to engage with those remembrances in direct, visible, and critical ways. Protracted engagement with public symbols such as the Rhodes statue invites a critical reading of this particular kind of curriculum – the memorial in place. This certainly is the kind of thinking that keeps in place memorials and burial sites of colonials in countries such as Zimbabwe and Zambia, where the argument is made that these representations are part of a nation's history: you cannot blot out what you don't like about the past. What you can do is to invite critical involvement with those 'curricula' in ways that transform their essential meanings.

In short, this conception of decolonisation means seeing the same set of problems differently, and using new theories, perspectives, and methods to engage with the resident curriculum such that, states Pillay, 'a decolonised knowledge project asks questions about the work that the disciplinary forms of knowledge do to reinforce unequal power relations or inhibit our thinking about certain objects of knowledge in particular ways'.[26]

Decolonisation as encounters with entangled knowledges

This kind of thinking about decolonising knowledge is relatively new and promises an advance on the rather staid criticisms of the (post)colonial curriculum. Here knowledge is not neatly separated into the neat binaries of 'them' and 'us', 'coloniser' and 'colonised', the 'metropole' and the 'South', 'the West' and 'the rest of us'. Instead, our knowledges, like our human existences, are intertwined in the course of daily living, learning, and loving. Even scientific discovery is the product of 'interwoven' knowledge between the coloniser and the colonised.[27] Hard as we might try, we cannot escape our entangled lives, which are invariably reflected in what we know and how we know it. This reality of entangled knowledges is especially valid in post-1994 South Africa, where former enemies quite literally breathe down each other's necks in shared social spaces such as schools and universities, and engage with the same troubled knowledge contained in the curriculum.

Decolonisation as the repatriation of occupied knowledge (and society)

This conception of decolonisation assigns to the curriculum enormous power to disturb not only settled knowledge but also settler society. Its most powerful arguments come from those involved in the struggles of indigenous peoples for control over their original land and their lives within an occupied country such as the US or Canada, where Native Americans are marginalised in public discourse simultaneously as 'at-risk people' (in sociologies of upliftment) and as 'asterisk people' (in bureaucracies such as a government census).[28]

Supporters of this 'hard version' of decolonisation are particularly incensed by the proponents of the additive-inclusive model of curriculum, for 'this kind of inclusion is a form of enclosure, dangerous in how it domesticates decolonisation'.[29] Under the repatriation approach, curriculum is invested with much more ambitious ends, which include 'repatriating land to sovereign Native tribes and nations'.[30] From this perspective, the demands of reconciliation and decolonisation are incommensurable, for to reconcile 'is about rescuing settler normalcy, about rescuing a settler future'.[31] Put bluntly, decolonisation is not about pampering settlers and affording them innocence through an accommodationist curriculum in educational institutions. Rather, its aim is to raise consciousness about the need to give back stolen land, end contemporary forms of slavery, and topple the internal imperialism that continues to keep indigenous people in subjection.

That is the sense in the 'decolonisation of curriculum' debates; now the non-sense.

Decolonisation of curriculum? A closer look

The fundamental problem with the recent call to 'decolonise the curriculum' is its rhetorical value in student politics, which is far removed from a sincere desire or commitment to change the curriculum in places of learning. In other words, there is a great deal of energetic and sometimes anxious flag-waving going on, for that is what is intended – to signal public standpoints for change with much less concern about the change itself. This subject of political symbolism has enjoyed some degree of consideration in curriculum theory.[32]

Nor is this rhetorical flourish around curriculum change something new. In every decade since the 1970s there have been similar political flashpoints in South Africa that turned attention to the curriculum. Examples include the work of the South African Committee for Higher Education (SACHED)[33] in the 1970s, the People's Education movement of the 1980s,[34] and the National Education Policy Investigation (NEPI)[35] in the early 1990s.

In these political moments, the themes of decolonisation (if not the word itself) were heard in the public square – purge the curriculum of offensive characters and ideas, make the curriculum more relevant to the lives of ordinary people, distance the curriculum from imperial Europe, recover African knowledge, install African heroes, and include African achievements in the curriculum. These recurrent themes are being raised again now, and will be raised again in the future at a time of social or institutional crisis. In such political moments, both past and present, the decolonisation flag is raised and lowered without sustained engagement on that most fundamental question in curriculum theory: 'What knowledge is of most worth?'[36]

To the current call for curriculum decolonisation, academics at South African universities responded with uncharacteristic enthusiasm. They offered all kinds of proposals that soon made the decolonisation of curriculum sound like *everything*, rather than careful deliberation on 'the what' of teaching and learning. For example, in an attempt to summarise the standpoints of the more vocal student protestors on the issue, Suellen Shay, dean of the Centre for Higher Education Development at UCT, identified six elements that protestors felt must be addressed in a programme of action: an undergraduate curriculum that is 'fit for purpose'; real-world relevance; the suppression of student voices; the domination of ideas by powerful groups such as white men; oppressive teaching; and the reproduction of inequalities through the curriculum. In other words, decolonisation as everything: 'Some of these challenges may fit more or less appropriately on the "decolonising the curriculum" agenda. Perhaps it does not matter: they are all important.'[37]

Particularly astounding is the protestors' dramatisation of the perils of the resident curriculum by pitching it as a celebration of 'white supremacy'. This is a rhetorical and dishonest appeal among student protestors and their allies in the academic community – another example of the tendency to 'catastrophise' (grossly exaggerate events or possibilities as unbearable 'realities'). In fact, there is no curriculum this side of apartheid that teaches white knowledge and experience to the exclusion of black knowledge and experience. The so-called cleansing of the curriculum, where decolonisation meant little more than erasure of the most offensive content in syllabi, took place even before the end of apartheid, and whatever vestiges remained would be cleaned up, so to speak, in the early years of democracy.[38]

The former white universities, particularly those that identify as liberal, started their transformation of curricula a long time ago – think of the curriculum debates at UCT in the 1990s[39] – and have continued to do so before (and after) the most recent calls for decolonisation of institutional knowledge. Most of these institutions have African studies or gender studies units or centres; organised sites for lesbian, gay, bisexual, transgender, queer or questioning, and intersex (LGBTQI) staff and students; and African-oriented research and teaching agendas that criss-cross the continent from Mali to Mozambique and Nigeria to Namibia. New courses in African film and media studies dot the institutional curricula. Every faculty or school of education in South Africa offers extensive reading lists that include works by scholars of Africa and the diaspora. South African universities have achieved award-winning innovations and research in many spheres of public health, ranging from innovative treatments of HIV/AIDS to managing infectious diseases such as tuberculosis. But you would not know about all these accomplishments from the rage around decolonisation. It is as if nothing has ever changed, as if every faculty, school, department, and centre on a university campus is caught in the grip of a colonial past and tied to the apron strings of a colonial present. This is, of course, the non-sense underpinning calls for the decolonisation of curriculum. The very fact that decolonisation's most articulate advocates work on South African campuses makes the point.

This does not mean that every academic department in every South African university has transformed or decolonised the curriculum according to the demands of protestors. As I showed in my book *Knowledge in the Blood*, the institutional curriculum does not change in the same way as flipping a switch turns darkness into light. The process of curriculum transformation – even in highly authoritarian societies – is necessarily uneven, untidy, and uncertain in its outcomes. The suggestion that human beings can instantly transform an undesirable curriculum in order to produce brand-new ideals belongs in the realm of science fiction, not serious scholarship.

Yet to claim with dramatic flair an unbroken continuity in the possession of curriculum knowledge from apartheid to democracy is to deny a whole tradition of critical scholarship then and now. Even under apartheid, critical scholars brought the colonial subject to its knees, whether through Jakes Gerwel's rethinking of Afrikaans, Allan Boesak's profession of Black Theology, Charles van Onselen's social histories of subjected persons, André Brink's anti-apartheid literature, Eddie Webster's sociology of labour, or Chabani Manganyi's psychobiographies of black lives – and on and on. Whole departments in sociology (Wits), anthropology (UCT), political studies (UP), media studies (UKZN), education (SU), and the humanities (UWC) have transformed over the years to establish new critical traditions already flagged in the early 1990s through collections such as *Knowledge and Power*.[40] Time did not stand still until today's new generation of students discovered the word decolonisation.

University leaders know this, of course, but they need to be seen to be responding to yet another round of public attacks on 'management', who are dismissed as deaf, recalcitrant, and obstructionist when it comes to student complaints. And so they set up committees, task teams, and other initiatives. The Curriculum Change Working Group at UCT was one such responsive committee called into life. Here is the official explanation of why this working group was formed:

It is the recognition that some of the injustices in our universities are lodged at the heart of our curriculum that made the call for decolonizing the curriculum one of the most persistent demands of the student movement and staff, particularly the Black Academic Caucus (BAC). The University's draft Strategic Plan 2016–2019 commits the University to expanding the scope of transformation. It foregrounds the critical role of curriculum as a *driver of change*.[41]

It is painful to see the UCT establishment bowing and scraping to these student demands for curricular change when in fact this university has done more than any other institution to revise and even radicalise its curriculum offerings. Examples include the recovery of the South Africa–Mali Timbuktu Project led by Shamil Jeppie; 'whiteness' studies inaugurated by Melissa Steyn (now at Wits); and the reinterpretation of the South African War inspired by historian Bill Nasson. But curriculum-change committees like UCT's are about *containment* of student discontent. Any attempt to put on the table what institutions actually do with regard to curriculum change would be met with howls of protest – the point is to bury academic works in play, not to praise them. And so UCT's working group genuflects in the direction of ideological and curriculum truisms for purposes of appeasement:

> The university is a place where ideas are contested. As such it should respond to the tensions that have surfaced in the post-Apartheid dispensation with new ideas for tackling the critical and urgent issues related to inequality within universities and society more broadly. As part of these debates we need to interrogate the ways in which race, class, gender and (dis)ability interface with our disciplines, and the environment in which we must all collectively teach, learn and live. We should also interrogate the hegemonic Eurocentric influences on global thinking about the content and foundational knowledge of many disciplines.[42]

With regard to curriculum change, the truth is that it is unlikely that universities like UCT will actually do much more than undertake their usual routines of curriculum review and renewal.

Nativism versus decolonisation

At the heart of the protest movement's most popular understanding of decolonisation – namely, the 'hard version' of Africanisation – sits a dangerous nativism often expressed in racist terms. The African envisaged here is not white or different shades of black. It is unapologetically the black African, to the exclusion of all other South Africans. This nativism is particularly hostile to white citizens as individuals and as a group, regardless of their origins, and to black persons who do not espouse a particular ideological narrowness as Africans. When the hardcore nativists say 'Eurocentric', they intentionally refer to white South Africans in a cruel playback of apartheid's use of referential terms such as 'European' and 'Native' for white and black citizens respectively.

This disfiguration of Africanisation into some form of racial essentialism is a danger that Frantz Fanon himself anticipated. Wits scholar Achille Mbembe notes that Fanon saw in Africanisation 'an inverted racism, self-racism' in which 'there is a shortcut from nationalism to chauvinism and eventually racism'.[43] This is not the Africanisation of Ngũgĩ wa Thiong'o or Harry Garuba. It is a crude and dismissive racism, a negative appropriation of a worthy term, as Max Price and a colleague point out in their statement on the call for decolonisation 'in its most radical form':

> This version of decolonisation is thus profoundly about race, and pitches black liberation against 'whiteness' conceived as some homogenised form of identity defined mainly by the happenstance of pigmentation. As such it risks polarisation as it implicitly rejects nonracialism as a form of co-option that is necessary if we are all to embrace transformation as a shared commitment.[44]

On campuses across South Africa, decolonisation quickly lost any sense of historical precedent or conceptual nuance and simply became a handy, racialised weapon to silence racist whites (by definition) and black compradors who stood in the way of a sharpened racial grievance against everything in its sight; the curriculum was simply one of those targets. When vice-chancellor Sizwe Mabizela therefore says, 'I still have to understand what the difference is between those terms – decolonisation and transformation', he is not alone. *Decolonisation*, it is now clear, has become the radical replacement for that ANC keyword *transformation*. The new word is supposed to do what the old one did not: namely, radically change society itself. But of course words do not change society. They can be used, however, to position a new movement as more radical than the incumbent movement. Moreover, invoking the language of decolonisation is at best a distractor from the challenges of producing, acquiring, and using knowledge to advance our understanding of a complex world and to deeply transform our communities. These challenges have nothing to do with decolonisation and everything to do with broken public schools, failing health-care systems, and corrupt government.

Curriculum and the educational transaction

A school or university teacher has the task of making the curriculum intelligible to students. The curriculum in itself is dead until it comes alive in the teaching and learning process. What inspired teachers do with that curriculum can provide students with critical insights into racism, inequality, poverty, imperialism, and underdevelopment. Incompetent or indifferent teachers can render the best curriculum inaccessible and leave students alienated from the learning process itself. The symbolic value of the curriculum matters little when its transactional value is undermined by uncaring, uncommitted, and incompetent teaching.

Moreover, teachers do not 'deliver' the curriculum to student minds in the way Domino's delivers pizza to your front door. Teachers *interpret* the curriculum to students on the basis of their own experiences, backgrounds, politics, and preferences. The advocates of decolonisation do not dwell in this space for too long, for their concerns are more limited: what to 'put into' the curriculum through the extension of, engagement with, or exclusion of whatever content is already in place. In any case, the question arises: who will teach the decolonised curriculum?

The academics who populate the lecture halls, studios, theatres, laboratories, and senates of South African universities are men and women socialised into their disciplines through postgraduate training, research cultures, and conference participation over many years. Most were trained as disciplinarians – that is, in the structures and routines of their specific disciplines or fields with particular theories and methods that inform their academic practice. Of the existing class of South African professors, most have worked on both sides of 1994, under apartheid and since democracy arrived in the land. Many academics see students the way their professors and lecturers saw students – as young people who need to be instructed in the discipline and treated as junior partners in the educational transaction. The point being made here is the unspoken expectation on the part of some activists that a decolonised curriculum handed over to lecturers for 'delivery' to students would wonderfully transform student–teacher relationships, change stand-up lectures into havens of Socratic teaching, and interpret the decolonised curriculum in ways that unmask white supremacy and racial inequality. Anyone who thinks this is even remotely possible across the diverse and entrenched cultures of teaching, learning, and assessment in universities clearly has not worked with academics.

An additional problem with the 'decolonisation of curriculum' position is the insistence on outdated terminologies of 'centre and periphery' or 'North–South' in an intensely globalised world and networked society. This is not to deny that the world order still privileges the rich developed world over impoverished developing nations. But those hierarchies have been and are being challenged through the rise of new powers (Japan and China, for example) and strategic realignments (such as BRICS, the association of Brazil, Russia, India, China and South Africa). Moreover, some South African institutions sit comfortably at the upper end of world rankings, whatever their limitations.

To fixate on the system of knowledge production as one in which Europe dictates the terms of engagement with a weak and submissive Africa is more non-sense. The terms of co-operation between European and South African universities are nothing like the colonial situation, even taking into account the discrepancies between investments and productivity in higher education on each side of the divide. And in several fields of study, South African universities and individual scholars are world leaders, attracting interest from students in the West who wish to study here under the intellectual authority of African scholars, and from overseas professors seeking partnerships with local universities. The insistence on a hierarchy of the powerful North and the powerless South not only plays into a sense of educational victimhood and emotional dependency, but denies the power and authority of South African intellectuals in many of these relationships.

The point here is that we South Africans have a choice in how we frame ourselves in relationships with international scholars. Surely our best option is to produce the kind of scholarship that addresses social and intellectual challenges at home, remains competitive with knowledge partners in other parts of the world, and works co-operatively to solve intractable problems affecting the planet, from climate change to HIV/AIDS to crop production. These efforts call for a very different kind of mindset from one that replays a language and politics from the 1960s in a globalised century where interdependence is key to planetary survival.

Bodies of knowledge

While the call for the decolonisation of curriculum on the part of protesting students might be viewed as a useful wake-up call to accelerate the transformation of universities, it is fundamentally misguided. The underlying conception of South Africa as a postcolonial state simply does not apply in the context of a constitutional democracy that endows all citizens with shared rights and a common national identity. Moreover, when wielded as a crude instrument of black nationalism, the call to decolonise curriculum and society is not only offensive; it is dangerous in a country still struggling with the racial, gender, and class inequalities of a very present past.

Of the contending conceptions of decolonisation, the most fitting point of departure – politically, educationally, and strategically – would be active engagement with entangled knowledges. This approach recognises the extent to which rival knowledges are tied up in 'entangled bodies' – living human beings who are globally interconnected and highly interdependent. It requires a much more sophisticated curriculum practice than interventions that, in the popular Africanist version, simply exchange the curriculum of one group for that of another. To re-hash(tag) the outdated language of oppositional binaries is to remain trapped in a discourse that is anachronistic, on the one hand, and without real chance of success as a curriculum-change strategy, on the other. Decolonisation is a simplistic application of a troubled construct to a much more serious set of challenges currently facing South African universities – and the world at large.

Chapter 8

Shackville and the Rise of the Welfare University

From the west I saw fly
the dragons of expectation,
and open the way of the fire-powerful;
they beat their wings
so that everywhere it appeared to me
that earth and heaven burst.
– From an Old Norse poem, translated by Thomas Wright
(1884)

To understand the roots of the perpetual discontent on South African campuses in the post-1994 period, and how this disgruntlement fanned the current wave of protests into such a destructive force in 2015–2016, it is important to grasp a largely unnoticed but consequential sea change in the culture of higher education institutions. That gradual but forceful change was the emergence of the 'welfare university' in South Africa. The change was made visible through a ubiquitous culture of routinely and forcefully presenting university leaders with demands for services related to students' material, social, and financial well-being. In brief, the protestors were acting on their belief that the university, as a state-run institution, was obligated to undertake student welfare support measures. If it did not do so, protest was the logical response.

Welfare: responsibilities and expectations

In 1998, the distinguished social historian Charles van Onselen commented on the growing welfarisation of the South African university, warning that 'government is in danger of confusing its welfare and educational responsibilities to the detriment of both'.[1] The shift towards the welfare university came about with the threefold increase in national student enrolments (0,4 million to 1,2 million in 21 years), including a huge percentage of poor students.

In the context of this rapid growth, 'massification [brought] previously excluded problems onto campus'[2] and along with it the struggles and conflicts besetting poorer communities. Thus the social problems of poverty as well as the protest politics of the poor moved seamlessly from community to campus. In Van Onselen's words:

> What we are currently witnessing is not so much a classical manifestation of 'student unrest' released by unrealistic expectations in the wake of a largely peaceful and successful political revolution, but an insistent plea for the alleviation of acute rural (and urban) poverty and distress via a youth cohort that is acutely aware of its responsibilities to the extended family, and which senses that it can most readily articulate its demands in educational rather than social terms.[3]

At UFS, we conducted a random, informal survey on the family welfare status and expectations of 200 black UFS students. Half of these students were from the urban Bloemfontein campus; the other half were enrolled at the rural Qwaqwa campus some 300 kilometres away. The Bloemfontein students are more diverse in terms of socio-economic status, while almost all the Qwaqwa students are from poor families of the eastern Free State and northern KwaZulu-Natal. The three survey questions were posed individually and answers were reported anonymously. The chief findings were:

- On the Bloemfontein campus, an unexpectedly high 76 per cent of the students reported that they came from a family that was a recipient of at least one government grant. On the Qwaqwa campus, 67 per cent of students indicated that they are from a welfare-supported family.
- Students were asked whether the state has a responsibility to ensure that *every* student is fully funded for university studies. (Note that the question did not single out poor students or students who could not afford higher education.) In response, 60 per cent of the Bloemfontein students, and a massive 85 per cent of Qwaqwa students, agreed that this is in fact the duty of government.

- Moreover, on the Qwaqwa campus 82 per cent of students believed that government also has a duty to provide for the basic needs of students – such as transportation and food – beyond direct funding for tuition, accommodation, and books.[4]

One needs more data to be able to assess the full extent of such a demographic turn in the student population. But it is reasonable to infer that this new generation of poor South African students, such as those surveyed at UFS, are the first to enter university from families who raised them as children under the generous social welfare regime of the democratic government. The state spent no less than R121 billion on social grants in the 2014/15 financial year, which is almost half of the total spend on education in the same period (R246,1 billion) and more than four times as much as allocated to university transfers (R26,26 billion).[5] The consciousness of this new generation of students was therefore shaped by their own experience, or that of friends and family members, of growing up as children of welfare families in which the state *as an institution* lifted whole communities out of abject poverty. They thus view the university, like the welfare net, as an extension of the hand of the state.

The child support grant in particular, which constitutes 71 per cent of the social grant allocation, applies to children born after 1993, so it makes sense that the cohort of largely poor students now entering university in their early twenties were either beneficiaries of welfare families or bore knowledge of the government's welfare outreach into impoverished communities. Given that the number of households benefiting from some form of the social grant increased from 29,9 per cent of the population in 2003 to 45,5 per cent in 2015,[6] the spread of the welfare net must have affected a significant portion of the students who entered the gates of South Africa's public universities expecting education but also a whole lot more.[7]

In this respect it is important to note that many of us tend to think of the move from school to university as a life transition, a radical *change* from one level of education to the next. However, in terms of the new service function of public universities, we might well be seeing a radical *continuity* in the welfare expectations of students. It is not just that the majority of new university attendees are likely to come from families or communities whose social well-being is secured by the government. There are also students who went to lower-quintile schools in which being fed by the state was part and parcel of what those public institutions did. For these communities 'in usual circumstances', argues a new book on the student protests, 'the ANC is regarded as the caring parent who may not get everything right, yet "it will bring home the food at night"'[8] – sometimes literally.

In travelling around to hundreds of schools in rural and urban areas over the years, I have been struck by the prevalence of community women cooking food in massive pots in order to feed students during lunch breaks and, in some cases, even before school begins.[9] Of course, food for the poor was always part of the experience of school children in different regions of the country. I benefited from soup and milk, for example, delivered throughout the week to Sullivan Primary School in Steenberg by the Cape Flats Distress Association (CAFDA). The post-apartheid government would make feeding students a 'lead project' of the Mandela government's Reconstruction and Development Programme (RDP). And the National School Nutrition Programme, despite frequent threats of collapse because of corruption in places like the Eastern Cape, survives to this day as part of an elaborate government welfare scheme.

The point is simply that the continuity of welfare provision from school to university is now being strengthened along the education pipeline as poor students move through the system in large numbers with the expectation that their basic material needs will be satisfied during the transition from one level of education to the next. In this regard at least one study has shown that the child support grant itself has kept more children in that pipeline as 'the grant is associated with a higher probability of enrolment, especially for older children'.[10]

This does not mean that universities are the only institutions taking up the slack where government, the markets, families, and traditional networks of social support have collapsed. One of the key allies of universities are the churches and other religious organisations that students attend. At UFS, both small and mega-churches such as the Christian Revival Church (CRC) offer students not only spiritual support but also welfare support. CRC, for example, provides students with work opportunities, clothing and food vouchers, and three months of food support ('until they get on their feet') through something called the Storehouse, while 'home cells' also adopt students in order to provide for their needs and in this way alleviate personal poverty.[11]

Outside of the church, whole families rally around poor students, taking them in and feeding them as part of additional new networks associated with the university, from which hundreds of students benefit. Hardly a week goes by without people from the nearby community coming through my office to find out how they can work with and support students in personal crises; some black as well as white students were helped in Bloemfontein shelters, for example, as they struggled to make their way through the university. Thus, when a student leaves this kind of college-town environment, such as during university vacations, he or she is leaving behind not only the campus but also a delicate network of support that makes student days liveable.

To note the rise in social grants is decidedly not a judgement against the South African welfare system, which has proven to alleviate poverty and even, some argue, to decrease household income inequality.[12] Given the inequities resulting from the country's racially segregated past, it is especially important to understand welfare as a matter of political rights rather than acts of charity. My argument about the emergence of the welfare university is an explanation offered for the *expectation* among many incoming students that the public university, as simply another institution of the state, will do much more for them as citizens than simply offer the education necessary for a degree. The university is also required to take care of the social, emotional, physical, and even nutritional well-being of the students in its care. Consider, for example, one item from a list of protestors' demands at CPUT as the vice-chancellor battled to keep the institution open towards the end of the 2016 academic year:

Female student tax, as they must pay for female hygiene products each month. If CPUT can provide condoms they should provide female hygiene products as well.[13]

In some contexts, this kind of official demand in the midst of a potentially career-ending crisis for students would be laughable. But in the current climate, a demand of any kind that is not responded to could cue yet another potentially violent protest and continued campus shutdowns.

But let's take one step back. Not too long ago, parents sent their children to university on the basis of a very simple contractual arrangement. The young high school graduate would be taught by university teachers in adequate facilities (libraries, lecture halls, laboratories, and studio theatres) to acquire a degree in a particular field or profession with the reasonable expectation of finding a job. There were selection decisions at the beginning, some orientation on entry, and graduation at the end – and that concluded the university's obligation to the student. The number of enrolments was small, so there was a good chance that a qualifying student would obtain a bursary or loan, which would be paid back over time in cash or by virtue of public sector employment, as in the case of graduating teachers.

But in recent years South African universities have gradually taken on more and more social welfare functions that stretch way beyond what was previously expected from a modern university. One study found that 'academics and administrators have acknowledged spending gratuitous time on tasks [such as personal counselling] that are not traditionally their responsibility as well as solving problems [such as student transport] that are beyond the remit of the HEIs [higher education institutions]'.[14] In the language of the social welfare specialists, universities could be said to be taking the shape of residual welfare organisations, which 'come into play when the market and normal systems of support, such as the family and community networks, break down'.[15]

That said, universities have reconstituted themselves as a consequence of policy intervention, with the result that 'education form[ed] part of the welfare package'[16] and 'higher education became part of national welfare policies'.[17] Consider, for example, the planned lifting of the ceiling to qualify for funding from the National Student Financial Aid Scheme (NSFAS) from household incomes of R120 000 to R600 000. This move significantly widens the net of support for student assistance in the form of bursaries and loans. It also significantly alters the organisation of universities, which will now need to enlarge their financial aid offices, increase their personnel, and expand their advising and support functions. Moreover, it is not only the functional work of university administration that changes. What also changes is how staff, students (especially the recipients of aid), and the institution itself understand the character and essence of what a university is and what it does.

The question, then, is: Why are students protesting, despite the hefty increase in social benefits and student aid? Why do they not 'feel' the effects of the massive expansion in assistance in their daily lives? There are three main reasons for this. The first has to do with *adequacy*: there are simply too many students entering higher education to cater for all of them, even if the increase in NSFAS funding is, on paper, quite impressive. Students all too often hear someone in the financial aid office telling them, 'We have run out of NSFAS money; try again next year.' It is not that they do not qualify; it is simply that there are more students in need of assistance than has been planned for. But what the student experiences is the feeling of being let down: 'I played by the rules, I did what was expected, and now you tell me it is not enough.' A mortal fear sets in: 'I am being told to go home; my future is over. I am doomed to be like those at home, permanently unemployed and stuck in a life of misery.' I have seen those faces of disappointment and fear; and for those who played by the rules, we made a plan and did what we could do. But funding inadequacy was a national problem, and no institution, even with the best of intentions, could resolve the issues on its own.

Which raises the question: is the problem of adequacy a failure of planning? Of course. But here two conflicting imperatives run headlong into each other. There is the rational imperative of common sense: you devise budgets against expected or planned enrolments. But the imperative of the politicians is to demonstrate that the poor now access higher education in greater numbers than ever before; this announcement is a point of pride in the president's annual State of the Nation address. What is not said is that the relentless political push to expand the system lacked punctilious administrative attention to what would be needed to financially support the growing numbers of poor students now entering higher education. For South African politicians, this attention to planning for implementation is a discipline lost in the politics of the immediate. For example, the ANC-led government opened two new universities – in such political reasoning, each province must of course have one – with an enrolment of little more than 1 000 for both of them together, and with no economies of scale in the foreseeable future.[18]

The second reason for students' continued discontent has to do with *efficiency*. It is now well known that the NSFAS has, in effect, given up on the crucial function of collecting loans made over the years, with the result that graduating students in general have simply stopped paying back the money. And there is the embarrassing fact that some universities simply do not manage their NSFAS allocations efficiently, which means that each year some portion of NSFAS funds is returned to the head office rather than every cent reaching students in need. There is also, sad to say, the uncomfortable suspicion that at least one university, under severe financial duress, might have spent its NSFAS allocations on staff salaries.

In relation to student performance, poor and desperate students may experience frustration and anger when they show up at the financial aid office and are told, 'You did not keep your part of the bargain. You failed too many modules to qualify for another year of support.' Here inefficiency is reflected in the high dropout and repetition rates, and the time-to-degree statistics for the majority of undergraduate enrolments. But what the student experiences is rejection, the frustration of being turned away despite doing his or her best with an inadequate school education. This challenge is what two university leaders at Wits University call 'managing the pedagogy of under-preparedness'.[19]

The third reason that students do not 'feel' the benefit of a welfarised bursary scheme is the problem of *sufficiency*. As funded students, they get the NSFAS grant, but it is not sufficient to meet the full costs of studying at university. The three standard costs – tuition, accommodation, and books – might well be completely covered, but students with no other money at all need to cover other expenses as well. These include food; visits to the doctor; trips to a distant home between semesters; unexpected departmental costs (such as field trips for geology students or teaching-practice transfers for education students); remittances sent home for unemployed parents and siblings; and personal items from sanitary towels to toothpaste and soap. A poor student brings *nothing* to university except his or her talents, and whatever NSFAS might put into a student's account, it is not sufficient to cover the range of that student's needs.

Often hidden from view is the 'coming of age' costs[20] for undergraduate students entering university at ages seventeen or eighteen. They are likely to date and even find their life mates on campus. This requires having money for going to the movies or a local dance, for buying a birthday gift or a meal out, or for taking a romantic trip off campus. For students in the former Afrikaans universities, entering a residence means spending money on the uniforms of that 'res' and on dressing up for the 'formals' with other residences. It is often assumed that all students come from families with this kind of discretionary funding, which leaves poor students embarrassed and desperate because they want to participate and be truly part of campus or residence life.

The poor student, then, might express the problem of sufficiency this way: 'You might be funding us, but you have no idea what it is to be a student.' Indeed, the lack of additional funding (beyond tuition, accommodation, and books) causes many students to drop out – the proverbial straw that breaks the camel's back. Of course, it is also true that students with the basic triad of funding often do survive the three or more years of undergraduate education by finding ways of supplementing this basic support. For example, they work part-time jobs off campus, the top academic students work as paid tutors in their departments, and others are supported by friends and extended families to bridge the sufficiency gap during their years of study. But the overriding expectation of the cohort of poor students is that all their costs should be covered.

At the everyday level, some universities have made proactive efforts to address observed needs in the student body. Examples include the No Student Hungry (NSH) programme or the University Preparation Programme (UPP) at UFS. And then there are the demands. In response to other demands, student welfare support actions at UFS have accumulated in recent years to include the following:

- After-hours transportation for students in evening classes
- Student feeding programmes

180

- Free health programmes
- Counselling and support programmes
- Out-of-term accommodation arrangements
- Transportation arrangements for talented recruits to and from home
- Funeral support services
- Medical student minibus service between campus and hospitals
- Spiritual support services
- Stipends for talented recruits
- Occasional winter meals
- Out-of-pocket payments by staff to students
- National and international bursary fund recruitment
- Open-door policies in senior team for student consultation
- Invitational morning breakfasts for students
- Special taxi terminus with covered parking for students
- In-residence computer facilities
- Wi-Fi facilities
- 'Study locks' for all-night studies
- Special textbook purchases
- Social worker service
- Loan laptops
- Referrals for special surgery or general hospital care from the university's medical school staff
- Assistance with off-campus accommodation
- Staff and private mentors on request for individual students
- Career network opportunities
- Teaching and learning support services including writing facilities
- Free registration for honours and full-time master's and doctoral studies (funded via council-approved funds)
- Work opportunities on campus
- Free refrigerators on loan to residence students on request

To see how these welfare functions come together in the life of a campus citizen, consider the real-life story of a poor UFS student with a potentially catastrophic ailment. Sipho (not his real name) is from an impoverished township called Thaba Nchu about twenty kilometres from campus. He comes from an extremely poor family in which his father was absent and his mother unemployed. Sipho grew up with extreme depression. When his mother died, he climbed onto the roof of the family's little house in order to jump to his death. But he survived, although with a serious leg injury. Since he could not afford health care, Sipho simply continued to live with the upper-leg ailment. Somehow he made it to university, where one of my colleagues noticed his limp. He was referred to the campus social worker, who sent him to the campus nurse. The nurse noticed that the leg was rotting away and needed far more serious attention than her office could provide.

The social worker, a friend of my family, mentioned this student's case to my wife, who asked that I find out how we could support Sipho. I made a call to the university's medical school to ask that they treat the young man as a matter of urgency. The dean made the necessary arrangements and Sipho received a free operation that not only fixed his leg but gave him hope. In my office afterwards, I could hardly recognise the joyful and confident young man. What had happened to heal Sipho would have been nearly impossible in his other world. Through a series of networks of caring campus persons – principally the nurse who had become close friends with the young student – a most unlikely healing could take place. Sipho knows this and expressed his gratitude for what had happened since he was, by all accounts, likely to lose his leg by amputation if he had been sent to one of the district hospitals. Our university medical staff were determined to save the leg. Within this labyrinth of many helpers is another beautiful South African story: except for my family, all the other helpers and healers were white folk.

The combination of student support functions varies in scale and scope from one university to the next. What is incontestable is that an intricate welfare net has been created that goes far beyond the basic contract of providing teaching that enables students to acquire competence marked by the attainment of a qualification. Even that extension of the contract into an expanded welfare support system is in itself uninteresting; after all, universities should be places of care and compassion especially in a country with so much poverty and inequality. What is significant is the fact that the welfare function is demanded, with a direct connection to the spiralling unrest on campuses.

The anthropologist James Ferguson drew attention to the change of thinking among South Africans about social assistance and the new politics that might flow from programmes of direct distribution.[21] With 15 million South Africans, or 30 per cent of the country's population, on government grants, Ferguson observed a growing expectation of official support in a country where 'service delivery ... [was] increasingly understood as a state responsibility to a deserving citizenry'[22] and expressed as 'a politics of rightful share'.[23] This expectation that material needs must be serviced was, however, based not on labour and reward but on 'such things as citizenship, residence, identity, and political loyalty'.[24] And no event better demonstrates this 'politics of rightful share' and its emotive appeal to racial identity and residency of citizenship than the so-called Shackville protests that erupted on UCT's Upper Campus on 15 February 2016.

Shackville

The postgraduate student sitting at my desk was a combustible mix of anger and anxiety. 'I need accommodation *now*,' he insisted. I anticipated the unhelpfulness of the usual response that the university could only accommodate about 20 per cent of its more than 32 000 students in the few campus residences; that undergraduates, and especially first-year students, enjoy priority in residence placement; and that applications should be made way in advance of the academic year to be considered in fairness to others. Something else in his insistence had caught my attention, which was that he *expected* the university to provide him with a place of residence. And so I asked him: 'Does the university have an obligation to provide you with a place to stay?' He looked stunned, mumbling as he tried to respond, but he could not answer.

I understood his anxiety, especially as he was a Zimbabwean student who would experience even greater difficulty finding finances for his studies or hospitality towards the foreigner while competing with South Africans for limited resources. He also knew that I would make a plan for him, even as I recalled a warning from one of my registrars that spending South African taxpayers' money on an international student was illegal. But to me that was less of a conundrum than the fact that this student, like his South African counterparts, *expected* to be accommodated.

This expectation is what energised the so-called Shackville protests at

UCT, where an unexpected upturn in the number of applicants who actually showed up to register created the ideal opportunity for protestors to seize on yet another example of 'institutional racism,' as Max Price recalls:

Max Price: We did not miss any classes [as a result of the Shackville protests], we did not have to close the university, but I think they [the protestors] were angling for a fight and it was going to be one issue or another. At Wits they targeted registration and financial exclusions, but here [at UCT] we gave them something on a plate, which was accommodation problems.

[In 2016] we were caught unprepared for a much larger number of students coming into university and returning than we had before. We always 'over offered' places because we know there's a lot of students, about 20 per cent, who do not take up their places or they move out. We know from experience that student applicants would not take up offers if they had residence options elsewhere, so we try to offer residence to as many people as possible.

What we normally do is we have a waiting list, and we accommodate people on the waiting list on mattresses in common rooms for the first two weeks and they eat in the dining halls. And as the returning students – who only come back a week after the first-year students come for orientation – don't pitch, then we offer places in res to the first-years.

But for some reason we had many more returning students coming, many more first-years taking up offers, and we quickly used up all of the transit accommodation we had, and we found that we weren't really in touch with who was looking for accommodation. Our systems weren't working well. We were hiring beds in backpackers' places which were not really suitable. So we gave the activists a cause which they could pick up on and rally around, and they could put out the message and mobilise people around that . . . I don't want to suggest that there wasn't a real issue. There was a problem that needed to be fixed and that we didn't handle well, but I think that it need not have become a violent conflict unless there was a group looking for confrontation in the first instance.

If you look on the UCT website, you'll see an article by the previous SRC president Ramabina Mahapa. It's a long article and in the last
paragraph he describes this strategy of making demands and then,
when concessions are made, making more demands until, as he
says, the university can give no more, and then the university will
bring on the security and the police, and that will then escalate and
the aim is to change the government. And he actually said that.

The accommodation crisis quickly became a focal point for organising
one of the most violent episodes in the student protest movement at
UCT.[25] In February 2016 a group of students erected a wood-and-iron
structure on the Upper Campus to protest the 'UCT housing crisis'. The
protestors' charges quickly turned racial – it was black students who
were denied access to accommodation, which privileged American and
European students (actually, only 2 per cent of foreign students were in
residence, according to UCT).[26] It was black students on the waiting
list, nobody else, was the activist complaint.[27]

It is important to bookmark at this point what exactly UCT was
being pushed into under the guise of addressing black poverty alleviation. Residences were now under pressure to become exclusively black,
thereby losing one of the most important functions of a residential education: bringing diverse students into the learning commons that a
residence provides. The UCT management's response to what was essentially race baiting on the accommodation question was correct: 'It is
important to have people from other parts of the world [together in
res]. That is what a university is about. It exposes us to other ideas.'[28] This
noble idea – what the university is about – was about to be shafted in
favour of a narrowly nativist agenda that privileges welfare above education 'to the detriment of both', as Van Onselen would put it.

The university management proceeded to ask the students to remove
the shack since it occupied a campus road, causing a backup of traffic on
the M3, a major bypass running below Upper Campus. The shack,
argued the UCT leadership, 'interferes with the freedom of movement
of other staff and students'. By the time the 5:00 pm deadline came for
moving the shack, the protestors had moved to a female residence
(Fuller) and helped themselves to food since they were 'forced to go to

185

class hungry' and were left without accommodation. And then things turned violent. The students removed treasured artworks from two residences (Fuller and Smuts) and Jameson Hall and started a bonfire of 'symbols of the coloniser' as part of the 'decolonisation project'.[29] The fact that at least one of the artworks was created by a black artist as part of an anti-apartheid project did not matter. The flames leaped high as the cameras clicked.[30]

Around this time police and security demolished the shack and dispersed the students. What followed was the torching of a car on Upper Campus and a shuttle bus on Lower Campus. Fleeing students were arrested and charged, sparking further protests demanding their release. Thus continued what had become a familiar pattern of grievance, protest, violence, arrests, protest demanding the release of arrested students, a new round of grievances, and so on.[31]

In response, the university doubled its efforts to find additional accommodation off campus and to set up a hotline to deal with students' residential needs. Instead of simply making the contractually adequate explanation that residences were full, UCT (as well as every other university) was pushed more deeply into assuming a welfarist rescue posture. In the process, that sense of obligation to satisfy basic student needs such as shelter became further entrenched in the South African university. Put differently, the university had become part of an extended welfare system from community to campus in which the expectation to satisfy student needs is now part of the normative culture of the post-apartheid university.

The demand for uninterrupted residence occupation was also to become a flashpoint for student protests at UFS during 2015–2016 in particular. Here the issue was the standard practice of clearing the residences during the long June and December holidays and shorter university vacations. There were three rather straightforward, rational arguments for this long-standing practice.

First, during holiday periods the university would undertake a thorough cleaning of the residences, including spraying all occupied spaces to prevent lice, cockroaches, and other specimens from making a home there. Second, this was the ideal time to carry out essential maintenance work such as fixing roofs or painting hallways, especially in the older residences. Third, during these times the university provided residential accommodation to various outside groups: major political parties holding their annual conferences (the ANC and EFF, for example, were accommodated, the latter after major universities elsewhere turned them down); community groups holding school winter and summer camps; teams visiting for national sporting competitions; religious groups gathering for their spiritual conferences; and so on. Opening up this accommodation to outsiders brought in millions of rands every year, and these monies were directly invested in lowering the costs of residential education for our students – which partly explains why UFS has one of the lowest fee structures in the country.

This was explained to students and student leaders over and over again, but it became clear that there was a real problem. Many students in residence had nowhere else to go. Some could not afford a trip from Bloemfontein to distant places such as Durban, Polokwane, or Mthatha; the cheaper option was to remain on the university campus. Others did not want to go home, for there was nothing there but isolation, poverty, the distress of unemployed parents and siblings, and the need to find some kind of work; the university provided a shelter from domestic stress. Yet another group knew that the relative quiet of the res enabled them to study without the noise and interruption that would take place at home. And what so many students would not actually say was that in the enclosure of a well-fitted campus they were more likely to find food, medical care, psychological counselling, uncrowded accommodation, and general well-being than was possible in the impoverished communities from which they came. Often a student returning from holiday would tell me, 'I could not wait to get back.'

The result? As in the case of UCT, the pressure of responding to these real and overwhelming needs of students pushed UFS further into financial peril – we gave up the very income that could lower students' fees and refurbish their dwelling places. But we also played our part in institutionalising the welfare function by offering out-of-term shelter to poor students.

The vice-chancellors themselves spoke directly about this gradual welfarisation of the South African university.

Ihron Rensburg: We agreed that we would set aside resources from the operating budget to help those who don't qualify for state aid from NSFAS, to the best of our ability. We put in place a meal scheme. That meal scheme now supports 3 500 students, serving two meals, twice a day. And it's a great partnership with Gift of the Givers [a charitable foundation], in which they leverage basically what we put in. So, we put in R12 million this year, and they leveraged it up to R24 million through their networks. It's really an excellent partnership.

We also put in place an inter-campus bus system. Why is that important? As you implied earlier, the student body has shifted and is shifting at UJ, with many more poor students coming in from the poorest schools. They arrive at university and they struggle to pay the bills. Many of them come from out of town; they live downtown and in Hillbrow, Doornfontein, and Berea. They must make their way to the Soweto campus or to the campus in Kingsway. To pay for taxis is probably going to cost them R500 or R600 a month on top of their fees and their residence costs downtown. And so the agreement was to find resources out of our operating budget to make it possible for us to run sixteen or seventeen buses between our campuses. I'm just using this to illustrate.

There were three or four other things that we agreed on since 2007 into 2016 and beyond, as a protocol with whoever was on the SRC. Of the average 9 per cent increase [in fees] per year over this period, 3 per cent is set aside to finance these initiatives. And this is why there was no debate or argument, because from the point of view of the SRC and the operators of the SRC, SASCO, and its allies, they were accomplishing things.

But you have to look at the big picture, at what has happened to fees over this period. So yes, you may set aside 3 per cent out of 9 per cent. And with this money you do altruistic things, very good and important things that we're proud of with the student leaders. But you look at the big picture and you see that fees at UJ have increased in this period from a base of R15 000 in 2007 to R32 000 in 2015. I'm talking average fees, excluding residence and other related costs. So, what then happens in October/November [2015] is the SRC group is outrun, outmanoeuvred, because they are comfortable with these arrangements. They're happy with the deal each year. In fact, we signed the agreement on a 9,5 per cent increase with the SRC in early October.

And then comes late October and the drama that then happens where the minister [Nzimande] agrees with the vice-chancellors on a 6 per cent adjustment with a top-up from the state. [The protestors reject the increase] and three days later the president announces something else [a zero per cent increase].

At Rhodes University the vice-chancellor also noticed the shift in the composition of the student body and knew that this would require some kind of institutional response.

Sizwe Mabizela: I was under no illusion regarding the challenges, particularly regarding the change in the student demographic profile and the issues of transformation. And I was aware of the fact that we are getting more and more young people who were ill-prepared for higher education, who come from poor and working-class backgrounds, who would need a whole range of support. And so I prepared myself for that psychologically.

At Rhodes we have to deal with many social needs of our students. There are students who can't afford food, and students who can't afford [sanitary] pads and so they're asking that we stock pads for women. Students are demanding things that have never been part of the mandate of a university. So we have this changing student profile in terms of social class and economic background which poses an incredible challenge to which the university has to respond.

This shift towards supplying students' material needs in response to changing demographics became a focal point of new demands even on the more privileged campuses. For example, over many decades the Students' Health and Welfare Centres Organisation (SHAWCO) at UCT has done sterling work taking privileged students from the health sciences into service-disadvantaged communities of the Cape Flats.[32] Now disadvantaged communities are coming onto campus demanding services – such as accommodation and transport. The university was being pushed into a new and challenging position – the need for an internal SHAWCO, in a manner of speaking.

It is not simply that students received bursaries and loans to enable them to study at university. It is no secret that some portion of this funding would be expatriated to the domestic economy to enable students' family members to survive hardship at home. This is one of the main reasons students prefer that bursaries be paid into their private accounts and not held in university cost-centres where money is centrally controlled and directly transferred to meet specific obligations such as tuition, accommodation, or even textbook purchases. By having direct control over their money, students could cover a range of personal living expenses and ensure that an unemployed mother could benefit from the bursary or a sibling could pay off school fees. As Van Onselen noted in his prescient analysis:

> For thousands of black South Africans, access to tertiary education has become the difference between having a roof over your head and being homeless, between being fed for a part of the year or starving, between owning some clothing or being decked out in rags, and between meeting your social commitments by sending home small amounts of cash to your family, or joining the ranks of those who are fully employed.[33]

This use of student funding is not something new, as generations of South African students would attest. But the sheer scope of the phenomenon has grown with the majority of today's poor students studying at a time of high unemployment and stalled economic growth. The biting hardships of rural and township life come with students to universities that, in the words of a visiting scholar from the Netherlands, 'do not look like there is no money, no matter what you tell the students'.[34]

There is another factor contributing to this acute hardship. A growing number of students do not qualify for bank loans because their parents have been blacklisted by financial agencies and are therefore not able to access funding to support their children. Many students have come through my office and shared what for them must be embarrassing information that their father or mother was blacklisted. The burden of financial exclusion shifts onto the student, with the consequence that young people coming to university in the hope of making a fresh start now have to suffer as a result of financial decisions made by their parents under obviously tough conditions.

It is simply not fair to entangle an entire family unit in debt with little hope of escape. The situation is particularly difficult to accept given the overwhelming evidence that women on welfare who go to university are able to go off welfare on graduation.[35] If there is one simple thing that can be fixed through agreements with financial institutions, it is that children of defaulting parents should be able to secure loans without being penalised for the financial status or obligations of a parent.

The welfare university and the academic project

Welfarisation narrows the scope of a university's ambitions for its academic project. For example, as I addressed a group of protestors after receiving the latest memorandum of demands, one student kept interjecting, 'F1 must fall!' At the time, this made no sense to me. Why would a student complain about UFS's signature study-abroad programme, the so-called F1 Leadership for Change initiative? This programme exposes selected first- or second-year students to brief immersion experiences at universities in Asia, Europe, and North America where they learn in comparative contexts about race, identity, citizenship, conflict, and leadership. For the protestor, I concluded, the F1 programme was 'a nice to have' – not something essential to the immediate and pressing material needs of students.

The welfare university narrows down the curriculum to focus on the bread-and-butter survival concerns of students. Regardless of the source of funding, whatever else enriches the academic programme of an academically ambitious university, such as students from abroad, comes to be seen as *uitspattig* (exorbitant), irrelevant to immediate demands. This sense of what is real and immediate to 'my needs' is inherently subjective and outside the traditional academic enterprise. As one UCT lecturer shared on her Facebook page, 'I am still grappling with decolonization especially in light of seeing one militant standing outside the Oceanography and Physics Building saying it should go.'[36] To this student, oceanography must have seemed a far way off from *terra firma*.

This is a critical tipping point for South African universities. With the relentless pressure on strained budgets to expand the welfare function of higher education, the university's ability to maintain a respectable academic standing is in jeopardy. A university operating under steadily declining subsidies cannot conduct world-class scholarship and research innovations applied to addressing real human problems when slim budgets are redirected to address urgent problems of student survival. Under such conditions, a university's competitive edge begins to falter. Something as simple as having budgets to enable top academics or young aspirant scholars to attend international conferences is vital to the careers of professors and students, as well as the reputation of a university. Yet it is those very budgets that university managers begin to reduce when other pressing priorities are brought to the table, especially when those demands are backed by threats to destabilise or disrupt the institution.

Consider the long-standing and legitimate complaint on campuses about worker outsourcing, which in previous years not only delivered more efficient services but also enabled universities, in the face of precarious budgets, to reduce costly overheads and devote attention to their 'core business' – namely, the academic project. Nonetheless, every vice-chancellor agrees that outsourcing is unjust and that giving workers full-time permanent jobs is the right thing to do. Yet, regardless of *how* insourcing is done, and within whatever time frames, the dilemma from a university leader's vantage point is this:

> Someone, however, will have to pick up the tab for this. At the University of Cape Town (UCT) for instance, the executive has intimated that the additional costs of insourcing will have to come from the upper end of the current staff payroll ... which may compromise other positions, especially in the academy ... And of course a plethora of ongoing service management, budgeting and logistical modalities will return to the agendas of management and executive meetings, yet again squeezing out the core business of learning and teaching, research, innovation and the application of knowledge to improve the social and economic prospects of the society.[37]

The demands of the welfare university therefore require a reorganisation of a university's operational budgets. But it is not only that money shifts across portfolios. The energies of the university leader also move in the direction of supporting student welfare. For example, in more than 100 talks I gave around South Africa during nearly seven years at UFS, every appearance required that the inviting organisation would deposit anywhere from R5 000 to R50 000 into the account for our No Student Hungry programme. But as the number of hungry students grew every year – at last count, 60 per cent of UFS students were found to be 'food insecure'[38] – the need to raise more funds to serve the three campuses also escalated. Whereas funding from such talks might previously have supported a physics education programme or a paediatric incubator for premature babies, all this income now goes towards meeting the immediate needs of students for nutritional well-being.

The focus and intensity of the 2015–2016 protests have made clear the limits of altruism. Whatever universities were doing, often at considerable sacrifice on the part of individual staff members and the academic project as a whole, was not only insufficient but often treated with contempt. The student protests highlight the need for systemic solutions to the problems of hunger, poverty, and inequality. The protestors know that the university cannot single-handedly solve these problems in an instant. What universities can do is prepare highly skilled graduates who can alter domestic economies and lead social change. But that solution is too far off into the future. The students want the change *now*, and to make their case they targeted the most vulnerable of institutions in the social welfare chain: the public university. The tragedy is that irrevocable damage was being unleashed on a fragile and immensely valuable national asset.

Chapter 9

University Leaders and the Anti-social Media

Twitter is a great place to tell the world what you're thinking before you've had a chance to think.
– Chris Pirillo, blogger

Many South Africans tend to regard the media as independent, reliable truth-tellers who simply report what they see. If it's in print, it must be true. Reporters typically pride themselves on their professionalism: their duty as journalists is to faithfully inform the public about what happened to whom, where, and why. News proprietors are likely to claim that they do not interfere with the work of their editors, and editors tell themselves that every journalist has the right to report the story 'as it happened', provided some basic rules are followed.

A story that appears in print must have been fact-checked with more than one source, and a person accused of something illegal or dishonourable must have the right to respond within reasonable deadlines. There is a Press Code for journalists and an Ombud where complaints of unfair treatment can be lodged. In other words, there are checks and balances in the system to prevent journalistic abuse. Thus, if it's in the news, it must be true.

Now consider these two reports on the same incident.

Version A: A group of black students protested peacefully on a rugby field and were badly beaten up by racist white students in the spectator stands. Bodies were lying everywhere and black protestors were stretchered off the field. This university is clearly racist and has not dealt with white supremacy and the racial problems that continue to plague the institution. Management allowed the match to continue despite the assault on black bodies. Because management would not listen to the protestors, they did the only thing left for them to do, and that was to go onto a rugby field to make their point and force management to deal with the workers' concerns. Students have the right to protest, and while there might have been a rugby match on the evening in question, they did nothing wrong and hurt nobody.

Version B: A group of students and workers, led by the SRC president, marched across campus and attacked the police with stones, injuring some of the officers. The SRC president had ignored a decision by students and members of the SRC not to proceed with this march. The protestors then forced their way into the precincts of the rugby stadium, breaking down a fence and slamming a loudhailer into the face of a white woman student, who was left injured. They invaded the sports pitch while the rugby game was in progress, causing a dangerous situation. The spectators, including families with children, came to spend an evening watching rugby. After pleading with the protestors to leave the field, some of the spectators, led by parents and outside visitors, and including white and some black students, attacked the protestors to force them off the field. This was not racism; the same thing would happen if protestors tried to interrupt a soccer match.

Both these narratives appeared in different media reports in varying amounts of detail, and are presented here as composite accounts compiled from social media, print and television sources, and campus accounts by students, staff, and the university management. Depending on which newspaper you were reading, some media opinion favoured Version A, popularised by the SRC president in a string of interviews over the days following the incident. His version became the truth as he tirelessly reiterated the narrative of innocent blacks and racist whites aided and abetted by management. From some media quarters, it was 'management' that was not disciplining the white students who are so clearly visible in the cellphone camera and televised footage from the event.

For others in the media, this was a straightforward interruption of an official university event and the task of management was to discipline the SRC president and those who broke up the game. Their reading of what happened leaned in favour of Version B. This group of newspapers would complain that 'no action' had been taken by the management – against the SRC president in particular – proving that university leaders were quite happy to suspend or expel white students from campus, but were soft when it came to black students.

How can two composite media accounts of the same event render the facts in such markedly different ways? At a very basic level, this phenomenon is often explained by analogy with a traffic accident. Two witnesses appear in court with different accounts of the same event based simply on where they stood in relation to the car accident, physically and sometimes also perspectivally. Physically, because a view from behind the cars involved in the crash yields different information from a view from the front. Different information will also result depending on when a witness turns his or her head in response to the sound of crashing metal. Perspectivally, because white middle-class suburban dwellers are much more likely to have a negative view of a black taxi driver involved in an accident with his overloaded minibus than would a fellow taxi driver who, observing the collision, sees an expensive luxury car driven by a bejewelled white woman. The facts, as a social science lecturer might explain to students, do not speak for themselves.

Making up the news

None of these observations are new in academic journalism. Since the days of landmark works such as *Covering Islam* by Edward Said (1981) or *Manufacturing Consent* by Edward Herman and Noam Chomsky (1988), those who study the media have shown how the 'facts' emerge from and are shaped by a complex web of social, economic, and political interests in every society. This is especially true in times of crisis, as captured in the old adage that 'the first casualty of war is truth', and in an age where the very notion of *embedded journalism* (the alliance between media and military in which journalist are attached to fighting units in an armed conflict) is hardly called out as an oxymoron.[1]

On a university campus, especially in times of institutional crisis that arise from highly emotive issues, such as rape and racism, the truth often takes a hammering. Two examples from recent history demonstrate the role of the media in bringing accusations against universities and pressure on their leaders in times of crisis.

In March 2006 a group of male students (white) from North Carolina's Duke University lacrosse team threw a party to which they invited two exotic dancers (black) to perform. By the end of the evening, one of the dancers would accuse three white members of the team of a brutal gang rape. In addition to prominent academics and a zealous prosecutor, the local, national, and even international media descended on the case with blaring headlines suggesting the guilt of the three students. Campus protests included banners calling for the castration of the young men, and the media frenzy fed a public appetite for justice long before the evidence was in. One senior editor of the *New York Times* offered this explanation for the feverish media coverage:

> It was white over black, it was male over female, it was rich over poor, educated over uneducated. All the things that we know happen in the world coming together in one place and journalists, they start to quiver with a thrill when something like this happens.[2]

In the course of time it became clear from DNA evidence, the contradictory testimony of the accuser, and several errors, if not deliberate deceit, in the investigation process that the rape did not happen. The North Carolina Attorney General declared the three students to be innocent and decried the rush to judgement and the failures of the investigation process. In the meantime the reputation of the university had been shaken and the futures of the young men placed in jeopardy. Several reports on the event would identify the media, and the *New York Times* in particular, as one of the culprits in the scandal.[3] While the Durham County district attorney was disbarred and convicted of contempt, the media, with barely an apology, lived to report another day[4] – as they would six years later in another university rape case more than 170 miles away.

In September 2012, a third-year student at the University of Virginia named 'Jackie' told an inquiring reporter from *Rolling Stone* magazine that she had been gang-raped on campus by seven boys at a fraternity party. After seven more interviews with 'Jackie,' the reporter, Sabrina Rubin Erdely, went to print on 19 November 2014 with a headline that was clear about what happened and the broader cause being pursued: 'A Rape on Campus: A Brutal Assault and Struggle for Justice at UVA'. The story went viral, with the online version of the article attracting more than 2,7 million views.[5] By early December of the same year, and following further conversations with 'Jackie', the reporter started to have doubts and reported this to her editors. The story was retracted, causing massive reaction across the country.

Following a detailed investigation, the distinguished *Columbia Journalism Review* called the whole affair 'a story of journalistic failure that was avoidable'.[6] The *Rolling Stone* team acknowledged that they were 'too deferential to our rape victim'[7] and therefore did not press harder for more information or pursue those named as involved directly and indirectly in the reported rape case. In the meantime, irreparable harm was also done to the reputation of the university and its leaders, but there is hardly any reference to this fact in the many reviews and reflections on a falsely reported rape at the University of Virginia.

University leaders in a media storm

I had occasion to deliver the Nelson Mandela Lecture in March 2014 at Pennsylvania State University, and the organisers arranged for me to meet the acting president of this renowned academic institution. As a sitting vice-chancellor, I had a special reason for wanting to meet the generous and well-liked leader who took over after the president was fired. Penn State was not only a top academic school; it was also the home of the famed Nittany Lions, one of the most successful teams in the history of college football. They were led by Joe Paterno, an American-style folk hero renowned for his skills and achievements as a coach. Because of his team's success, Paterno brought in millions of dollars in revenue and much more in reputation to this university in a small city called State College.

Then tragedy struck. In 2012 Paterno's assistant coach, Jerry Sandusky, was found guilty of sexually assaulting dozens of young boys. Some of the assaults took place at Penn State facilities, including the shower room used by the football team. Paterno and several university officials – including the president – were accused of being aware of complaints about Sandusky's molestations but doing little to stop his predatory behaviour. Amid a major uproar from students, staff, and alumni, Paterno and the president were fired.

The acting president took me to the window on the upper floor of his ample office and drew back the curtains. 'As I looked out of this window,' he said, 'there were hundreds of national and international media camped out on those lawns below.' I remember that shivers ran down my spine as he said this, for it brought to mind my own experience, although on a much smaller scale, of opening the blinds of my own office early one morning in October 2009, and seeing the media arrayed across Red Square on the UFS campus.

The media had hyped up the event as 'high noon' on campus. It would be a metaphorical shoot-out between the fiery leader of the ANC Youth League, Julius Malema, and me, the outspoken UFS vice-chancellor who had just pardoned the four white students involved in the racist Reitz scandal and invited them back to campus to complete their studies. The media were salivating at the expected clash of two well-known public figures. Malema came to meet with university management, agreed with our decision to bring back the offending students, and left the meeting room to address the buoyant crowd and say of the vice-chancellor, 'He is one of us.'

I heard what sounded like a disappointed roar from the crowd. After waiting a few minutes, I opened the blinds at my window for the second time that day. There was not a soul left on Red Square. I sank into my chair, emotionally drained and overwhelmed. My cellphone rang. It was Malema: 'I told them, Prof.'

No matter how tough he or she might appear in public, a university vice-chancellor quails at the appearance of a negative media report on a controversial campus event, such as alleged misconduct by a lecturer, the rape of a female student, a racial confrontation between white and black students, or the disruption of classes by protestors. There is a reason for this stress reaction. The vice-chancellor is the public face of the institution, the leader of the university, and the person held responsible for any incident regardless of what has led up to it. In the minds of critics, the vice-chancellor is to blame. Those who already hold hostile views about the incumbent seize the opportunity provided by the critical event to point an accusatory finger at the leader. In reporting on the current crisis on university campuses, the media do not allude to 'institutional failure' or limit their reporting to perpetrator behaviour; they invoke the names or actions of the vice-chancellors themselves.

But a vice-chancellor may experience stress for many other reasons. A vice-chancellor takes personal and managerial responsibility for the safety of staff and students, for the integrity of university degrees, for the protection of public property, for the reputation of the university in relation to its various publics, for the estimation of the alumni about their treasured university, and for the well-being of all campus citizens. A vice-chancellor is especially attuned to the needs of vulnerable groups on campus, such as women, LGBTQ students, staff and students with disabilities, those from minority religions such as Muslim and Jewish students, black students on former white campuses, white students as demographic minorities on campus, poor students, and international African students at times of xenophobic attacks in surrounding communities. When any one of these campus citizens gets hurt or humiliated, it is for many vice-chancellors a personal matter; and when the bad news is reported in the media, it sometimes feels like personal failure. That is why throughout the interviews with the eleven vice-chancellors they would often comment on their decisions and actions in personal terms: 'I do not know what I could have done differently.'

Exacerbating the university leaders' stress level is the fact that they often have information the media do not. Sometimes the frustration is about not being able to make that information public, as in cases where the privacy of a student or the integrity of a faculty member is involved, or when a sensitive investigation is under way. The university lawyers would advise – and that is all they can do – against sharing that information beyond the vice-chancellor's office because doing so could compromise the inquiry. As the media heat intensifies, the university leader learns a difficult lesson: the management of that very human instinct for personal or institutional self-justification. You have to sit on your emotions and tell yourself that eventually the truth will come out. In the meantime, your reputation takes a battering and the institution is hung out to dry.

There may be only one thing worse than the media working with incomplete information. That is when the media twist the information they have in hand to suit a prejudiced agenda. In my book *Leading for Change*, I detailed numerous cases of how one newspaper, *Volksblad*, systematically led a campaign against UFS based on the perception that blacks had taken over and destroyed the language, culture, and identity of the institution. And the paper did this by publishing extremely racist views of some Afrikaans alumni and community members in letters to the editor. The only reason *Volksblad* got away with this institutionalised racism in the attacks on the local university and its leaders was that the letters appeared in Afrikaans and in an isolated region of the country.[8]

But there were other cases that went beyond Afrikaans newspapers attacking transformation at their local universities (*Volksblad* at UFS or *Die Burger* at Stellenbosch University). Sometimes the conflict between the university and the media became very personal, as in the astounding case of the owner of Independent Newspapers, Iqbal Survé, and the vice-chancellor of UCT.

Max Price: So our situation was particularly complicated from the media point of view by a personal conflict between me and Iqbal Survé. The story was basically that there was a *Cape Times* report on a fishery scandal involving Sekunjalo [an investment holding company co-founded by Survé] after which Survé fired Alide Dasnois (then editor). He said it was because she failed to lead the paper with Nelson Mandela's death. [It was wrapped around the paper instead.]

A lot of people at UCT as well as alumni were writing to me and saying that Iqbal is not someone who should be representing the university in senior positions. He was the chair of the advisory board of the Graduate School of Business, and he was also on the board of governors of our foundation. Our executive discussed the matter and we thought that we should ask him to step down from those positions – not criticise him publicly, but just say we did not want him to be the public face of the university through those structures. I went to see him in early 2014 and he was mortally wounded about this, and it became an argument in which he said that I don't understand how much he's done for the university, black alumni, and other matters. And I said to him, 'You know, the main thing is it doesn't serve the university to have someone who is very controversial in a position like that. You can be controversial in other kinds of positions.'

Anyway, we agreed that I wouldn't ask him to resign in any written record, but that based on the discussion we had he said he would step down at the next meetings of these two bodies. Those bodies only meet once every six months and it turned out he didn't step down at the next meetings. I don't go to those meetings, but I found out about a month later that he hadn't stepped down. So I made an appointment to go see him again to ask what was going on.

Quite 'perfect storm' like, I had invited Alide Dasnois to give a graduation address at the end of 2014. And by absolutely unplanned coincidence, it turned out to be the graduation of Iqbal's daughter and he was present and his family were present in the audience. We don't publicise graduation speakers beforehand; it's just in the programme. No one knows in advance. I didn't know Iqbal's daughter was graduating until she sat in front of me and I capped her and I recognised her because I know his family. And of course, I realised Iqbal would be in the audience somewhere.

That night I wrote to him to say, 'I'm sorry, I want to just tell you that I had no idea your daughter was graduating. This was probably embarrassing for you and I would not have wanted your daughter to be embarrassed in any way. Just want to assure you that this was not intended.' I received a letter from him the next day, but I have evidence he backdated it to the day before the graduation. I could tell from the fingerprint on the electronic document that it was only written after the graduation. In the letter he resigned from all positions in the university but claimed it was as a result of years of frustration with the lack of transformation which he could no longer be associated with. The letter was a tirade about how he was going to react, how I was worse than any of the apartheid rulers because I was so dishonest, and how the university wasn't transforming and this was all my fault.

And from then on it seemed to me as if he waged a campaign to get rid of me and some of it's been very public and explicit. There was a session we had here which the black alumni organised where he was on a platform with me and he basically said to the alumni: 'You've got to remove this management team because nothing will change until you do.' The session is available on YouTube. So that's what it's been about.

It appears as if he sent a message to the *Cape Times* in particular, and perhaps others in the Independent group such as the *Cape Argus*, to present stories about UCT in a way that would discredit its management.

I believe he's also been paying for the lawyers and senior counsel for some of the [arrested] students, but particularly for Chumani Maxwele, whom we've been trying to prosecute.

We weren't going to prosecute Maxwele for any of his protest activities, but he allegedly harassed and verbally assaulted a lecturer, and that I thought needed disciplinary action. We needed to defend that lecturer.

Chumani challenged the suspension orders and disciplinary cases, including appealing to court. Each time he had senior counsel arguing the case. And we think [the senior counsel] came from Iqbal because Iqbal approached one of my friends to ask that he act for Chumani in the case against the university and my friend turned him down. So I believe he's been a direct agent in this battle and that's turned what should be quick internal disciplinary matters into public, high profile, court battles, often going on appeal and consuming much time, energy and money. When I first wanted to take Iqbal on by revealing the other side of the story behind his supposed self-initiated resignations over the lack of transformation, one of my council members said something to the effect that 'you don't pick a fight with someone who buys ink by the barrel'. You can't win a fight against someone who owns the newspapers.

[In retrospect] the one thing I would have done differently would have been to counter Iqbal right from the start and put a question mark against the *Cape Times* reporting. Although some people know that the reporting is full of rumours and they wonder why it's so biased, they don't have the full story.

More than one independent journalist and media columnist would comment on the blatantly biased, persistently negative, and unusually personalised attacks on both UCT and Max Price by the Independent Newspapers. The veteran journalist Max du Preez offered this:

> Reading the *Cape Times* every morning the last few months was like watching a huge train smash in slow motion. I have never in my long career in journalism seen such a deliberate attempt at destroying a newspaper. My suspicion is that the new owners are using the paper to fight the ANC's battles for the 2016 local elections for them, and afterwards it will be closed down and incorporated into the *Cape Argus*. The last few weeks the newspaper's main theme, dominating the front page, has been the middle-aged poo-chucking UCT student Chumani Maxwele's fight with the UCT administration. This morning's banner headline was again: 'Apartheid-style UCT lashed'. On several occasions the reporting on the matter completely twisted the UCT management's statements. The reporting is generally poor and the decisions on what to cover and what not and what to give prominence to are bizarre. What a tragedy to see such a once proud newspaper being killed off.[9]

What appears to be a highly personalised pursuit of a university vice-chancellor by the owner of a newspaper and his editors and reporters is unusual even by the erratic standards of political reporting in South Africa. Much of the entanglement between the media and universities is, however, more routine and less visible than in the case of the war between Survé and Price.

The dance of the media and the protestors

A protest event does not simply happen. It is produced and performed by live actors, and then portrayed by the media in a particular way to consumers of the news. Chumani Maxwele does not show up in the dark of night to quickly deposit excrement over a university statue and then run to evade notice or arrest. Rather, the event is planned and the choice of defilement is not an accident in Western Cape protests. In their book *Shit Matters*, Lyla Mehta and Synne Movik demonstrate how and why poo matters in the social protest movements of Asia.[10] So too in South Africa, where 'the most graphic illustration of inadequate service delivery is surely sanitation. The problem is simple and immediate: it stinks.'[11] Over time poo would become part of protest performance in and around Cape Town with one outlet in mind – the event is *made* for media. If it is true that the lead protestor's legal and other costs are bankrolled by an owner of the Cape Town media establishment, then of course its journalists will enjoy front-row seats, so to speak, to the song-and-dance performance.

The metaphor of a dance, along with other performance terminologies, is not accidental in studies of social movements in general and student protests in particular. Nor is the invocation of theatre and theatrical performance meant to demean or diminish acts of protest; in fact, these images of protest are used by scholars broadly supportive of movements for democracy and social change. Marcelle Dawson, for example, describes South African social movements in relation to 'demonstrations, dress, slogans, murals, songs, radio, dance, poetry and political theatre' that make up protest actions.[12] On the other side of the world, in the discredited rape-case allegations against Duke University's lacrosse team, Anna Turnage frames the debacle using dramaturgical metaphors of scene, act, and tragic frame.[13]

The political theatre constituting a South African protest event is high drama and media spectacle as in few places in the world. There is singing and there is marching. There are choice slogans and there are banners. There are threatening hand-held weapons such as knobkieries and spears. ('Merely cultural weapons,' the protestors dismissively explain.) There is dancing and its particular struggle version, the toyi-toyi. There is usually the burning of tyres and, in particularly violent performances, the torching of vehicles and the looting of stores.

'Which part of a motor vehicle,' I would sometimes ask my students, 'most vividly represents the brutal connection between South Africa's past and present struggles?' The students are always puzzled. 'The tyre carries heavy symbolic freight,' says cultural studies professor Helene Strauss, not only as a terrifying memory of necklacing (of suspected police informers under apartheid) but now also 'in spectacles of promise and disappointment' during protests in the democratic period.[14]

While all of this is happening, camera phones are clicking and journalists run from one scene to the next with photographers in tow, recording every event. Sometimes a new phase of dramatic performance kicks in to draw further attention to the plight of the protestors. Sometimes a man will drop his pants and reveal his buttocks. One or more women might remove their tops and bare their breasts.[15]

And when armed security personnel push back against the threat of violence, a group of protestors, keeping an eye on the trailing media, might move towards them with flowers. The message is, 'We come in peace'. Yet, not long previously, bricks had flown in the direction of police and security, who then rushed forward to disperse or arrest students. Tear gas fills the air, wet cloths cover faces, a protestor is seen being dragged towards a police vehicle – all of this as verbal abuse and stones are hurled at the authorities. Cameras click away as this spectacle of South African protest politics reaches fever pitch. While the protests, arrests, and further protests escalate, media houses receive real-time video and still footage of events. These are instantly placed online and in print for immediate consumption. Just another rough day in 'Protest Nation',[16] a little dot on the southern tip of the African continent that some commentators describe as 'the protest capital of the world'.[17]

It is easy to imagine that such an emotive spectacle would be read in many different ways by the media as well as the general population. This is especially so because the media in South Africa are not one thing. The Afrikaans media are products of the Afrikaner nationalist period in the twentieth century. For decades the English liberal press has represented the white English establishment and reflected their changing values. The black press represents an often confrontational response to the white nationalist press. Even newer media hold a particular ideological line. *Business Day* will speak for the interests of capitalist business enterprises and the free market economy, while the *Sowetan*, *City Press*, and the *Sunday Independent* represent black opinion articulated by some influential black columnists. With its long struggle history, the *Mail & Guardian* generally takes the side of the underdog and holds a persistently critical view of the government, as in the old days.

Each news outlet has, to borrow from Anna Turnage, 'an orientational perspective'.[18] This in itself is not news to students of the media, but such an understanding sheds light on how the student movement is read by the vast majority of the South African media, where 'repertoires of protest', as described above, 'frame demonstrations, protests and dissent through an ideologically inflected lens and one known to be attracted to spectacle and theatre as well as conflict, controversy and deviance'.[19]

With few exceptions, during the 2015–2016 protest season the media sided with the students. Their cause was just whether it was the toppling of colonial symbols or the pursuit of free higher education. Government was unreasonable and unresponsive in the light of university demands. University leaders were inept and needed to be 'present' and listen to the students; in fact, if only they listened, the problems could be solved. Youth voices shouted from the front pages of the newspapers, with moving pictures of impressive, well-dressed student leaders perched on a stand with microphone in hand addressing the crowds. Cameras clicked as vice-chancellors were bowed before their students, a clear victory for the masses. Editors were breathless in their praise of the movement, going so far as to allow students to compose special issues of a newspaper and declaring 2015 'The Year of the Student'.[20] After all,

> in a society trapped in a leadership quagmire, where somebody probably stands for something yet nobody stands for anything, a flame has flickered to life. Thousands of young people rose up, stood together and challenged the establishment – from their campuses, the streets, Parliament and the lawns of the majestic Union Buildings, they made their voices heard. They brought down a symbol of exploitation and privilege, exposed the prevailing racism on their campuses, and fought against fee increases in higher education. When all else is being sucked into a bottomless pit, the youth of the nation raised their fists and reminded us what true leadership is.[21]

University leaders had decidedly mixed feelings about this uncritical praise of student protests. To a person, they valued the mobilisation for free education for poor students, and the former activists among them admired the students' idealism and ambition, which reflected their own generation's struggles against the brutal apartheid state. But they were troubled by what was being ignored in these heady celebrations of student protests – and deeply disappointed, even dismayed, when their academic staff sided with students in the heat of the actions. What exactly was being ignored, and what danger would this spell if the media continued to fortify student protestors' positions through an unconditional validation of what they were actually doing to other students, personnel, and facilities for learning?

The dark and dangerous side of the student protests

What received only fleeting attention in the media was the angry and violent turn the student protests took near the end of 2015 and in the course of the 2016 academic year. This is not to say that 2015 was completely non-violent and that protests 'suddenly' became violent. What was different was the sheer ubiquity of violence, its deadly intensity, and the accumulating costs – mounting to millions of rands – in damage to university property.

Petrol bombs were found in offices and residences on campuses. Buildings and vehicles were torched. A vice-chancellor's office was petrol-bombed. A staff member was held hostage. A worker died. The social media were loaded with racist and violent postings against other students, staff, university leaders, opposition parties, and, of course, the government. Firm statements were made against those who dared to continue classes, with threats of disruption, violence, and worse. It was lewd, crude, and personal. Lies and distortions mixed freely with what was accurate and true. An activist declared himself to be taken hostage, only to be exposed as a liar. What went unreported was the protestors' constant provocation of campus security and their unfounded allegations of being threatened with sexual assault by armed guards; this was catastrophising the crisis at its best.

Of course the media reported on the violence, but without a hint of condemnation. Journalists were attracted to the spectacular events, and images of smoking tyres and burning buildings appeared online and in print in daily media reports. In much of the journalistic narration, the violence depicted how angry the students were, not how deadly the protests had become. The death of a university worker as a consequence of student protests received passing coverage compared with images of topless women protestors or tear-gassed students. Even the torching of a building in which three security guards were trapped (on CPUT's Bellville campus) was given relatively short shrift:

> Three security guards, feeling threatened by protesting students who had surrounded the building, were trapped in the burning office and left for dead in the early hours ... A supervisor came to their rescue, pulling them free. One of the guards had lacerations on his head after being struck by a stone. All three were treated for smoke inhalation.[22]

There was another narrative that the students sold to the media and the public: the protests were peaceful until campus security was expanded. This, of course, was an open-faced lie. Protestors had been dragging students from classes, attacking and insulting non-protestors, threatening lecturers in their classrooms, launching water bottles at vice-chancellors, and burning buildings. It was only then, and under duress, that university leaders called for reinforcements to protect life and property on their campuses. But in the student account, happily parroted by the media, it was security that *instigated* the violence. To vice-chancellors on site, it was a media battle they were losing no matter what was said, and what took the media control out of their hands was the new platform called social media.

The 'sunny-side up' version of the new social media

The initial studies of the impact of social media on the South African student protests were ecstatic about the medium and the message, drawing on 'the romantic register'[23] of heroic writings on the student movements of the 1970s and 1980s. There were heady references to the Arab Spring and the Occupy movements. A new referential authority came into all these writings, that of the Berkeley sociologist Manuel Castells and his seminal text *Networks of Outrage and Hope*. This 'internet-age student movement in South Africa' was not only about campus but also about country, and great inferential leaps were made to the future of society itself.[24]

Thus '#EverythingMustFall', hailed another publication, from costly education to colonial institutions.[25] Heroes were being made and exalted, from the poo-throwing Chumani Maxwele at UCT, alleged by the university to have racially harassed a female lecturer, to the Hitler-adoring Mcebisi Dlamini, the SRC president at Wits,[26] who led some of the most violent protests in the long history of this university. The hashtag revolution was upon us and the possibilities were endless. The 'fairy tale' of a peaceful transition from apartheid to democracy had finally been trashed. The Fallists brought us back to reality.[27]

The ambition attached to protests that was carried through social media was endless. Students could now 'frame their protest as not just the need to lower the tuition fees for their studies but, rather, as dissent to the structural inequality they feel that applies to their lives'.[28] The revolution was irreversible thanks to the social media, as posted images of revolutionaries 'cultivate the African student spirit' and 're-imagine a future worth living for through these struggles'.[29]

Even within student politics and media organisations, Twitter activism was reshaping democracy, as demonstrated by #RhodesMustFall. Twitter overcame problems of the digital divide by broadening youth participation in politics, challenging existing ways in which citizens produce memory, and even setting the agendas for news making in the mainstream media. In the view of some commentators, student uses of the social media were uniformly positive and affirming of marginalised voices, and uplifting when it came to transforming universities themselves. And of course what 'the Twitter discourse' effectively did was to play 'a key role in public perception of the movement'.[30]

These 'sunny-side up' accounts of student protests no doubt derive from the dazzle of new technologies and the marketing spin these tools could generate in the hands of a spanking-new generation dubbed 'millennials'. With unbounded courage and optimism, they were creating new economies from the Silicon Valley to India and promising new politics from North Africa to Chile. In South Africa, the revolution now had a new face: the impatient student rejecting the struggles of an older, withering generation in favour of an angry new politics buoyantly carried by a brand-new medium.

The anti-social media

Virtually every university student, from the richest to the poorest, has a cellphone. This means that almost all students have access to real-time communication from other students and that, in a crisis, their first bits of information come not from university management but from student leaders or agitated protestors. That simple fact has changed everything in traditional media management by a university administration, as Max Price describes.

> **Max Price:** I think one of the things that is very different now, and this goes back to Rhodes Must Fall, is the use of social media. And certainly as a management team, as an establishment, the university, we still do not know how to do social media communication in crisis situations. And where the students run rings around us is in their ability to get messages out, and to get a particular message out, and to counter other messages.
>
> We are still sitting not knowing, not having a strategy, and it's not that we haven't been looking for advice. I've called in some experts to try to ask, how should one deal with this? We're not the first people to have to confront this, and yet I don't think the experts' answers are the right answers [for our situation].
>
> So, the extent to which one gets involved in responding on blogs and on Twitter and Facebook, and whether you respond to the nonsense that gets put out, as an institution it feels like we should not. We were hoping that other individuals will present the counter view of the truth, but they're not, they don't, and so only one side gets put out. One of the things we need to figure out is how to fight this world in social media, and I think it's part of the reason we've been much less effective than we should have been.

Social media have a number of built-in features and capabilities that have outrun the capacity of university management to manage or respond to information outflows during a crisis:

- Anyone can report on a crisis via social media, at any time of day or night.

- Multiple platforms can be used simultaneously, including Twitter, Facebook, and Instagram, combining text and image.
- Crisis reporting massifies as hundreds, even thousands, of messages about events can go out from all over the campuses, into the community and across the country.
- Social media offer mainstream media a windfall of live stories they would never be able to solicit via traditional means, such as reporters on the ground. The old-fashioned news-gathering methods were too costly and too cumbersome.
- There is no editor, as in a traditional newsroom, to check on the veracity of what is being sent out.
- The communication is instantaneous: as soon as the messenger presses 'send', it's out there.
- Messages are re-tweeted or forwarded almost immediately to a second and third layer of potentially thousands of new consumers of the story.
- By virtue of character-count limits, social media deliver abbreviated accounts of what happened, leaving out crucial information even if the basic content is more or less accurate.
- It is extremely difficult to hold a social media messenger to account in a university's disciplinary code – there are too many offences, the law in this field is still young, and attempting to prove sender identity is to enter a maze of technical difficulties.
- Senders can conceal their real identities; sites can instantly go up and down.
- The sheer volume of messaging makes any form of control and accountability nearly impossible.
- Social media attention is transient. Any management intervention to set the record straight tends to be overtaken quickly by a new round of reports and incriminations.
- Social media messages are self-edited. An activist can edit a text-video tweet in such a way that only police reaction is shown – 'brutality' – and not student assault or provocation.
- The social media are brutal against naysayers. A student or staff member who dares to counter the preferred narrative of a crisis – such as police brutality on innocent students – is likely to be assailed

on social media, even threatened with personal violence, with such persons usually withdrawing from the space because of the personal and emotional abuse.

- Finally, the social media are relentless as a form of communication: no university management team has the time or resources to correct or respond to the constancy of electronic messaging.

In comparing activism from the 1960s with that of the current period, researchers have found that social media can make three significant impacts: it can act as an accelerant of student protests, instantly bringing together large numbers of activists; it strengthens weak ties among diverse individuals, often strangers, for purposes of action; and it helps distribute leadership since those connected by social media can now organise and take charge of protest activities wherever they are.[31]

Perhaps one of the most troublesome aspects of the new social media is the fact that messages or posts on complex issues are constrained by the 140-character limit of the tweet, along with the preference of the online 'reader' to scan rather than read anything lengthy so as to become familiar with the *content* of the protest issues and events. But ill-considered tweets and posts can do real harm, provoking anger and retaliation.

In South Africa, race is the unfailing flammable agent for provoking outrage and spurring action. This was evident in the infamous case of Penny Sparrow, a white estate agent from KwaZulu-Natal who compared blacks to 'monkeys' in a Facebook comment on the littering of the Durban beaches over the festive season. All hell truly broke loose. Sparrow's racist comment trended almost immediately, and the public outrage and vitriol that resulted were unprecedented. Eventually legal charges were brought against her.

Yet the social media have done more than attack racist individuals. They created in the popular culture a special kind of vigilantism – a form of public naming and shaming – as social media activist Jon Ronson reveals in this astounding piece of reflection:

In the early days of Twitter I was a keen shamer. When newspaper columnists made racist or homophobic statements, I joined the pile-on. Sometimes I led it ... in those early days the collective fury felt righteous, powerful and effective. It felt as if hierarchies were being dismantled, as if justice were being democratized. As time passed, though, I watched these shameful campaigns multiply, to the point that they targeted not just powerful institutions and public figures but really anyone perceived to have done something offensive ...

I also began to marvel at the disconnect between the severity of the crime and the gleeful savagery of the punishment ... Eventually I started to wonder about the recipients of our shamings, the real humans who were the virtual targets of our campaigns ... whenever possible I have attempted to meet them in person, to grasp the emotional toll at the other end of our screens. The people I met were mostly unemployed, fired for their transgressions, and they seemed broken somehow – deeply confused and traumatized.[32]

On campuses around South Africa, a perceived racial incident – whether or not racism is confirmed by a factual investigation – will light up social media screens with a vengeance. UFS has certainly had its fair share of this particular outrage and reaction. The Reitz incident of 2007/08 remains the event against which all subsequent racial incidents are bookmarked in all media forms. The words 'once again' would lead a racially tinged story eight or nine years later. Lingering on the campus and in the community is a hypersensitivity to any signs of racial friction, and when such signs are perceived the social media agents pounce with menace.

Such reaction is, of course, understandable given South Africa's long experience of racial subjugation and oppression under colonialism and apartheid. In a place of higher learning, however, university leaders confronting such incidents would reasonably expect to follow their usual routine: establish the facts, search for teaching moments in a crisis, engage in collective deliberation on what happened and why, and make thoughtful assessments of strategy for preventing abhorrent behaviour in the future. But none of these kinds of deliberative, rational actions were allowed in the emotionally charged environment of the Twittersphere. The accused were identified, charged, found guilty, and dismissed within one posting. The angry campus had become like the angry social media community. For here the physical violence of everyday life melded into the virtual violence of the social media, yielding the same effects as with any kind of personal violence: trauma, hurt, and humiliation. For the shamer, this was justified retaliation. Who cared about civil or criminal courts to resolve the matter? This was, in other words, a virtual vigilantism, the darkest side of the new social media.

University leadership: confronting the 'reality' of social media

So what did university managers actually do in the face of these new communication technologies? They stopped fighting and let social media 'happen', so to speak, and used their conventional platforms to put out management news. By the time they responded, however, they found that the protestor stories had already taken on a truth of their own. In football terms, vice-chancellors and their teams were playing defence all the time.[33]

But all was not lost in this new communication space. With more than 90 000 followers on my Twitter account and 5 000 followers on Facebook, I used a different tack: I communicated directly with students, staff, and the broader community on a crisis as it unfolded. The militant minority hated this, as did their off-campus supporters. The hate posts came in thick and fast, but I made ready use of the 'delete' button. After several months, the only persons receiving my real-time updates in a crisis were tens of thousands of followers, including parents, who got to know the other side of a critical story in numbers far outweighing the social media audience numbers of any student. It worked. The traditional media would come to me asking questions, and more balanced reporting would sometimes result. In addition, I was and remain a columnist for *The Times*. Every Thursday I would present my analysis and opinion on some burning issue in education, including the student protests. Column readers were another audience of thousands – many of whom messaged or wrote to me to tell me how much they looked forward to Thursdays to 'get the story' on what was going on. This really helped UFS in presenting its case to the broader world. But when a negative story broke, like the rugby park incident, it was important to describe the event with truth and remorse, and indicate what was being done to address the problem. After such a crisis, a new stream of hate mail would come through on Twitter. But the 'delete' button would once again do its work, allowing me to circumscribe the audience who received the institutional account of events.

Yet most vice-chancellors, by virtue of their age and lack of opportunity, are not adept in the use of social media. Few of them steer their institutions with a technology that relentlessly updates itself. As the social media revolution galvanised the protest movement, university leaders realised they were outgunned by thousands of students and many activists who could frame, tell, and retell a story before the vice-chancellor even got out of bed in the morning.

The traditional media, communication, or public relations offices of universities have been slow in retooling themselves in light of the new social media challenges and opportunities. Many still speak to journalists on the telephone or via email as the basic forms of communication. But there is another reason why a vice-chancellor might personally avoid going onto social media, and that is to prevent becoming the object of relentless personal assault. More than one vice-chancellor told me they did not want their children, who are social media users, to pick up deadly threats against them and their families online.

The historical register on which the South African media constructed its initial reporting of the 2015–2016 protests was the heroic struggles of students against apartheid in the 1970s and 1980s. For many in the media, the current protests were a resurrection of the revolutionary spirit of the youth. As was the case in the earlier struggles, a generational divide was evident between complacent elders and inspired youth. What today's students were doing was simply making real the dreams that earlier generations had fought for – even as they trashed one-time revolutionaries, such as Nelson Mandela, who in their strange narrative sold out to recalcitrant whites and monopoly capitalism. Little distinction was made between the jackboot of apartheid and the workings of a constitutional democracy. 'Voting helps but violence works,' ran the smoothly told narrative.

For a while the heroic student narrative held together in the 'orientational perspective' of the mainstream English media. Then the destruction and violence escalated, and public sympathy began to shift. Slowly some of the media changed their tune as they realised what was really driving the campus protests. Columnists led the charge as they recognised that 'a dangerous line was being crossed'.[34]

Imraan Coovadia, *GroundUp*: The student groups paralysing our higher education system have shown no qualms about their methods: destroying buses, cars, libraries, administrative offices, and works of art, manufacturing petrol bombs, looting sections of Johannesburg, harassing ordinary staff with clubs and threatening the children's crèche at the University of Cape Town.[35]

Judith February, *Daily Maverick*: Why is it that students involved in burning, barricading and intimidation believe they are above censure? Calling for disciplinary action is not condoning police or security brutality, yet somewhere, somehow, a line must be drawn in the sand. It might well be an unpopular or politically incorrect position to take but how can universities afford not to?

Some images on social media reflect the intolerance and have been entirely unedifying. In one, a senior professor of UCT's law faculty is seen fighting off students who appear to want to disrupt a class. The situation is unclear but there is shouting and taunting. What one sees next is the woman professor jumping on lecture desks engaging a fire extinguisher to ensure that she is heard while a group of students dances on desks, one holding a loudhailer.

In another video a student is seen standing on a desk in a lecture hall and hitting a fellow student with a sjambok. A daily newspaper in Cape Town carried a sobering image of a student standing on a library table at UCT forcing everyone to switch off their computers and leave the building.

Is this an institution of higher learning, one asks, and is this democracy's essence? It looks a lot like tyranny.[36]

The respected *City Press* editor, Mondli Makhanya, also weighed in:

Before South Africa gets bullied by the student movement, it should frame the conversation by asking the Fallists what they are offering society in return for all these things they want.

Their answer should begin with them demonstrating a love of knowledge – something that has been lacking in these 18 months of burning libraries, destroying laboratories and boycotting classes at the drop of a fedora – and an ambition to make South Africa great and cutting edge.[37]

In the early reporting of the protests, the university principals were simply extensions of the state apparatus: stubborn bureaucrats, unresponsive administrators, security-obsessed managers, and, in the colourful words of an academic activist, 'chief executives and tin pot dictators'. But with more analytical and balanced media coverage, the image of the university leader started to change, or at the very least to become more nuanced. Those in charge of our universities found themselves between a rock and a hard place: they were either to be pitied or blamed.[38] Being the head of a South African university had become a thankless task: trying to manage the demands of rival constituencies in the face of declining revenues and threats to lives and facilities. University leaders needed public support, but was it too late?

Chapter 10

The Test of Leadership and the Future of South Africa's Universities

God gave Noah the rainbow sign
No more water, the fire next time
– James Baldwin, The Fire Next Time

Lying just south of the equator, Tanzania would have experienced a typically hot and humid week in March 1996 when a group of researchers and administrators descended on the city of Arusha to participate in a workshop on university crises organised by the University of Dar es Salaam. The proceedings of the workshop, captured in a book of some 250 pages, present a depressing account of what had happened at the universities of East Africa since the days of independence. Chillingly, it is as if the conferees were writing the script for the demise of South African universities exactly twenty years later. Despite their origins in the Oxbridge universities, South Africa's elite institutions of higher learning are heading down the path of their East African counterparts. And for those who still cling to the notion that Mandela's country is somehow different from its neighbouring states to the north, more than one public intellectual has made the point that decolonisation means giving up on the idea of South African exceptionalism.[1]

Students in East Africa, the conferees complained, expected the universities to do everything for them, such that

> many universities organized their welfare on the same footing as is done in crèches or disabled people's homes. Some of the conflicts of the seventies were welfare conflicts and combined rising corruption in catering and other services with the withdrawal of some of the VIP treatment students were traditionally given.[2]

219

These universities were constantly in turmoil and 'the major factor was uncertainty and unpredictability caused by university conflicts and crises'.[3] New private universities sprang up to take advantage of the perpetual instability of the public universities. Better-off parents were sending their children out of the country even for their first degrees. Whether at the University of Nairobi in Kenya or the University of Dar es Salaam in Tanzania, staff members felt their reputations were slipping because of the ongoing crises. Frequent closures meant new curricula and innovative programmes could not be developed or got off the ground. As a consequence, there was a sharp drop in the quality of applicants to these universities – the best students went elsewhere. Extra classes had to be given and examinations were written under police surveillance. Fear and frustration meant these universities lost their best academics and could not attract the best scholars. Academic productivity slumped and staff members did consultancies on the side. The majority of students felt they wanted a degree, but with such frequent schedule interruptions attending classes was impossible.

There was more. The 'continuing underfinancing' of universities came to have a negative effect on academic staff, who saw for themselves 'the decaying physical facilities, insufficient pedagogical resources in classrooms and inadequate laboratories and libraries'.[4] In fact, the unwillingness and incapacity of the state to provide sufficient funding were a major cause of the university crises, especially in Tanzania.

Rapid expansion contributed to the crises, as did ongoing political conflicts and demands for welfare. The most violent strikes came near examinations, for 'it has been established that ... arson [and] violent destruction of property [are] carried out by students who are usually keen to have university closed so that either examinations are postponed or courses lengthened'.[5] Police were brought in to contain violence, but before internal consultations on the decision took place. When the university disciplined students, it sparked further student strikes and additional disruption of campus events.

Students felt academically inadequate, which compounded their misery. It was recommended that, in trying to cope with the student violence, 'universities should not be run as [military] camps' and should distance themselves from the authorities, for 'the universities and the state are too close for comfort'.[6] The appointment of cadres as vice-chancellors was given as one example of such collusion.

No, this is not a description of South African universities in 2016; it is a report on East African universities in 1996.

How South African vice-chancellors see the future

'I am scared' is how one of the more senior vice-chancellors expressed himself when asked about his view of the future. Ahmed Bawa is not a man given to hyperbole. He has been a leader of more than one South African university as well as of overseas institutions, and is known as a deep thinker. Over dinner after the interview, his head shook from side to side. 'It does not look good,' he said. The question I asked him and all the vice-chancellors I interviewed was, 'How does this movie end?', drawing on the words spoken by the character played by Nicolas Cage in the movie *Next*.

Ahmed Bawa: I have to say that I'm not very optimistic. I think that we're very much at the top of a slippery slope. We're at the point now where I feel that if we don't fix up three or four different things, we're in a fix.

The first thing, for me at least, is to try to understand how to get back to a funding regime which puts the universities in a situation where they can [survive]. The second thing that really bothers me is the [in]capacity of the state to intervene in [the crisis]. This has become an opportunity for those wanting instability, and unfortunately we've played into their hands because of the crisis and because we lack leadership. Because of crisis, we're in a situation where we are forced into making concessions which normally we would be opposed to. So, for example, for 2017 we're talking about the fee increase and yet it's going to be a decision that will have to be taken nationally.

Now, one has to say that this is not very different from what goes on in other parts of the world. But having said that, the question is, what does it do to our system if we go down that route [of continually making undesirable concessions]? Are we, as a result of what is happening, reshaping our notions of institutional autonomy? It's just a question of time before we discover that it's all gone too far. I am really concerned about that, and clearly these concerns are going be a large part of my thinking and work [as head of USAf] in the next period of time.

Max Price's view of the future is more optimistic, but he expressed it before intense protest activity and disruptions temporarily shut down UCT towards the end of 2016:

Max Price: Well, I'm an optimist, so the ending that I write may have no relationship to reality or to a kind of dispassionate analysis. But in my view, we will get through it; universities are strong and most universities are strong institutions. They have long histories. We go through crisis and we'll get through it on the other end. It will take us some time to recover because I think damage has been done, particularly to reputation globally. I think that #RhodesMustFall and the social movements have overplayed their hand, particularly on our campus with the violence, and yet on many campuses their support is relatively small.

So, coming back to the question of where does this end up, I hope that by dealing with the real issues we can persuade the vast majority of students that we're serious about transformation and that we will control an unacceptable version of the protest.

Tyrone Pretorius shares Ahmed Bawa's gloomy analysis of the future, but adds that the students have a new dilemma – how to stop the accelerating train of demands.

Tyrone Pretorius: I don't see it ending in the foreseeable future because one of the keys to the #FeesMustFall group on our campus is the constant shifting of the goalposts. And that's deliberate, that there must not be a resolution. I always tell my colleagues when we have staff assembly that the issue with insourcing/outsourcing is a prime example of why they [the protestors] don't want a resolution. We can insource tomorrow, and I promise you the day after insourcing they will find something else because there is, as I said, different interests in #FeesMustFall that cannot let this just die out. There's no symbolism at UWC that must be broken down that you can rally around – maybe just the curriculum, but there's no statues. Since there's nothing really concrete to rally students around, the goalposts need to shift constantly.

My own sense is that [the students] do not know how to end this gracefully. They don't know. Some of them really believe in the nobility of what they stand for. But my own sense is even those who believe in the nobility of the cause do not know how to end this.

Beyond the strife on individual campuses, there are broader political and structural impacts on universities that make the future bleak, says Ihron Rensburg.

Ihron Rensburg: Just look at the financial, the economic outcome for 2016. If the state finances a 7 per cent increase, there is still a gap of 3 per cent on average. Universities will then have to find between 2 and 3 per cent. What does that mean? We cut back. At UJ we had to cut back R60 million in operating expenditure. Can we do it next year [2017]? Not sure. Can we do it the year thereafter? Crisis. Can we do it for the next 20, 30 years? The spectre of Makerere University [Uganda] comes to mind.[7]

Consider the democratic, postcolonial moment [in other African countries] and look what has happened to our premier African institutions. What comes to mind is the spectre of South Africa's twelve leading research-productive institutions going down that track and becoming effectively like the University of Zululand or Fort Hare, institutions that are struggling and which the state has not really picked up in the two decades since democracy. That spectre now faces all of us because of a political decision in late October 2015 that there would be no fee increase. So how does that particular story end? We simply have to have a fee increase for 2017. It's non-negotiable.

Prins Nevhutalu raises the possibility of private higher education as an inevitable future response to the crisis in the public universities.

Prins Nevhutalu: I imagine that Wits, UCT, and Tukkies [UP] can secede and become private institutions in order to protect what they have. Less so Stellenbosch – Stellenbosch will continue flying the Afrikaans flag. Wits and UCT may actually opt to say to the minister: 'You're not giving us money; our quality is eroding. Therefore, in order for us to maintain this we need to get out from under you and we'll find a way of funding ourselves. We can fund ourselves and then you create a higher education of poor quality for the poor.'

You know about primary and secondary education in this country. Quality education is for the rich, private, and former white [Model C] schools. The poor get garbage. We would be lucky to get to that stage where perhaps you and I one day also establish our own private university and make it such a good-quality institution that we can charge whatever because people who value education are prepared to pay a premium price for it.

People are prepared to pay a premium. And poor, black parents pay. If you look in many of the townships, every morning they travel. They pay fees when there is a no-fee school just next door. They commute, they bus their children to the old Model C schools, so that they can at least get better education. So I think we are likely to get to that stage where we may have a chronically underfunded higher education system which would lose its quality and only cater for the poor. The rich can go into private schools, private universities. They can send their kids overseas. It will be unfortunate because that's not what this country fought for. It really would be unfortunate if that happens.

The proposals that are being mooted for this fee-free system include a graduate tax. But you probably would have to increase the tax base by 5 per cent, yet that's not going to be feasible since the number of graduates is so few: you will not be able to collect enough money. If you go and tax businesses more, what are the chances that they will leave and go somewhere else where they do not have such a high taxation bill? We have to tread very carefully on this one.

We can get to a stage of no return and we've seen it happen in Africa. We have seen how a UCT today can become a horrible institution in a few years' time. Makerere [University] is one example. And so I think the citizens of this country need to understand that while there is a public good for higher education, there is also a very big private good for themselves and they must pay for it. When you say government must pay, it's indirectly saying let's tax those who are working very hard. Let's tax them harder, and the group who are supposed to be taxed grow thinner and thinner and shrink. Perhaps there has to be a special compact which allows us to build institutions that are going to ultimately empower this country. You can't build when you don't invest.

South Africa's future, says Sizwe Mabizela, will be determined by what happens not only in universities but also in the school system.

Sizwe Mabizela: This movie has to end soon. Yet what is happening in our higher education system reflects what is happening in our society more broadly. There is a sense of disenchantment, a sense of discontent with what is happening. People are frustrated. They say 22 years after the advent of democracy there has really been very little change; there is corruption and people are frustrated. It doesn't help the crisis in universities when the governing party itself is in a state of chaos. So the university crisis reflects what is happening in this country. But at some stage it will have to end.

I think one of the critical decisions that will have to be taken soon is what happens with the fees in 2017 and beyond. The zero per cent fee increase [in October 2015] was, in my view, a poor decision. We need to move on from there, and this is the year when we need to confront that challenge. People have to understand that they have to pay for higher education. Those that can afford to pay have to pay, and those that cannot afford to pay must be assisted by the state. This notion of universal fee-free education is completely untenable. No country can afford that, much less a developing country. You can tax citizens of this country, but the tax base is about 4 million people and it won't be long before that tax base will collapse. It's just unsustainable. Almost a third of our compatriots are on social grants. That's an untenable situation.

In the short term, those that can afford to pay for higher education should pay, because if we have another year of a zero per cent fee increase, you may as well just forget about the current funding arrangements for higher education. We'll just have to start from scratch and come up with a different mechanism of funding universities, because after two years there's just no way in which you can start to enforce fee increases . . .

The solution to the challenges facing our public higher education system is not just additional funding. It's a fundamental rethink that is required. We need to reimagine our education from early childhood right across to university. What we have at the moment is not working, and we're busy putting a band-aid here and there and we are not confronting what we should be doing. Just throw everything off the table, start from scratch. What should happen with early childhood education? What should happen with foundation phase? What should happen with intermediate phase? Those are the three critical levels where you lay a solid foundation for a young person to be successful in life.

At the moment we spend inordinate levels of resources at Grades 10, 11, and 12 when young people still lack foundational knowledge in the starting grades. They can't read, their numeracy is weak. So if I had my way I would say let's allow ourselves a 20- or 30-year time horizon. Let's put aside all the experiments we have tried for the past 22 years. Let's go back to the drawing board.

There are other things we can do as well. How do we ensure better articulation between Grade 12 and university? Shouldn't we be looking at what was once proposed as a four-year degree programme, because at the moment there's such wastage at university level? And of course we need to look at how we can create a multiplicity of education and training opportunities for young people so that we invert this pyramid: have more young people at TVET colleges and fewer at universities, and have a system that articulates better all the way from early childhood to university.

Anything short of that is not going to deal with the fundamental challenges confronting higher education. Unfortunately, politicians are not interested in that. In terms of what we invest in education, we invest far more than what other countries do; but in terms of the returns, it's absolutely abysmal. And of course, coupled with that, [we need to] pay attention to the content and pedagogic knowledge of our teachers because they are very crucial in making this whole thing work. How do you make sure that you have teachers who are competent and capable and are able to inspire hope? Because for me, that is one of the things that education should do. Inspire a sense of hope that tomorrow will be better than today. How do we build such a system?

And if you can fix education, you'll then start to tackle issues of inequality, unemployment, poverty. Those are our three core challenges. The solution is quality education for every young person. And there's no better investment that any country can make than ensuring that its young people have access to quality education.

It is this quality of education that is threatened by the crisis, as Derrick Swartz emphasises in his view of the future.

Derrick Swartz: I think the net effect of this [crisis] will be a slow but quite profound slide in the university's ability to support its mandate, thereby defeating the very policy objective of the government, which should be a rich irony. That has been a problem of much of sub-Saharan Africa since the 1970s: the massive increase in numbers in the system was followed by a long multi-decade slide in the overall quality of education. And the middle classes, of course, leave the institutions and study at private universities or go abroad, and literally entrap the working-class and poor students in substandard, low-quality, mass-produced higher education institutions producing graduates for an economy that is unable to absorb them.

Of all the interviewed vice-chancellors, Lourens van Staden has had the most extensive experience in other African universities, and so his assessment of the future focuses sharply on our northern neighbours:

Lourens van Staden: I'm not saying we should have fee-free education, because that could lead to disastrous implications, if you look what happened elsewhere in Africa. I worked as a consultant in Central and Eastern Africa for the Africa Institute at about nine universities. And I spent a bit of time in Makerere University; it used to be a good institution, but when I spent time there things were not good. And the same decline happened at the University of Zimbabwe after the 1980s when things changed, as well as at Dar es Salaam in Tanzania and the universities in Kenya and Zambia. My visits there happened just before Madiba was released. Things here are almost there.

Cheryl de la Rey, like her vice-chancellor colleagues, addresses the question about the future by looking at the relationship between funding and enrolments, which will determine the fate of universities.

Cheryl de la Rey: At the moment the fees issues is a big question mark. So we've got the Fees Commission established by the president.[8] Our university and myself, on behalf of the university, went and gave evidence because it is a legal commission. We made a submission and then they called us to do a presentation.

And my argument was that the concept of tuition fees as a revenue stream is both reasonable and rational. I agree that poor, academically deserving students should be funded by the state. But why would we want free university education [overall] when school education is not free? Why would we want free education for all when it's often cheaper for parents when their kids come to universities compared to what they pay for them to attend the local school? So rationally it makes sense to continue with the concept of a tuition fee for university education.

Of course there's a lot to be done on the state financial aid scheme and looking at affordability of higher education, but I think the decision has to be made politically in the end. You can hypothesise as much as you wish, but at some point we're going to have to make a decision. Otherwise, we are looking at a situation which we've seen in many other countries, other postcolonial societies, where you have huge enrolment increases without public investment.

So how does the movie end?

Having listened to my colleagues with the perspective of a comparativist, and by bringing to bear my own knowledge and experience, I can now sketch the outlines of the likely future of South African universities. History tells us that universities in post-independence Africa self-destruct as a result of three major forces acting on these institutions: a decline in government funding, a steady increase in state interference, and the normalisation of chronic instability.

The decline in government funding

This is the well-narrated story that every vice-chancellor has told, in different ways, throughout my interviews with them: every year universities receive less state subsidy in real terms than ever before. With less money in their budgets, universities are forced to cut back on their operational expenditures, leaving staff demoralised and the physical plant poorly maintained. Innovation suffers, and for the top institutions, the ability to compete with universities at home and abroad starts to decline. The capacity to attract top postgraduate students – the research engine of the modern university – through competitive bursaries begins to lag.

For wealthy institutions overseas – such as Stanford or Harvard – the cutbacks on operational expenditures are usually temporary, thanks to the large endowments of these universities. Budgeting decisions are based on the inevitable rise and fall of earnings on billions of dollars in investments, and private universities can raise millions of dollars in one funding campaign cycle. In South Africa, the costs of delivering university education are shared among the beneficiaries of that education (mainly government and students), and the deterioration in the state subsidy has no upside. That is, once government cuts back, it continues on that trajectory.

The numbers are all too familiar to university leaders. The state subsidy for university education decreased sharply from 49 per cent of institutional funding (in 2000) to 40 per cent (in 2012). Meanwhile, student tuition fees as a source of university funding rose from 24 per cent to 31 per cent over the same period. How did this affect students? In the period 2010 to 2012, student debt skyrocketed from R2,6 billion to R3,4 billion. The system was beginning to sag under its own weight and it was not surprising that the top universities would feel the massive blow first. Wits University's state subsidy would be reduced to a mere 27 per cent of its total revenue, which meant one thing only: the remaining 73 per cent would have to be found elsewhere. And when a council decision leaked that Wits would raise its fees by 10,5 per cent, its current and future debtors rebelled, sparking a nation-wide uprising that became unstoppable throughout 2016.[9]

Because South Africa does not have many large corporations, foundations, and wealthy families that endow their top universities, the leaders of these institutions must turn to the only other reliable and available source of revenue: student fees. Without substantial and reliable state funding, a university cannot hire top-ranked professors, fund innovation, pursue international research partnerships, and generally build a strong academic platform. The academic project, the core of what distinguishes South African universities from its sister institutions elsewhere in Africa, is now under severe threat. And here is another consequence: at the very point that more and more students from other African countries are descending on South African universities as a better-quality option than their home institutions and a less expensive option than European or American universities, the higher education system is beginning to fall apart in the last country on the continent to break the shackles of white political domination.

The decline in government funding has affected different universities in different ways. The worst-funded universities are little more than rural teaching colleges offering low-quality degrees – and sometimes selling them off – with the weakest academic staff profiles and the least-prepared students from the poorest schools. These universities had long ago entered the spiral of chronic protests on a seasonal basis, often at the beginning of the academic year and when 'financial exclusions' kick in. At some campuses, such as Butterworth in the Eastern Cape (part of Walter Sisulu University) or Soshanguve in Pretoria (part of the Tshwane University of Technology), there are almost weekly running battles between campus security, police, and the students. The residences are shut down and then reopened as the campus gates become revolving doors for learning on unpredictable teaching calendars.

These waves of protests, violence, and closure have largely been ignored by the general public, in part because they have become routine, in part because they happen out of sight in rural areas or outside the boundaries of the city, and in part because it is the black poor and not the middle classes who are affected by these protest repertoires. The tragedy of these so-called universities is that the black poor are still being fed a microwaved diet of Bantu Education barely distinguishable in quality or impact from what was offered in apartheid's colleges. Poor black students, many with undoubted potential, are being failed over and over again in these marginal institutions. Nobody notices – and members of government could not care less. Their children are enrolled at the former white universities.

The black universities have therefore been the first to suffer from the reality of declining state revenues. For years they have been waiting for a post-apartheid bailout that has never arrived. Infrastructure has crumbled. Management is generally weak and every position hotly contested. Funding decisions have raised eyebrows, such as diverting bursary funds to meet payroll. The integrity of degrees remains under threat as all kinds of unscrupulous practices – such as sex or cash for degrees – make news headlines from time to time. Libraries are seriously understocked. Residences are overcrowded, often shared with students who are not registered occupants. Research performance is low in volume and quality. Few staff hold PhDs and there are seldom any research chairs or meaningful research funding. Council meetings are lengthy and heated events where the distinction between governance and management has long dissolved in contestations around every issue; few vice-chancellors stay very long. Situated in poor communities, these campuses are the target of factional and political interference ensuring turbulence around everything from tender allocations to staff appointments. The last thing demanding attention in these campus ecologies is the academic project.

These universities are even more susceptible than the top ten academic institutions to the immediate effects of the decline in government funding. But since they have been operating in constant crisis for years, such campuses simply continue in survival mode from month to month with bailouts from government, overdrafts from banks, and shady accounting practices that invariably lead to the appointment of an administrator to sort out managerial collapse. For the black universities, the funding crisis is not new, which explains why many of them were largely unaffected by the 2015–2016 protests for long periods of time.

For their part, the top ten universities are now being threatened in a very serious way, and for the first time, by the funding crisis. Even in this group there is an upper tier with relatively strong reserves, such as Stellenbosch University and the University of Pretoria. The rising academic institutions, such as UWC, are most immediately endangered by the crisis of funding; having built up its academic status by recovering from financial crisis and then investing in major research programmes, UWC is a black university that defied the odds. But its financial position has always been relatively weak; UWC could go down more quickly than it shed its apartheid birthmarks. If the student protests and instability continue, UWC will find itself slipping into the financial and operational quagmire that engulfs the bottom ten universities.

Although it is a historically white university, Rhodes University could be the next to fold under the financial and political crisis. It is a small institution (only 7 519 students; 64,2 per cent black in 2014) with growing numbers of poor students from the Eastern Cape and without the financial stability once offered by a largely middle-class enrolment. Unlike mega-institutions such as the University of Johannesburg, Rhodes cannot 'massify' itself out of financial difficulties. It is situated in an impoverished city with a failing infrastructure, as demonstrated by Grahamstown's water crisis that resulted from years of political misman-agement and municipal incompetence. So interdependent is the city and the campus in this fragile community that the university could not even open a new residence – for which it had received government funds – since there is no municipal capacity to manage the added efflu-ent. When students refused to pay off debt – one of the many threats coming out of the protests – a university circular fuelled rumours in the media that Rhodes was on the verge of collapse.[10] It may be only a matter of time.

What turned the financial crisis into disaster is that students and workers on various campuses added insourcing to the many demands placed on the desks of the vice-chancellors. Now the leaders' problem was not simply managing the declining state subsidy and the protesting students' demand for 'free higher education for all'. Leaders also faced the demand to insource contract workers, which for each university would mean finding additional millions of rands on an annually recurrent basis or risk interminable protests. Soon after UCT, under great pressure, agreed to insourcing, it made arrangements for reneging on salary increases (which the staff rejected), offering early retirement, and introducing the prospect of future layoffs. A serious crisis has been compounded and several universities are now even more susceptible to collapse.

In other words, the continuing underfunding by the state had unleashed from different quarters – students, workers, and external political opposition – an alliance acting in concert to force anxious universities to make concessions that would send them further down the road to ruin. But financial duress in itself is not sufficient to collapse all 26 public universities in the short to medium term. The unprecedented interference of the state in the affairs of public universities is the second nail in the institutional coffin.

Creeping state interference

South Africa's more established universities have a proud tradition of resisting government interference in the management and governance of these public institutions. In its traditional formulation by Thomas Benjamin Davie, a former UCT vice-chancellor, academic freedom means 'our freedom from external interference in a) who we shall teach, b) what we teach, c) how we teach and d) whom we teach'.[11] Since then scholars have debated the meanings of academic freedom (especially freedom of speech) and institutional autonomy (relationship between government and university),[12] but I want to focus here mainly on the state and higher education.

As the major funder of universities, or most of them anyway, government has a reasonable interest in how taxpayers' money is spent within public institutions. Government should have an interest in how many universities operate and in which regions of the country. Through macroplanning, government should decide on the numbers of engineering schools, medical programmes, teacher education facilities, and so on that make sense in terms of national development needs. Universities accept such guidance from the government. But what happens when steering becomes interfering?

Before 1994, the distance between the apartheid government and the liberal universities was crystal clear since the former pursued racist policies in admissions, appointments, and resource allocations. Yet it has always been a mistake to assume a benevolent state *after* apartheid. Indeed, the post-apartheid government has interfered in university affairs in a number of significant ways.

For example, the government pressures universities to extend its influence within their governing bodies. Universities rightly limit the number of government appointments to their governing body to what higher education law allows: three to five members. Invariably those external appointments are political activists or union members allied with the ruling party. Seldom are independent experts appointed, let alone members of the political opposition. Ministerial appointees, as they are called, are often political emissaries commissioned to particular universities for specific purposes. They are not open appointments based on expertise alone. When some universities informed the minister of higher education that they would stick to three ministerial appointments, they were threatened and told that their positions would be rejected and revisions to their institutional statutes not approved. If these were strictly professional appointments, without political mandates, there would have been no problem.

There is, however, one particular case where the minister can override a university's authority, and that is in the appointment of an administrator. After a failed attempt to enforce an administrator on one university, the Higher Education Amendment Bill was passed in May 2016 to empower the minister to instruct a council how to act and, if it refused, to dissolve this highest decision-making authority of a university, thereby 'infringing the right to academic independence'.[13] The minister's office was unbowed by these incursions into institutional autonomy and its seizure of universities, for these are merely 'public institutions . . . subject to the national imperatives of a developmental state'.[14]

Government also interferes with universities on transformation. In and of itself, government enquiry into changes in student and staff demographics is a reasonable action in relation to public institutions. But Zuma's government went far beyond its authority by setting transformation targets and demanding that these be achieved. A pompously named Ministerial Oversight Commission on Transformation

(MOCT) duly delivered an 'equity index' to measure transformation at universities, a crude reductionist exercise which was rightly dismissed by many in the academic community.[15] Commissions investigating racism and other forms of prejudice were enthusiastically launched. These actions assumed that institutions themselves did not care about transformation and were not driving the process with serious intent. This was nonsense, but it boosted the political image of ministers as taking charge of recalcitrant institutions. But the minister of higher education went even further by publishing institutional rankings on transformation achievements – a less than subtle blame-and-shame game in which, not surprisingly, the university led by the MOCT chairman topped the rankings.

A political rallying point inside universities and from government itself is the need to address the dearth of black professors, a campaign inspired by a series of thoughtful articles in the media by UCT academic Xolela Mangcu.[16] All over the world, creating a diverse professoriate in countries with histories of racial inequality and oppression remains a major challenge. No matter how hard institutions try to correct this wrong, it takes time, money, strategic commitment, and a good dose of patience; and in a place like South Africa, where the pipeline from school to university is exceptionally weak, it is difficult to raise a productive generation at appreciable speed. But there are few more effective ways to rally hard-line nationalists than by asking the accusatory question, where are the black professors?

I do not know of a single vice-chancellor who would not give an arm and a leg for ten black professors in chemistry and mathematics or in architecture and anthropology. But they are simply not there, and they are unlikely to emerge unless the school system is fixed and professorial salaries are raised. And neither of those is likely to happen under a government that simply does not recognise the scale of dysfunction in poor schools and does little about an institutional crisis in which nobody wants to pay the costs of the higher education that would make this possible.

So what do institutions do, especially when government holds out the funding carrot at the wrong end of the professorial pipeline? They take shortcuts to obtain the money and the prestige that come with additional funding for preparing black and women professors. It is astounding to observe how black nationalists play the same tragic game that white nationalists played in the apartheid period. In order to boost racial self-esteem, they advance their own kind to professorial positions with the slimmest of curricula vitae and without the weight of scholarship (research publications, scholarly books, funding grants, students supervised and graduated, international esteem, and so on) that normally counts for a professorship anywhere else in the world. The black universities play this game as if they are merely following a predetermined historical script, while the white universities, under huge pressure from government, have begun to make those same compromises of principle, especially when black lecturers took to the press during the 2015–2016 crisis period. There is nothing that damages the reputation and credibility of a university more than fake professors. All the postcolonial conditions are in place to ensure that South Africa plays the game like everybody else.

This assumption that 'government could do it better' feeds into the current student politics with a vengeance. The ruling party's young student cadres play this card at every university management meeting. Their argument is simple: government needs to intervene in this situation because universities are 'using autonomy' as a smokescreen to remain white. Universities should be whipped into shape and their whingeing ignored when it comes to hiring and promoting black professors.

A student leader at UFS, generally a reasonable fellow, told me he had a solution for the black professor problem. I was alert, eager to learn how we could accelerate the process beyond the successful Prestige Scholars Programme that I had inaugurated to prepare new PhDs for the future professoriate. 'I was in the senate the other day,' the student said, 'and I saw all these white professors. Why don't we simply replace them?' I sank back into my chair. 'Well,' I said, 'even if South Africa's labour laws allowed us to do that, who is going to teach medicine, the sciences, and humanities at the levels required?'

Nevertheless, Blade Nzimande, higher education minister and general secretary of the Communist Party, certainly had no qualms in coming up with his own interventions in this regard. First was his relatively innocuous decision to set funds aside for preparing black and women academics for senior positions. But then he also decided to set up his own National Institute for the Humanities and Social Sciences for this purpose, despite the work being done in this area by the independent Academy of Science of South Africa (ASSAf) and in the universities themselves. This straightforward interference caused a stir among academics; they saw the breach of autonomy behind the smiling face of authority.[17] One academic raised the question of 'whether the humanities and social sciences community intended to hand over the future of [these fields] to regulation by a government ministry'.[18] And then there were the frightening phrases in the minister's rationale for his own academy: to break the authority of 'hegemonic ideas' and to rally 'progressive academics' behind the cause. Since when does a university single out ideas, let alone academics, on the basis of a preferred ideology?

There are many other ways in which government has breached the autonomy of universities, from the setting of enrolment targets, to taking away the authority of individual universities to manage their student applications, to the illegal pronouncement of the president on fee increases (the zero per cent decision). It is not only that interference in the operations of universities has become routine. It is that in the mind of government, public universities are more and more seen as no different from public entities such as the South African Broadcasting Corporation, Eskom, and South African Airways, whose corrupt and mismanaged operations have caused massive losses to the public purse. For their part, universities over the years have learned to become adept at managing government interference. But they would inevitably knuckle under with the third and final nail in the institutional coffin.

Chronic instability

The third and most determinant factor in the future of South Africa's university is chronic instability. From February 2015 onwards, we have witnessed the spread of increasingly disruptive and destructive protests that have made the university teaching calendar as unpredictable as the school calendar in the union-controlled schools of the country. It is not just that the protests have become seriously violent, already claiming victims and with damage trending towards R1 billion. It is also that these acts are now routinely justified as necessary and retaliatory violence, not only by militant students, but even by some academics in the former white universities.

Just as economic markets value stability in the political economy of a country, so too do those who teach and learn on university campuses appreciate predictability. When, as in 2016, an academic timetable is constantly changed in the hope of restarting classes after forced shut-downs, students and professors lose faith in the institution to provide a high-quality education in a secure environment. For top academics who choose the life of the mind, a university salary is certainly not the main attraction; if anything, academic compensation drives many of the talented into the private sector or into more competitive positions in the civil service. For others, the academic world offers serenity, collegiality, freedom to pursue ideas, and the opportunity to inspire young minds through education. For students serious about academic and social pursuits, a place at university is an ideal opportunity for them to be fully themselves, to test ideas, to challenge authority, and to prepare to make a difference in the larger world. For students, the university is a sort of gap period between the restrictive environment of high school life and the routine obligations of occupational life. It is also a space for social, cultural, and political expression. What most students do not want or expect is an unstable or dangerous experience in which their academic studies are constantly threatened by violence, with class schedules chopping and changing in response to the latest protest action and reaction.

By way of comparison, student protests in South Africa seldom carry the range of activism agendas overseas, which include protests around university investments in fossil fuel companies, academic freedom of speech, institutional governance, presidential candidates and policies, and intolerance in the academic community. While there are common issues in what has been called a global 'renaissance of student activism'[19] – such as campus racism, cultural symbols, and the costs of tuition – South African protests are mostly about the capacity of the state to provide for material needs and about the kinds of decisions, such as fees and fee increases, that place obstacles in the way of fulfilling material objectives. #RhodesMustFall and the quest for symbolic transformation were an aberration on the campus protest scene and, not surprisingly, short-lived. It was #FeesMustFall that gained traction, for it spoke to immediate, real, and visceral needs – the politics of the stomach, in South Africa's lexicon.

The key to understanding the future of South African universities through a comparative lens is that university protests elsewhere, from the Occupy movements in the US to Canada's 'Maple Spring',[20] come to an end. In African universities, and now South African universities in particular, the protests persist and the instability becomes chronic. And the institutional game-changer after 2015 is that the chronic instability that was once limited to a few of the historically black universities now threatens to characterise the top research universities as well. In other words, what we are now witnessing is a full system meltdown in process. Universities can manage sporadic protests with their minimal security arrangements. But institutions of learning cannot survive never-ending protests that create instability in the educational environment and place lives and facilities at risk.

The effects of underfunding, interference, and instability

What happens to public universities when these three forces – underfunding, state interference, and instability – act in concert? The evidence from the African experience is consistent from east to west and north to south. Here I will highlight three effects on South African universities.

First, the students who can afford to do so will leave the university. Parents send their children to university for two reasons – quality education and personal safety. Both of those former certainties are under threat and there seems to be no resolution in sight. When a university loses four weeks to militant student protests, with fellow students intimidated and dragged out of classes, a student with options will go elsewhere. As already indicated, this is to the detriment of our public universities. And since South Africa has very strict controls over the establishment of private higher education institutions on home soil, most of these fleeing students will study overseas.

Second, the professors who can afford to leave will take jobs outside the country. Top-rated academics may receive multiple job offers from universities in Australia, New Zealand, Europe, Canada, and the US. These are professors with A, B and upper C ratings from the National

Research Foundation and whose academic capital makes them prime recruits around the world. What these academics want from a university, more than anything else, is an environment of relative calm in which they can pursue their research, teach their students, and make a contribution to society free of constant harassment and the uncertainty of a turbulent environment. When top professors leave in numbers, the academy is further 'juniorised', and the big losers are the masses of students deprived of the best academic teachers.

Third, the academic facility begins to disintegrate, even collapse. This starts with an inability to replenish library stock and renew critical journals against a weak rand; the maintenance of buildings is postponed until the costs of restoration become prohibitively high; laboratory equipment and computer software become out of date; and donors' trust in the university as a promising investment begins to dry up. When budgets don't balance – declining subsidies coupled with students' inability to pay fees versus rising costs of salaries, electricity, supplies, property taxes, interest on loans, and so on – something has to give, and the shortfall will be all too evident on the public university's balance sheet.

Do the militant minority of student protestors even care that they are in the process of destroying the few top academic institutions left on the continent? Frighteningly, it seems not. The logic of the militant minority is that unless everyone can get free education right now, then no one should – and if that means razing universities to the ground, so be it. What was built up over a century could very well be laid waste in a matter of two to three years.

Explaining the end of the South African university

Why are South African universities so fatally susceptible to underfunding, interference, and instability? Why can't these 26 institutions simply ride the wave of crisis posed by these difficult challenges and live to fight another day? There are two critical explanations for the inevitable decline of South Africa's public universities: the special vulnerability of these fragile institutions, and the institutionalisation of violence within them.

Inherent vulnerability

The first explanation lies in the university's inherent vulnerability, which takes a number of forms: ideological, organisational, physical, and academic.

Unlike other public institutions, universities are supposed to be open-minded spaces in which students and academics are free to do what they want, think for themselves, and experiment with unpopular ideas. This cultural understanding of the university is particularly profound at the English liberal campuses such as UCT and Wits, which explains their immediate vulnerability to violent protests. It also accounts for the deep ambivalence within these campus communities to the idea of expanded security and an on-site police presence. This ambivalence has proven costly and remains unresolved. But the point is that when students sensed this *ideological vulnerability*, they attacked not only buildings but the security system itself.

Academics coined phrases like 'the securitisation of universities', and students made opportunistic arguments that 'the millions spent on security could be used to pay student fees', while both students and staff argued that the presence of police *provoked* violence. Yet that lofty commitment to liberal university ideals was violently assailed by illiberal student and worker ideals in which immediate material demands dashed the romanticism that comes with high-minded notions of what a university stands for.

Insourcing is a concrete example of how something that could not be accomplished in the broader society could be forced upon liberal universities as vulnerable institutions. For years the ANC and the ANC-led government, the South African Communist Party, and the Congress of South African Trade Unions (COSATU) campaigned vigorously against 'labour brokering' in the broader society. Despite all the political rhetoric, short-term contract employment remained the norm for millions of workers. There is a simple reason for this: insourcing made no business sense, and companies could easily ignore politically grounded claims to the contrary. But in the small, intense, organised spaces of the public universities, the outsourcing campaigns led by students and workers could wear down management day after day until they gave in in order to save the academic calendar. A private company can walk away from this kind of threat; a university cannot. Hence campuses became 'islands of welfare [surrounded by] a sea of economic inequity'.[21]

The close and intense aggregation of thousands of 18- to 22-year-olds in unconstrained post-school environments that not only encourage self-expression but offer organised associations (cultural clubs, political parties, green movements, debating societies, and so on) and more than enough targets for discontent makes universities the ideal settings for protest and revolt. In the confined spaces of the university, complete strangers cohere for purposes of intimacy, worship, study sessions, and of course politics. Add to this the fact that students bring to university memories of the heroic struggles of their parents' generation and you have all the tinder needed for a full-on conflagration. The kind of uprisings taking place on campuses today would be impossible in any corporate, NGO, or government office where these same students hope to find work after graduation. Such behaviour would be regarded as aberrant and would quickly lead to dismissal. At university, it seems, you can get away with murder. You can burn campus property and, at places like UCT, be readmitted via an institutional reconciliation process. Many outside observers find institutional accommodation of this kind reprehensible; yet most campus citizens understand how this happens within *organisationally vulnerable* places like the university. As the UCT vice-chancellor explained, in the context of vulnerability you sometimes make decisions that override even matters of principle.

The students discovered not only the ideological and organisational vulnerability of university campuses, but also their *physical vulnerability* in the face of protests. Some called it guerrilla tactics: a relatively small group of students would spread across large campuses disrupting classes, intimidating lecturers, and setting fire to buildings. Students and staff were warned not to react to provocation for fear of stoking violence. Campus security were instructed to handle the protestors with care, intervening only when absolutely necessary. And official university communiqués emphasised the right to protest – with the caveat, of course, that the rights of others be respected. The protestors hardly paid attention to 'the rights of others'. They knew that they could shut down a campus at will even when campus security was strengthened by private security. And they did.

There was one more kind of frailty that would weaken universiti
the face of disruptive protests, and that was *academic vulnerability*. A
university delivers its academic programme in a time-constricted nine
months of the calendar year. In that period an enormous amount of academic content must be taught, learnt, and examined. Any disruption of
the academic business cycle, so to speak, could threaten the graduation
of tens of thousands of students and the welfare of millions of families
dependent on an earning graduate. When the university is threatened by
violent protests, university leaders freeze. Their overriding concern in
such crises is, 'How do we protect the academic year?' and, by extension,
'How do we maintain the integrity of our degrees?' And since government subsidy depends on future enrolments and graduation rates,
vice-chancellors are simultaneously concerned with financial impacts
and institutional image – will parents redirect their children to more
stable universities? This academic vulnerability was starkly revealed in
the latter months of 2016 as academic programmes on campuses around
the country were shut down, reopened, shut down, and reopened once
again.

The institutionalisation of violence

The studies of university protests around the world indicate that in
almost all cases violence is rare, relatively non-threatening, and brief. At
most of the postcolonial African universities, violence has seldom been
part of student protests, and when it is, such incidents are episodic in
nature, with violence mostly aimed at the police. The universities in the
rest of southern Africa, have rarely experienced prolonged student protests, let alone sustained violent protests on campuses. In South Africa,
however, violent protest is no longer exceptional and fits the textbook
definition of institutionalisation: 'routine, something repeatable, predictable, and sustainable'.[22] How did this country at the foot of Africa
come to be so violent in its social culture, institutional behaviours, and
its student protests?

The violence of contemporary South Africa cannot be understood
outside of the country's violent history over the centuries. To explain the
destructive violence of today as if it arises out of a vacuum of time and
space is to ignore that simple but powerful maxim attributed to

Mahmood Mamdani: 'The present is not its own explanation.' The violence, in other words, comes from somewhere in our past.

Neither our violence nor our history starts with colonialism. For centuries the territory that would become modern-day South Africa was racked by violence, from the Mfecane (the violent crushing of subject chiefdoms between 1815 and 1840) to the slave trade, leaving South Africans (and indeed all Africans) a legacy of 'endemic violence which cuts across the precolonial, colonial and postcolonial epochs'.[23] From South Africa to Zimbabwe, the region's identity was formed through violence.

What colonial intrusion did was to make violence normal, to impress violence onto the systems of control and domination over African people – from the courts and the law to the routinised repression of subjugated peoples. Whether it was the Anglo-Zulu War, the South African War, or any number of frontier wars, South Africans remained swamped in violent conflict through the years leading up to Union in 1910. The successive Union governments, as well as the apartheid governments after 1948, regularised violence in every state institution as a way of keeping black people – and the minority of white resisters – in subjugation to laws of political repression and economic exploitation.

The long years of apartheid rule also served to entrench violence in the South African psyche. The victims of apartheid – and those who struggled against it – are not relics of the past. They are living human beings bearing the scars of apartheid's brutality, and they are everywhere: in corporate offices, on the streets, inside government buildings, and on university campuses. Many of them teach and lead us, even as the new generation of students contemptuously dismiss their life-and-death struggles for freedom. These embodiments of apartheid's violence look normal, on the outside. But they, and all South Africans, have been traumatised directly and inter-generationally by the violence of apartheid.

The violence of apartheid was directed not only against an imagined terrorist or communist threat from the outside. It was also used against a people on the inside: the violence of white government against black families, of white institutions against black lives, of white people against black people. Apartheid violence was up-close and personal. It was the white policeman throttling a black activist, smothering a fellow citizen with a wet bag, raping a woman resister, burning black bodies while enjoying a braai, shooting youth from the inside of a police van, throwing activists from police buildings, or hanging them in their cells. This kind of intense interpersonal violence went on for decades.[24]

What made the apartheid years different from the experience of our neighbouring countries was both the longevity and the intensity of state-sanctioned violence. We were the last of the African nations to experience the end of white rule, following Zimbabwe (1980) and Namibia (1990), and right up to the end the violence escalated in a desperate attempt to prevent the inevitable. During the transition to democracy, no place saw more intense violence than KwaZulu-Natal, where the contestation between the Inkatha Freedom Party and the ANC, fuelled by the security forces, caused the death of thousands of black people. Again, the violence was personal, relentless, and deadly, pitting families and communities against each other.

South Africa's new democratic government, led by Nelson Mandela, was born amidst this violence in the wake of events such as the Boipatong massacre,[25] the Bhisho massacre,[26] and the assassination of struggle hero Chris Hani.[27] The violence of the state against its citizens would continue into the democratic era, perhaps most tragically marked by the Marikana massacre of protesting miners at the hands of police. In terms of corruption, violence, and the disregard for citizens, the behaviour of police and security forces has changed little from the past. The protest culture established over decades of anti-apartheid resistance – whether from exile camps or township streets – simply continued into the post-apartheid period. The burning tyre was the symbol tying together two periods of protest, just as the rubber bullets connected the official response on both sides of the democratic transition.

This 'everydayness' of violence, then and now, is part and parcel of South African life, and university campuses are no longer immune to the ordinariness of events in the broader society. As more and more poor students access university through an expansion of enrolments, they bring with them their direct and daily experiences of protest and violence in urban and rural township life. Using protest and violence against the authorities, such as municipal managers, and against public institutions, such as municipal offices, is perfectly normal. When students' demands are not met on campus, the vice-chancellor and the university are seen as simply another kind of public authority, and therefore fair game for violent protests. But something else very important has come onto campus as part of students' experience of violence in their communities.

The violent cultures of South African communities have always intermeshed criminal and political violence. The reactive political violence against apartheid's police blended with criminal violence against suspected *impimpi* (informers). The image of the anti-apartheid icon Winnie Mandela telling an angry crowd that 'with our boxes of matches and our necklaces we shall liberate our country' might have sent shivers down the spines of fair-minded citizens, yet it legitimised the collapse of the distinction between violent resistance against the apartheid state and vigilante action against ordinary citizens suspected of being informants. In the same way, decades later the utterances 'We will kill for Zuma' (2008)[28] and 'Take up arms for Zuma' (2016)[29] are not mere rhetoric by populist politicians, but the continued settling in the public mind of violence as a worthwhile cause for achieving certain functional ends.

Over and over again the student protestors would come to imitate the politicians and the police in making meaningless the distinction between criminal and political violence. Worse, students and academics would come to justify violence in campus protests even as buildings were being burned down, shops looted, security posts set alight with campus security inside, and a campus worker died as a result of inhaling the fumes from a fire extinguisher wielded by a marauding student.

How does anyone justify violence? The first major book on the #FeesMustFall phenomenon included a 'Student Protester Glossary of Terms' in which violence is defined as follows:

> Violence is an experience of structural oppression. This experience can translate into physical violence, emotional and psychological violence through violent words, institutional processes, actions and behaviour that are directed at black people in order to dehumanise them. A reaction to this violence is not violence itself, but a defence against dehumanisation.[30]

This is a highly irresponsible construct of violence. By this vague definition, anything can be violence – as long as it is racialised. Note that black people are the subjects of violence, not women, the disabled, intersex persons, or foreign nationals. Violence is defended without any constraint on scope or terms. For a militant student, this means 'anything goes'. And the term 'institutional processes' is so broad that virtually anything a university does can be dismissed as violence – and 'defensive violence' is therefore justified. The legal, ethical, and moral bumbling notwithstanding, this is an example of how violence was justified on campuses in the 2015–2016 period.

My central contention is that the inability to make the connection between the violence that animates community xenophobia (or any other reactionary violence) and that which drives campus protests (or any other violent demonstrations in South Africa) has led to dangerous and misleading ascriptions applied to student activism in the present period. Student identities and criminal identities are completely fluid and interchangeable in, for example, the violent intimidation of non-protesting students, staff, and management; the burning of property on the Wits campus; and the looting and burning of shops which occurred in the nearby streets of Braamfontein. They are the same actions committed by the same people with the same twisted logic of violence.

For this reckoning with violence to settle in the conscious or unconscious minds of the protestors, they need to frame their target in particular ways. This is called *race branding*, which means setting a group apart as the enemy, as Mahmood Mamdani explains in his estimable work *When Victims Become Killers*.[31] The African foreign national is the enemy coming to steal what is rightfully yours – your commerce, your livelihood, your women. The white university is foreign and therefore must be decolonised from its occupation by settlers and its habitation by their colonial artworks and curriculum. This framing of the enemy as foreign does not have to be true; it only needs to be available as justification of a process in which the victims of racial violence become the perpetrators of the same violence. Once that framing is done, the next step is simple – kill the foreigner or burn the university.

References to anti-colonial literature are used to justify such retaliatory violence, with frequent citations of the works of Frantz Fanon, the influential philosopher-revolutionary. Native violence – as opposed to settler violence – is 'the violence to end violence, more like a utopian wish to close the chapter on colonial violence in the hope of heralding a new humanism'.[32] Protestors disregard the fact that Fanon was responding to the violence of colonial rule before independence and democracy. For them, the symbolic violence that black students on white campuses experience every day – things like 'institutional processes' – justifies the assault on property and people; it is, after all, a defensive position against 'dehumanisation'. Yet another layer of writings in social psychology justifies violent protest as a form of reasonable, even sweet, revenge.[33] Those protestors who consciously draw on these supporting literatures view violence by students as 'a derivative outcome, a result of a prior logic' of violence, as Fanon would have it.[34]

When protest violence and ordinary criminal violence blend into each other, rational, logical thought around action against people and property may disappear in the moment of confrontation. However, student protestors have ready recourse to a script premised on a strong *identity politics* and projected onto protestor placards, songs, and rhetoric. The struggling native must be asserted against the imposing cruelty of the foreigner. Black bodies, black lives, and black oppression are posited against whiteness, colonial curricula, and the settled foreigner. You cannot act violently against that which is your own; you need to distance yourself from that which you claim distances itself from you.

In summary, then, violence has become institutionalised in the everyday routines of South African universities, first in the historically disadvantaged campuses and now in the upper tier of privileged institutions. As more and more students from poor communities engulfed in protests come onto university campuses, they bring with them experiences of the normalisation of disruption and violence from their daily struggles at home. They act in the shadow of a long history of violence that has assumed an everydayness in the lives of battered communities. They have learnt that, more often than not, there is a causal connection between levels of disruptive violence and the chances of getting what they want. And when they cannot get what they want, the protests escalate quickly into destructive and dangerous cycles of violence that have laid low even the top universities in the country.

When does a university cease to exist?[35]

What does all of this mean for the future of South African universities? In a nutshell, there is no future. The forces of underfunding, interference, and instability, acting together, are collapsing public universities rendered impotent through an incessant violence which, however justified, is razing to the ground the last of the continent's most competitive research institutions. It is like watching the collision of two fast-moving trains on a single track – the ambition of university leaders to create world-class institutions undermined by the determination of university students to break these institutions in the quest for an elusive social justice in the face of an unresponsive state.

In the absence of moral leadership at the centre of government and through a woeful misreading of the anti-colonial literature, public universities have been made the singular targets of a retaliatory violence for the ills of society and a revolution that never happened. The great irony of this misguided violence is that the blame for the enduring and systemic effects of apartheid has been laid at the doors of the very institutions that could have been harnessed to overcome them. Not understanding the fragility of these institutions – or perhaps because they did – the violent protestors are taking the public universities apart, ensuring that nothing will be left for the reconstruction of society. The fatal error of some of the most militant agitators is the belief that 'decolonised universities' can be built from the rubble of the predecessor institutions.

My analysis does not mean that there will not be an array of buildings called 'the university'. Post-independence African institutions have remarkable capacity for self-delusion. Doors will be opened, and closed. Junior lecturers will teach. New professors will be promoted on the slimmest of criteria, raising eyebrows. Buildings will skip maintenance cycles and once-grassy landscapes will be neglected. Masses of poor students will pour onto campuses without money to pay and with government having exhausted its once optimistic financial aid schemes. Classrooms will be overcrowded, with limited innovations or investments in new technologies for teaching and learning. Pass rates will decline sharply or be artificially raised. Libraries will become tired warehouses as they quickly run out of replacement and renewal capacity for books and journals. Computers and computer software will not be updated according to required schedules. Top research chairs and appointments will slowly disappear as declining funds are channelled to support mass teaching. Racial and class diversity will gradually be lost in almost all universities. University managers will be reduced to conflict-management tasks; the best potential scholar-leaders will no longer apply for vice-chancellor positions, for these are reputation-busting jobs.

All of this will happen as classes start up and then end, resume again to be disrupted once more, and then start up and shut down again. And all the while, institutions will pretend that they are universities while in fact they are now simply poor, mass-based, black training colleges offering degree certificates with declining market validity. In the meantime, funding from government will continue to decline, the Department of Higher Education and Training will hire more administrators to 'intervene' in failing institutions, and hardly a week will go by without class disruptions and another violent run on these 'universities' for failing to satisfy all the material needs of angry and impoverished students.

There is another loss, incalculable and irreplaceable, that further diminishes the chances that the future of our universities can be saved. This is the exit of deeply wounded and disillusioned men and women from their jobs as vice-chancellors, some even before their contracts have expired. Among them are some of the best available scholars, leaders, and managers of these vexed institutions called universities. They were the institutional pivots on which the future of higher education would revolve in such turbulent times. Yet during their tenure they were screamed at, humiliated, threatened, intimidated, punched, held hostage, and vilified – with their families – even as they tried to prevent public universities from disappearing into the abyss. In late 2016 I reached out to one vice-chancellor who had been physically assaulted by students. He was grateful for the words of solace, but I could sense the deep emotion in his words: 'I am trying desperately to prevent our university and higher education from stepping off the precipice.'

Some vice-chancellors have come to feel that they were thrown under the bus by the South African government. Over the years Minister Nzimande injected the notion of free education into his speeches and railed against outsourcing, but when students and workers came to collect the cheque, the vice-chancellors were left to take the rap.

Vice-chancellors as university leaders have become the final casualty of the collapse of South Africa's universities in a struggle that was not theirs and inside a system that did not care. The violent protestors not only burned buildings, incinerated libraries, and jeopardised the life chances of desperate students who wanted to return to class; they attacked the very humanity of academic leaders charged with ensuring the sustainability of the public university as a national asset.

A ray of hope

It is unlikely that the stand-off over free higher education will be resolved through a political settlement between the ruling party and the warring opposition, or through fiscal redemption whereby the government miraculously conjures up the money required on a sustainable basis. It is more likely that the government will either enact force or continue to abscond, leaving the public universities at the mercy of those inflicting terror on institutions, with property, lives, and leaders being collateral damage in an unending conflict.

But there is one remaining glimmer of hope. There is a reason that these institutions are called public universities. They belong to all of us, the ordinary citizens of South Africa. When ending apartheid looked impossible, ordinary people rose up against the might of the white nationalist state and brought a terrorising power to its knees. It is possible to salvage our universities if ordinary citizens once again reclaim the public in our public universities. This means religious communities, employers of graduates, alumni of universities, non-protesting students, civil society organisations, parents, civic leaders, and respected icons coming together on two principles: the right to free higher education for the poor, and the right to education for everyone. Those two minimal conditions should set the ground for a vigorous public activism that reasserts the value and importance of higher education and its institutions in the life of a nation, in the prospects for democracy, and in the welfare of communities. This activism would be as much an educational intervention as a political intervention to stem the bleeding in public universities.

Such broad-based civic action constitutes a realistic project. Government can and should instantly provide fully funded education through grants for poor, first-degree, first-generation students without any obligation to pay so that these graduates can contribute to lifting their families out of poverty without the burden of debt. It might be necessary even to enact laws that force the state to meet the standard of adequacy in such provision for all poor students. The rest of the financial arrangements for students should combine grants and loans for second-generation and second-degree students so that they do pay back a portion of their earnings to ensure a sustainable cycle of funding for successive generations of students in need of support. And the middle classes and wealthy must pay so as to relieve the burden on government coffers and enable the cross-subsidisation of students with financial need.

Solidarity of community action would also reinstate the value of education and higher education in public life. In a country where more and more youth have lost faith in education, it is crucial to demonstrate by a sustained and inspired programme of activities in poor communities how further and higher education can change lives and alter futures at the individual and collective level. Here powerful and repeated testimonies of graduates from the poorest communities can alter public perception of post-school education. These messages should simultaneously take an unambiguous stand against violence and destruction in education, and show the effects of disrupting classes and burning facilities on opportunities for learning and advancement.

All of this will be difficult to achieve with a corrupt and unresponsive government in place, and without a moral consciousness at the highest levels of leadership. But even if this situation does not change soon, it is important to remind communities that, as in the past, governmental leadership is no substitute for civic and community leadership in education and society. In other words, a progressive programme of action that supports the poor in the quest for free education but underlines the terms of a disciplined learning environment can be established whether or not the government we desire is yet in place.

More than ever before, our chances of establishing revitalised South African universities that are well resourced and well positioned to prepare the next generation of leaders in the sciences, the humanities, and society at large depend on a calibre of university leadership that is both compassionate in speaking to the student heart and competent in leading our universities in a demanding world of teaching, research, and public duty.

This is our fire, our time of testing, perhaps even 'the fire next time' that James Baldwin warned his country about.[36] We must deal with injustice without losing our humanity. We must repair (reparation) what was wronged even as we reconcile what remains divided (reconciliation). Any other path will destroy both campus and country. We are being tested 'as by fire', and even though buildings might have been burned and material losses suffered, we are a resilient people and our spirits will not be broken.

We have come through the fire before. We can do it again.

Notes

Preface

1. For example, see McGregor, K. (ed). 2015. 'Thoughts and experiences of African university leaders'. *University World News*, 6 March. http://www. universityworldnews.com/article.php?story=20150306095945342. See also Council on Higher Education. 2016. *Reflections of South African university leaders, 1981 to 2014*. African Minds & Council on Higher Education: Cape Town. http://www.che.ac.za/sites/default/files/publications/Reflections%20of%20 South%20African%20University%20Leaders%201981-2014.pdf.
2. Typical is George, B. 2009. *7 lessons for leading in crisis*. Jossey-Bass: San Francisco.
3. Wang, J., and Hutchins, H.M. 2010. 'Crisis management in higher education: What have we learnt from Virginia Tech?' *Advances in Developing Human Resources*, 12(October): 552–572.
4. Mills, R.W. 2004. 'University presidents and their leadership: Crisis scenarios at institutions of higher education'. PhD thesis, Oklahoma State University.
5. Bass, J., and Newman, J.I. 2013. 'Too big to fail: The Penn State scandal and the crisis of the corporate university'. *Journal of Issues in Intercollegiate Athletics*, special issue: 22–40.
6. Coleman Jr, J.E., et al. 2008. 'The phases and faces of the Duke Lacrosse controversy: A conversation'. *Seton Hall Journal of Sports and Entertainment Law*, 19(1): 181–220. http://scholarship.law.duke.edu/cgi/viewcontent. cgi?article=3056&context=faculty_scholarship.
7. Hurst, J.C. 1999. 'The Matthew Sheppard tragedy: Management of a crisis'. *About Campus*, 4(3): 5–11.
8. Boin, A., and 't Hart, P. 2003. 'Public leadership in times of crisis: Mission impossible?' *Public Administration Review*, 63(5): 544–553.
9. 'Introduction' to Bataille, G.M., and Cordova, D.I. (eds). 2014. *Managing the unthinkable: Crisis preparation and response for campus leaders*. Stylus Publishing: Sterling, Virginia, p. 3.
10. Jansen, J.D. 2015. *Leading for change: Race, intimacy and leadership on divided university campuses*. Routledge: London.

Introduction

1. In no doubt much more sedate environments, this is an approach taken by political theorist and university president (Wellesley, Duke) Nannerl (Nan) Keohane, who, in her book *Thinking about leadership* (2010, Princeton University Press), examines what university leadership feels like 'from the inside'.
2. James March and his colleagues referenced the 'boundedness' of managers by human and organisational limitations, and the role of ambiguity in university

254

leadership. Clark Kerr and others took the position that university 'presidents make a difference' and this showed in Kerr's very directive leadership of the large University of California, Berkeley. See: March, J., and Simon, H. 1993. *Organisations*, 2nd edition. Blackwell: London; March, J. 1974. *Leadership and ambiguity*. McGraw-Hill: New York; Kerr, C. 1984. *Presidents make a difference: Strengthening leadership in colleges and universities*. Commission on Strengthening University Leadership: Washington DC.

3. James March quoted in Martin, T. 1985. 'Comparative reflections on leadership in higher education'. *European Journal of Education*, 20(2/3): 143–159, 145.
4. Ibid., 154, 150.
5. The best narration of this generational complaint against the anti-apartheid struggle heroes is captured in Wa Azania, M. 2014. *Memoirs of a born free: Reflections on the rainbow nation*. Jacana Media: Johannesburg.

Chapter 1

1. Jansen, J.D. 2012. *Letters to my children: Tweets to make you think*. Bookstorm and Pan Macmillan: Johannesburg, p. 111 (tweet no. 87).
2. I account for Botman's leadership in the final chapter of my 2015 book: Jansen, J.D. 2015. *Leading for change: Race, intimacy and leadership on divided university campuses*. Routledge: London.
3. Poplak, R. 2016. 'Trainspotter: Adam Habib – the rock, the hard place, and the cruel beauty of an uncaring universe'. *Daily Maverick*, 14 October. http://www.dailymaverick.co.za/article/2016-10-04-trainspotter-adam-habib-the-rock-the-hard-place-and-the-cruel-beauty-of-an-uncaring-universe/#.V__SoqMaIqQ.
4. Mills, R.W. 2004. 'University presidents and their leadership: Crisis scenarios at institutions of higher education'. PhD thesis, Oklahoma State University.
5. See Glenn, I. 2016. '"Standing up for injustices"? – Nine notes on #FeesMustFall'. *Litnet*, 28 September. http://www.litnet.co.za/standing-injustices-nine-notes-feesmustfall/.
6. See Horowitz, M.C., Stam, A.C., and Ellis, C.M. 2016. *Why leaders fight*. Cambridge University Press: Cambridge.
7. Useful references in this regard are: Convington, P.D. 2013. 'Institutional crisis readiness as perceived by small college and university senior student affairs officers at NASPA member institutions'. PhD thesis, University of Nebraska; Zdziarski II, E.L. 2001. *Institutional preparedness to respond to campus crises as perceived by student affairs administrators in selected NASPA member institutions*. Texas A&M University: College Station; and Larson, W.A. 1994. *When crisis strikes on campus*. Council for the Advancement and Support of Education: Washington DC.
8. Burnett, J.J. 1998. 'A strategic approach to managing crises'. *Public Relations Review*, 24(4): 475–488, 476.

9. See Thoroughgood, C.N., and Padilla, A. 2013. 'Destructive leadership and the Penn State scandal: A toxic environmental perspective'. *Industrial and Organizational Psychology*, 6(2): 144–149.

10. Keohane, N. 2010. *Thinking about leadership*. Princeton University Press: Princeton, New Jersey, p. 12.

11. See Brown, P.A. 2008. 'Presidential leadership: Understanding the influence of academic disciplines'. *Public Purpose*, April/May: 9–13; Del Favero, M. 2005. 'The social dimensions of academic disciplines as a discriminator of academic deans' administrative behaviour'. *Review of Higher Education*, 29(1): 69–96; Goodhall, A.H. 2009. *Socrates in the boardroom: Why research universities should be led by top scholars*. Princeton University Press: Princeton, New Jersey; and Whistle, W. 2014. 'Do college presidents matter? An analysis of the effects of college presidents on retention and graduation rates'. MPA/MPP Capstone Projects. Paper 28. University of Kentucky, Lexington. http://uknowledge.uky.edu/mpampp_etds/28.

12. Jim Spillane is perhaps the foremost authority on distributed leadership and the construct of 'stretched-over leadership'; see Spillane, J.P. 2010. 'A distributed perspective on school leadership and management'. In *International encyclopedia of education*, 3rd edition, vol. 5, edited by E. Baker, P. Peterson, and B. McGaw. Elsevier Science: Amsterdam.

13. Beaudan, E. 2002. 'Leading in turbulent times'. *Ivey Business Journal*, May/June: 22–26. http://iveybusinessjournal.com/publication/leading-in-turbulent-times/.

14. George, B. 2009. *7 Lessons for leading in a crisis*. Jossey-Bass: San Francisco, p. 12.

15. Boren, M.E. 2001. *Student resistance: A history of the unruly subject*. Routledge: New York.

16. The detail reported here of US college student protests in 2015/16 is drawn from the excellent account by Wong, A., and Green, A. 2016. 'Campus politics: A cheat sheet'. *The Atlantic*, 4 April. http://www.theatlantic.com/education/archive/2016/04/campus-protest-roundup/417570/.

17. Soule, S.A. 1997. 'The student divestment movement in the United States and tactical diffusion: The shantytown protest'. *Social Forces*, 75(3): 855–882.

Chapter 2

1. The 'missing middle' is a term used during the fees protests to refer to students whose parental income is above the then NSFAS ceiling of R120 000 to qualify for government bursaries and loans, but still low enough to cause these students financial stress during their studies. Put differently, students in the missing middle are neither poor enough to qualify for financial support nor wealthy enough to pay for their own studies.

2. The Second Higher Education Transformation Summit was hosted by the minister of education, Blade Nzimande, from 15 to 17 October 2015 at Durban's

International Convention Centre. These summits bring together all stakeholders in higher education – students, workers, academics, managers – to discuss pressing issues on the university transformation agenda. At this second summit a serious rift opened up between the minister and his department officials, on the one hand, and student leaders, on the other hand. While the minister's speech spoke to transformation more broadly – with brief references to the funding of higher education which included corruption in SRC ranks – the rumbling elephant in the room was, for the students, the crisis in student finance. Several observers claimed that the dismissive attitude of the minister and his officials set fuel to the fiery student protests that would soon engulf the country's universities – starting at Wits University in Johannesburg while the Durban summit was still in progress.

3. Merten, M. April 2016. 'Higher education: Saving the "missing" middle'. *Daily Maverick*, 21 April. http://www.dailymaverick.co.za/article/2016-04-21-higher-education-saving-the-missing-middle/#.WBA-WqMaIqQ.

4. Council on Higher Education. 2016. 'Presentation to the Commission of Inquiry into Higher Education and Training: 22 August', pp. 5–6. http://www.che.ac.za/sites/default/files/CHE%20Presentation%20to%20Commission%20of%20Inquiry%20into%20Higher%20Education%20and%20Training%2017%20August%202016.pdf.

5. Ibid, p. 8.

6. Ibid., p. 6.

7. Jordaan, B. 2015. 'Unisa's open book tests make it easy to cheat'. *Sunday Times*, 2 August. http://www.timeslive.co.za/sundaytimes/stnews/2015/08/02/Unisas-open-book-tests-make-it-easy-to-cheat.

8. Council on Higher Education. 2016. 'Presentation to the Commission of Inquiry into Higher Education and Training: 22 August', p. 7. http://www.che.ac.za/sites/default/files/CHE%20Presentation%20to%20Commission%20of%20Inquiry%20into%20Higher%20Education%20and%20Training%2017%20August%202016.pdf.

9. PwC. N.d. 'Funding of public higher education institutions in South Africa'. http://www.pwc.co.za/en/higher-education/Funding-public-higher-education-institutions-SA.html.

10. Ibid.

Chapter 3

1. BBC News. 2015. 'Rhodes statue removed in Cape Town as crowd celebrates'. *BBC.com*, 9 April. http://www.bbc.com/news/world-africa-32236922.

2. I draw much of this information, with appreciation, from the account by Schmahmann, B. 2016. 'The fall of Rhodes: The removal of a sculpture from the University of Cape Town'. *Public Art Dialogue*, 6(1): 90–115.

3. Monuments expert Brenda Schmahmann, email message to author, 28 October 2016.

4. Ibid.

5. Says Schmahmann, 'The name was chosen to woo the Rhodes Trust from which, through a sleight of hand of Leander Starr Jameson, money had been found to start the university'; email message to author, 28 October 2016. See also Schmahmann, B. 2013. *Picturing change*. Wits University Press: Johannesburg.

6. Monuments expert Brenda Schmahmann, email message to author, 28 October 2016.

7. Schmahmann, B. 2016. 'The fall of Rhodes: The removal of a sculpture from the University of Cape Town'. *Public Art Dialogue,* 6(1): 90–115, 90.

8. Lloyd, J. 2016. 'The great debate: Quest to tear down statues over racism is intellectually vapid'. Reuters, 21 January. http://blogs.reuters.com/great-debate/2016/01/20/quest-to-tear-down-statues-over-racism-is-intellectually-vapid/.

9. Monuments expert Brenda Schmahmann, email message to author, 28 October 2016. See also Maylam, P. 2005. *The cult of Rhodes: Remembering an imperialist in Africa*. David Philip: Claremont pp. 43–46.

10. Lloyd, J. 2016. 'The great debate: Quest to tear down statues over racism is intellectually vapid'. Reuters, 21 January. http://blogs.reuters.com/great-debate/2016/01/20/quest-to-tear-down-statues-over-racism-is -intellectually-vapid/.

11. Garner, R. 2015. 'Oxford University risks "damaging its standing" if it pulls down Cecil Rhodes statue, warns Tony Abbott'. *Independent*, 23 December. http://www.independent.co.uk/news/education/education-news/oxford-university-risks-damaging-its-standing-if-is-pulls-down-cecil-rhodes-statue-warns-tony-abbott-a6784536.html.

12. For a high-quality photograph of MT Steyn in pink, and the rationale of the 'pink president' project, see http://www.cigdemaydemir.net/plastic_histories.html.

13. City Press. 2015. 'The Rhodes debate: How we can have the last laugh'. *News24 .com*, 29 March. http://www.news24.com/Archives/City-Press/The-Rhodes-debate-How-we-can-have-the-last-laugh-20150429.

14. Schmahmann mentions the interesting point that South Africa House falls under British heritage protection, so the options available to the embassy were probably limited anyway. Schmahmann, B. 2016. 'The fall of Rhodes: The removal of a sculpture from the University of Cape Town'. *Public Art Dialogue,* 6(1): 90–115.

15. Nelson Mandela and other anti-apartheid activists were arrested on Liliesleaf Farm in the Rivonia suburb of Johannesburg in July 1963, and stood trial later that year. Mandela and nine others had within their defence team the Bloemfontein lawyer Bram Fischer, who started his undergraduate studies at UFS before taking a Rhodes Scholarship to Oxford.

16. Wim Trengrove is a well-known legal expert in South Africa often called on as counsel for prominent politicians, including Nelson Mandela.

17. Brian Molefe is a powerful South African businessman who at various times served in chief executive roles for public sector entities such as Transnet and Eskom.

18. Frank Chikane was a leading cleric and activist in the anti-apartheid era and served as the director general in the Presidency under President Thabo Mbeki.

19. UCT's Trans Collective is a student-led organisation that prioritises the rights of transgender, gender non-conforming, and intersex students.

20. The quotations below are taken from an excellent profile of these two students: Pillay, D. 2016. 'Meet UCT's new student leaders'. *Times Live*, 21 September. http://www.timeslive.co.za/local/2016/09/21/Meet-UCTs-new-student-leaders.

21. Ibid.

22. Ibid.

23. Graham, S. 2011. 'Manyi under fire for coloured remarks'. *Mail & Guardian*, 24 February. http://mg.co.za/article/2011-02-24-manyi-under-fire-for -coloured-remarks.

24. Matentjie, T. 2017. 'The educational motivations and strategies of black middle-class parents in predominantly white schools in post-apartheid South Africa'. Forthcoming PhD thesis, University of the Free State.

25. Mahr, K. 2016. 'Protests over black girls' hair rekindle debate about racism in South Africa'. *Washington Post*, 3 September. https://www.washingtonpost.com/world/africa/protests-over-black-girls-hair-rekindle-debate-about-racism-in-south-africa/2016/09/02/27f445da-6ef4-11e6-993f-73c693a89820_story.html.

26. Fairbanks, E. 2014. 'A paradox of integration'. *New York Times*, 17 October. http://www.nytimes.com/2014/10/19/opinion/sunday/a-paradox-of -integration.html?_r=0.

27. Wa Azania, M. 2014. *Memoirs of a born free: Reflections on the rainbow nation.* Jacana Media: Johannesburg.

28. See Jansen, J.D. 2015. *Leading for change: Race, intimacy and leadership on divided university campuses.* Routledge: London. See also my forthcoming book *Making love in a war zone* (provisional title) to be published by Bookstorm in 2017.

29. Examples include the 2003 and 2007 Institutional Climate Surveys, University of Cape Town; also Ismail, S. 2000. 'An investigation into staff members' experiences of institutional culture at the University of Cape Town'. Research Report. Institutional Culture Working Group of the Employment Equity Forum, UCT; and of course the now prophetic and landmark study by Steyn, M., and van Zyl, M. 1999. '"Like that statue at Jammie stairs": Some student perceptions and experiences of institutional culture at the University of Cape Town in 1999'. Research Report. Institute for Intercultural and Diversity Studies of Southern Africa: Cape Town.

30. Ngwenya, G. 2016. 'The reaction to Penny Sparrow was not rational'. *Politicsweb*, 8 January. http://www.politicsweb.co.za/news-and-analysis/the-reaction-to-penny-sparrow-was-irrational.

31. Ndebele, N. 2016. 'They are burning memory'. Tenth Annual Helen Joseph Lecture, 14 September, University of Johannesburg.

32. Ibid.

33. Mbembe, A. 2015. 'Achille Mbembe on the state of South African political life'. *Africa is a Country*, 19 September. http://africasacountry.com/2015/09/achille-mbembe-on-the-state-of-south-african-politics/.

34. Nieuwoudt, S. 2015. 'Francis Nyamnjoh's STIAS Lecture: "Rhodes fell because of an illusion"'. Stellenbosch Institute for Advanced Study, 17 April. http://stias.ac.za/news/2015/04/francis-nyamnjohs-stias-lecture-rhodes-fell-because-of-an-illusion/.

35. Thaver, L. 2006. '"At home", institutional culture and higher education: Some methodological considerations'. *Perspectives in Education*, 24(1): 15–26, 8.

36. This complaint was removed from the Yale University website, and is reproduced here: http://www.freerepublic.com/focus/chat/3357552/posts. See also Rossler, D. 2015. 'Letter from the editor'. *Yale Herald*, 7 November. http://yaleherald.com/op-eds/hurt-at-home/.

37. Jacobs, A. 2016. 'Renaming the university'. *National Affairs*, 28 (Summer): 3–19.

Chapter 4

1. Salisbury Island, a ferry ride from the Durban coastline, was the founding home of the University College for Indians. Later housed on the mainland as the University of Durban-Westville, it merged with the University of Natal to form the current University of KwaZulu-Natal.

2. Fanon, F. 2004. *The wretched of the earth*. Grove Press: New York, p. 166.

3. Pithouse, R. 2016. 'Violence: What Fanon really said'. *Mail & Guardian*, 8 April. http://mg.co.za/article/2016-04-07-violence-what-fanon-really-said.

4. Fanon, F. 2004. *The wretched of the earth*. Grove Press: New York, p. 51.

5. Kamanzi, B. 2016. 'Demythologising campus violence: Towards a united front for free education?' *Daily Maverick*, 6 March. https://www.dailymaverick.co.za/opinionista/2016-03-06-demythologising-campus-violence-towards-a-united-front-for-free-education/#.WGxbAqMaIqQ.

6. For the senior management's explanation of the decision, including an apology, see 'Statement from the executive on the interdict and the police action on campus', 1 November 2015. https://www.uct.ac.za/dailynews/?id=9445.

7. This statement is not a defence of the illiberal character of liberalism at UCT and the surrounding milieu of a historically liberal Cape Town. The contradictions of a rather shaky commitment to liberalism deserve and have received scholarly attention. At the same time, the claim to and defence of liberal notions of the

university remain real both at a discursive level and in the ways institutions like UCT see themselves, and others.

8.   Kearney, P. 2009. *Guardian of the light: Denis Hurley: Renewing the church, opposing apartheid.* Continuum and UKZN Press: New York and Pietermaritzburg.

9.   Wicks, J. 2016. '11 UKZN protestors to stay in jail'. *News24*, 23 September. http://www.news24.com/SouthAfrica/News/11-ukzn-protesters-to-stay-in -jail-20160923.

10. Kruger, G. 2016. 'Max Price's submission to fees commission disrupted by fallists – UCT'. *Politicsweb*, 6 September. http://www.politicsweb.co.za/news-and- analysis/max-prices-submission-to-fees-commission-disrupted.

11. News24. 2016. 'Stick-wielding protestor whips at UCT student' (video). *News24*, 20 September. http://www.news24.com/Video/SouthAfrica/News/ watch-stick-wielding-protester-whips-at-uct-student-20160920.

12. For an interesting argument linking corrupt political behaviour and citizen behaviour, see Ellis, S. 2016. *This present darkness: A history of Nigerian organized crime.* C. Hurst & Co.: London.

13. TMG Digital. 2016. 'Transcript: Judgment of the Constitutional Court on #Nkandla'. *Times Live*, 31 March. http://www.timeslive.co.za/politics/ 2016/03/31/TRANSCRIPT-Judgment-of-the-Constitutional -Court-on-Nkandla.

14. African News Agency. 2016. 'SA National Civic Organisation welcomes investigation into Hammanskraal land issue'. *Mail and Guardian*, 26 May. http://mg.co.za/article/2016-05-26-00-sa-national-civic-organisation -welcomes-investigation-into-hammanskraal-land-issue.

15. I am grateful to Andre Keet for raising the construct of 'unmanageability' in our management (*sic*) meetings.

16. Sain, R. 2016. 'Student activist #VusiMhlangu arrested'. *IOL*, 6 April. http:// www.iol.co.za/news/crime-courts/student-activist-vusimahlangu -arrested-2005778.

17. Taken from quotes in Lukianoff, G., and Haidt, J. 2015. 'The coddling of the American mind'. *The Atlantic*, September. http://www.theatlantic.com/ magazine/archive/2015/09/the-coddling-of-the-american-mind/399356/.

Chapter 5

1.   Students' Academy. 2014. *Words of wisdom: Chinua Achebe* (ePub). Lulu Press: Raleigh, North Carolina.

2.   Mbongwa, K. 2016. 'The unheard voices: LGBTQ+ people in student movements'. *Daily Vox*, 31 March. http://www.thedailyvox.co.za/ unheard-voices-lgbtq-people-student-movements/.

3.   *Womxn* is a term used to counter the 'man' in 'woman', which, it is argued, makes women a subject of men. *Queer* is used to mean 'gay' or as a broader term

encompassing non-heterosexual groups including gay, bisexual, and transgender persons. *Transgender* is a term referring to persons with a gender identity other than the biological sex assigned by birth.

4.   Whittles, G. 2016. 'The rise and fall of Nompendulo Mkhatshwa, the Wits SRC president'. *Mail & Guardian*, 20 October. http://mg.co.za/article/2016-10-20 -00-the-rise-and-fall-of-nompendulo-mkhatshwa-the-wits-src-president.

5.   Vaccaro, A. 2012. 'Campus microclimates for LGBT faculty, staff, and students: An exploration of the intersections of social identity and campus roles'. *Journal of Student Affairs Research and Practice*, 49(4): 429–446.

6.   In the US, 'minority' is a political term referring to non-white citizens, especially African American and Latino communities, as demographic minorities in relation to the white majority community. Needless to say, a simple demographic definition of minorities cannot adequately express rapid changes in the numbers of 'minorities' in certain geographic areas of this large country.

7.   Ackelsberg, M., Hart, J., Miller, N.J., Queeney, K., and van Dyne, S. 2009. 'Faculty microclimate change at Smith College'. In *Doing diversity in higher education: Faculty leaders share challenges and strategies*, edited by W.R. Brown-Glaude. Rutgers University Press: New Brunswick, New Jersey.

8.   Quotation drawn from Rankin, S., and Reason, R. 2008. 'Transformational tapestry model: A comprehensive approach to transforming campus climate'. *Journal of Diversity in Higher Education*, 1(4): 262–274.

Chapter 6

1.   See the magisterial work by Giliomee, H. 2003. *The Afrikaners: Biography of a people.* University of Virginia Press: Charlottesville, pp. 268–272.

2.   In the heyday of Afrikaner nationalism after D.F. Malan's National Party took power in 1948, there emerged some very revealing publications of the *volk*'s ideological passions and practices with regard to education and upliftment. See Coetzee, J.C. 1951. *Die onderwys en opvoeding van die Afrikaner in die twintigste eeu.* Fakulteit Opvoedkunde: Potchefstroom.

3.   Jansen, J.D., with Koza, N., and Toyana, L. 2011. *Great South African teachers.* Bookstorm: Johannesburg.

4.   Taken from Els, R. 2016. 'Betogers verjaag rektore en plunder op kampus'. *Netwerk24*, 10 March. http://www.netwerk24.com/Nuus/Algemeen/ betogers-verjaag-rektore-20160310.

5.   See Mangcu, X. 2016. 'Students shouted me down'. *Sunday Independent*, 29 May. http://www.iol.co.za/sundayindependent/students-shouted-me-down-2027581. See also the student response: Bomvana, B., Mpemnyama, N., and Mtoto, M. 2016. 'UWC students respond to Prof Xolela Mangcu'. *Daily Vox*, 30 May. http://www.thedailyvox.co.za/uwc-students-response-xolela-mangcu/.

6. Van der Westhuizen, C. 2016. 'Anti-democratic element in student movements holds warnings for South Africa'. *The Conversation*, 30 June. http://theconversation.com/anti-democratic-element-in-student-movements-holds-warnings-for-south-africa-61448.

7. On YouTube as 'UCT talks: Heritage, signage and symbolism', posted on 16 March 2015. https://www.youtube.com/watch?v=4NgpJ00M5Ho.

8. Vice, S. 2010. 'How do I live in this strange place?' *Journal of Social Philosophy*, 41(3): 323–342. http://onlinelibrary.wiley.com/doi/10.1111/j.1467-9833.2010.01496.x/abstract.

9. See Villet, C. 2011. 'The importance of having a voice'. *Mail & Guardian*, 4 November. http://mg.co.za/article/2011-11-02-the-importance-of-having-a-voice. See also Hempson, C. 2011. 'The story of humility and silence'. *Mail & Guardian*, 20 October. http://mg.co.za/article/2011-10-20-the-story-of-humility-and-silence.

10. For a range of resources on actual and desired leadership behaviours in a crisis, see Cynthia Lawson, C. 2014. 'The power of leadership in at a time of tragedy'. In *Managing the unthinkable: Crisis preparation and response for campus leaders*, edited by G.M. Bataille and D.I. Cordovia. Stylus Publishing: Sterling, Virginia, pp. 37–46; Patterson, B.G., et al. 2007. 'Human crises'. In *Campus crisis management: A comprehensive guide to planning, prevention, response, and recovery*, edited by E.L. Zdziarski II et al. Jossey-Bass: San Francisco, pp. 255–282; DuBrin, A.J. (ed). 2013. *Handbook of research on crisis leadership in organizations*. Edward Elgar Publishing: Northampton, Massachusetts; Alden III, R.W., and Kafer, H. 2010. 'The provost's perspective: Campus-wide needs and responses'. In *Enough is enough: A student affairs perspective on preparedness and response to a campus shooting*, edited by B.O. Hemphill and B.H. LaBanc. Stylus Publishing: Sterling, Virginia, pp. 135–148.

11. Mills, R.W. 2004. 'University presidents and their leadership: Crisis scenarios at institutions of higher education'. PhD thesis, Oklahoma State University, p. 174.

12. Ibid., p. 175.

13. Msimang, S. 2016. 'UCT and #RMF: A burning issue'. *IOL*, 19 February. http://www.iol.co.za/news/uct-and-rmf-a-burning-issue-1986784.

14. Following the merger, North-West University had the somewhat unusual arrangement of having an overseeing vice-chancellor (Kgwadi) for the university as a whole, and rectors for each of the three campuses (Potchefstroom, Mafikeng and Vaal Triangle).

15. I borrow the term 'the greatest generation' from Tom Brokaw, the US journalist, who also has a 2001 book by that name, published by Random House.

16. This section does not contain a separate and lengthy discussion of the impact of the crisis on Professor De la Rey since she did not elaborate on the short responses given to this question.

Chapter 7

1. Wa Thiong'o, N. 1986. *Decolonising the mind: The politics of language in African literature*. James Currey: Oxford, p. 89.

2. Ibid.

3. Ibid.

4. The argument about a selective tradition appears consistently in Michael Apple's curriculum thought from his classic *Ideology and curriculum* (1979) to *Official knowledge* (2014, third edition), both published by Routledge, New York.

5. Mathebula, T. 2013. 'People's Education (for People's Power) – a promise unfulfilled'. *South African Journal of Education*, 33(1): 1–12. http://www.scielo.org.za/scielo.php?script=sci_arttext&pid=S0256-01002013000100002.

6. Jansen, J.D. 1991. 'The state and curriculum in the transition to socialism: The Zimbabwean experience'. *Comparative Education Review*, 35(1): 76–91.

7. The double meaning of the word 'settled' refers to the critics' view of 'settler knowledge' still occupying South African universities, as well as to the notion of established knowledge being bedded down, or settled, within the everyday routines and regulations of the older universities. See the chapter on curriculum in Jansen, J.D. 2009. *Knowledge in the blood: Confronting race and the apartheid past*. Stanford University Press: Palo Alto, California.

8. See Modiri, J. 2016. 'In the Fall: Decolonisation and the rejuvenation of the academic project in South Africa'. *Daily Maverick*, 16 October. http://www.dailymaverick.co.za/opinionista/2016-10-16-in-the-fall-decolonisation-and-the-rejuvenation-of-the-academic-project-in-south-africa/#.WA1Y26MaIqQ. See also Wild, S., and Nordling, L. 2016. 'Op-ed: Science is not un-African – but there is a prejudice towards African science'. *Daily Maverick*, 21 October. http://www.dailymaverick.co.za/article/2016-10-21-op-ed-science-is-not-unafrican-but-there-is-a-prejudice-towards-african-science/#.WA1Z_qMaIqQ.

9. Jansen, J.D. 1998. 'Curriculum reform in South Africa: A critical analysis of outcomes- based education'. *Cambridge Journal of Education*, 28: 321–331.

10. Jansen, J.D. 2004. 'The politics of salvation and the school curriculum'. *Verbum et Ecclesia*, 25(2): 784–806.

11. Jansen, J.D. 1998. '"But our natives are different!": Race, knowledge and power in the academy'. *Social Dynamics*, 24(2): 102–116.

12. In Jansen, J.D. 2009. *Knowledge in the blood: Confronting race and the apartheid past*. Stanford University Press: Palo Alto, California.

13. De Oliveira Andreotti, V., Steyn, S., Ahenakew, C., and Hunt, D. 2015. 'Mapping interpretations of decolonization in the context of higher education'. *Decolonization: Indigeneity, Education and Society*, 4(1): 21–40, 22.

14. Nyamnjoh, F.B. 2016. *#RhodesMustFall: Nibbling at resilient colonialism in South Africa*. Langaa Research and Publishing Common Initiative Group: Bamenda, Cameroon.

15. See, for example, the distinctions made between 'soft reform', 'hard reform', and 'beyond reform' in the 'social cartography' of curriculum decolonisation in De Oliveira Andreotti, V., Steyn, S., Ahenakew, C., and Hunt, D. 2015. 'Mapping interpretations of decolonization in the context of higher education'. *Decolonization: Indigeneity, Education and Society*, 4(1): 21–40, 15 (Table 1).

16. Prinsloo, E.H. 2016. 'The role of the humanities in decolonising the academy'. *Arts & Humanities in Higher Education*, 15(1): 164–168.

17. See Tselapedi, T. 2016. 'Political studies: An entry into "social science thought" in the South African academy'. *Arts and Humanities in Higher Education*, 15(1): 169–174; and Rijsdijk, I. 2016. 'The arts in contemporary South African education: Film and media studies'. *Arts and Humanities in Higher Education*, 15(1): 107–121.

18. Wa Thiong'o, N. 1986. *Decolonising the mind: The politics of language in African literature.* James Currey: Oxford, p. 93.

19. Ibid., p. 95.

20. Quoted in ibid., p. 9.

21. Ibid., p. 9.

22. Ibid., p. 71.

23. This proposal is made by scholars such as Harry Garuba. See Garuba, H. 2015. 'What is an African curriculum?' *Mail & Guardian*, 17 April 2015. http://mg.co.za/article/2015-04-17-what-is-an-african-curriculum/.

24. Ibid.

25. Pillay, S. 2015. 'Decolonizing the university'. *Africa is a Country*, 7 June. http://africasacountry.com/2015/06/decolonizing-the-university/.

26. Ibid.

27. This is implied in Sarah Nuttall's work on entanglement and given curriculum direction in two of my books in sequence: Jansen, J.D. 2009. *Knowledge in the blood: Confronting race and the apartheid past.* Stanford University Press: Palo Alto, California; followed by Jansen, J.D. 2016. *Leading for change: Race, intimacy and leadership on divided university campuses.* Routledge: London. On 'interwoven' knowledge, see Connell, R. 2016. 'Decolonizing the curriculum'. http://www.raewynconnell.net/2016/10/decolonising-curriculum.html.

28. Richardson, T. 2011. 'Navigating the problem of inclusion and enclosure in native culture-based education: Theorizing shadow curriculum'. *Curriculum Inquiry*, 41(3): 332–349.

29. Tuck, E., and Wayne Yang, K. 2012. 'Decolonization is not a metaphor'. *Decolonization: Indigeneity, Education and Society*, 1(1): 1–40, 3.

30. Ibid., p. 31.

31. Ibid., p. 35.

32. See, for example, Arnold, G.B. 2004. 'Symbolic politics and institutional boundaries in curriculum reform: The case of National Sectarian University'. *Journal of Higher Education*, 75(5): 572–593. Other authors on symbolic policies in curriculum and education include Hans Weiler, Stanford University.

33. Although SACHED was established in 1959 and admitted its first learners in 1960, it was during the 1970s that it launched a number of independent programmes and initiatives which expressly linked educational and political objectives as part of an alternative education strategy. See the fascinating account of the evolution of SACHED by E.P. Nonyongo (undated), available at http://www.c3l.uni-oldenburg.de/cde/support/readings/nonyo98.pdf.

34. People's Education was more of a movement expressed in different ways across the country rather than a singular structure controlling the alternative vision for education. See Reagan, T. 1989. '"People's Education" in South Africa: Schooling for liberation'. *Journal of Thought*, 24(1/2): 4–25; and Vally, S. 2007. 'From People's Education to neo-liberalism in South Africa'. *Review of African Political Economy*, 34(111): 39–56.

35. NEPI was established by affiliates of the ANC to explore policy alternatives to apartheid education between the period of the release of Nelson Mandela (1990) and the advent of democracy (1994). See NEPI. 1993. *National Education Policy Investigation: The framework report and final report summaries*. Oxford University Press: Cape Town.

36. This question was famously posed by the British philosopher Herbert Spencer about 150 years ago.

37. Shay, S. 2016. 'Decolonising the curriculum: It's time for a strategy'. *The Conversation*, 13 June. http://theconversation.com/decolonising-the-curriculum-its-time-for-a-strategy-60598.

38. Jansen, J.D. 1997. '"Essential alterations"? A critical analysis of the state's syllabus revision process'. *Perspectives in Education*, 17(2): 1–11.

39. See Jansen, J.D. 2009. *Knowledge in the blood: Confronting race and the apartheid past*. Stanford University Press: Palo Alto, California.

40. Jansen, J.D. (ed.). 1991. *Knowledge and power in South Africa: Critical perspectives across the disciplines*. Skotaville Press: Johannesburg.

41. University of Cape Town, Curriculum Change Working Group: Preliminary Conceptual Framework (undated).

42. Ibid.

43. Mbembe, A. 2015. 'Decolonizing knowledge and the question of the archive'. http://wiser.wits.ac.za/system/files/Achille%20Mbembe%20-%20Decolonizing%20Knowledge%20and%20the%20Question%20of%20the%20Archive.pdf.

44. Price, M., and Ally, R. 2016. 'Decolonisation must not be a black and white issue'. *Business Day*, 4 April. http://www.bdlive.co.za/opinion/2016/04/04/decolonisation-must-not-be-a-black-and-white-issue.

Chapter 8

1. Van Onselen, C. 1998. 'Closer to home: Student unrest and the welfare function'. In *Ironic victory: Liberalism in post-apartheid South Africa*, edited by R.W. Johnson and D. Welsh. Oxford University Press: Cape Town, p. 164.

2. Godsell, G., and Chikane, R. 2016. 'The roots of the revolution'. In *Fees must fall: Student revolt, decolonisation and governance in South Africa*, edited by S. Booysen. Wits University Press: Johannesburg, p. 60.

3. Van Onselen, C. 1998. 'Closer to home: Student unrest and the welfare function'. In *Ironic victory: Liberalism in post-apartheid South Africa*, edited by R.W. Johnson and D. Welsh. Oxford University Press: Cape Town, p. 164.

4. I am grateful to senior UFS student Sinoxolo Gcilitshana for the meticulous conducting of this survey on the Bloemfontein campus and to Teboho Manchu and Grey Magaiza for conducting the survey on the Qwaqwa campus. Note that in an earlier version of the survey, the framing of question 3 was confusing to respondents and therefore their responses might have been overstated. I thus made the decision to report only the Qwaqwa results for this question, where the distinction between core costs and basic needs coverage was more clearly made.

5. National Treasury. 2015. 'Budget 2015 highlights'. http://www.treasury.gov.za/documents/national%20budget/2015/guides/2015%20Budget%20Highlights%20Card.pdf.

6. Statistics South Africa. 2016. 'Facts you might not know about social grants'. 2 June. http://www.statssa.gov.za/?p=7756.

7. In the absence of hard data from groups like the National Income Dynamics Study, I am hesitant to make firm statements about the link between welfare receipt and university enrolments. This section of the book is therefore largely speculative about that relationship. Yet a broad conclusion is reasonable: that the average class status of students at UCT makes that link unlikely, even though the relationship is more likely to exist in the poorest universities, such as Zululand, but also in the 'mixed economic' universities like UFS. I am grateful to Jeremy Seekings for comments on the draft of this chapter (personal communication, 28 October 2016), advising caution about making firm connections between welfare receipt and welfare expectations.

8. Booysen, S. 2016. 'Two weeks in October: Changing governance in South Africa'. In *Fees must fall: Student revolt, decolonisation and governance in South Africa*, edited by S. Booysen. Wits University Press: Johannesburg, p. 35.

9. An image seared into my consciousness was the sight of high school students digging into food in a secluded office of a high school in Delft, as if they had not eaten for days. I would address their seniors minutes later about opportunities for study at UFS.

10. Eyal, K., and Woolard, I. 2013. 'School enrolment and the child support grant: Evidence from South Africa'. SALDRU Working Paper Number 125/NIDS Discussion Paper 2013/7. SALDRU, University of Cape Town: Cape Town.

11. Recorded voice note sent to me via WhatsApp by a youth leader in the CRC, 19 October 2016.

12. Cassim, A., and Bhorat, H. 2014. 'South Africa's welfare success story II: Poverty-reducing social grants'. Brookings Institution, 27 January. https://www.brookings.edu/blog/africa-in-focus/2014/01/27/south-africas-welfare-success-story-ii-poverty-reducing-social-grants/.

13. Joint Union Task Team (JUTT), Cape Peninsula University of Technology, Protest Situation: General Assembly, 21 October 2016.

14. Bokana, K.G. 2010. 'The attrition crisis in South African universities: How to keep students on the graduation path'. *Journal of Interdisciplinary Economics*, 22(3): 181–201, 187.

15. Patel, L. 2015. *Social welfare and social development*. Oxford University Press: Cape Town, p. 21.

16. West, A., and Nikolai, R. 2013. 'Welfare regimes and education regimes: Equality of opportunity and expenditure in the EU (and US)'. *Journal of Social Policy*, 42(3): 469–493, 484.

17. Pechar, H., and Andres, L. 2011. 'Higher education policies and welfare regimes: International comparative perspectives'. *Higher Education Policy*, 24(1): 25–52, 25.

18. Pillay, P. 2016. 'Financing of universities: Promoting equity or reinforcing inequality'. In *Fees must fall: Student revolt, decolonisation and governance in South Africa*, edited by S. Booysen. Wits University Press: Johannesburg, p. 258.

19. Fitzgerald, P., and Seale, O. 2016. 'Between a rock and a hard place: University management and the #FeesMustFall campaign'. In *Fees must fall: Student revolt, decolonisation and governance in South Africa*, edited by S. Booysen. Wits University Press: Johannesburg, p. 236.

20. Bokana speaks of 'onset of youth needs' under conditions of extreme poverty; see Bokana, K.G. 2010. 'The attrition crisis in South African universities: How to keep students on the graduation path'. *Journal of Interdisciplinary Economics*, 22(3): 181–201, 188.

21. Ferguson, J. 2015. *Give a man a fish: Reflections on the new politics of distribution*. Duke University Press: Durham, North Carolina, p. 60.

22. Ibid., p. 167.

23. Ibid.

24. Ibid.

25. A detailed account of the events around Shackville appears in a judgment of the Supreme Court of Appeal (SCA) to determine whether the high court correctly granted a final appeal against five appellants responsible for the violent protests. The SCA confirmed the ruling of the lower court. *Hotz and Others* v *University of Cape Town* (730/2016) [2016] ZASCA 159; [2016] 4 All SA 723 (SCA) (20 October 2016); available at http://www.saflii.org/za/cases/ZASCA/2016/159.html.

26. GroundUp staff. 2016. 'How serious is the student housing crisis?' *GroundUp*, 29 February. http://www.groundup.org.za/article/ how-serious-university-accommodation/.

27. Furlong, A. 2016. 'Rhodes Must Fall protestors burn UCT art'. *Daily Maverick*, 17 February. http://www.dailymaverick.co.za/article/2016-02-17 -groundup-rhodes-must-fall-protesters-burn-uct-art/.

28. UCT Acting Deputy Vice-Chancellor Anwar Mall quoted in GroundUp staff. 2016. 'How serious is the student housing crisis?' *GroundUp*, 29 February. http://www.groundup.org.za/article/how-serious-university-accommodation/.

29. Africa News Agency. 2016. 'Shackville erected at UCT to protest lack of housing for black students'. *eNCA.com*, 15 February. https://www.enca.com/south-africa/ shackville-erected-uct-protest-lack-housing-black-students.

30. Furlong, A. 2016. 'Rhodes Must Fall protestors burn UCT art'. *Daily Maverick*, 17 February. http://www.dailymaverick.co.za/article/2016-02-17-groundup -rhodes-must-fall-protesters-burn-uct-art/.

31. Mian, N. 2016. 'Protestors demand UCT drop charges'. *GroundUp*, 1 June. http://www.groundup.org.za/article/protesters-demand-uct-drops-charges/.

32. Favara, D.M., and Mendelsohn, S.C. 2012. 'The Students' Health and Welfare Centres Organisation: A review of the past 69 years'. *South African Medical Journal*, 102(6): 400–402.

33. Van Onselen, C. 1998. 'Closer to home: Student unrest and the welfare function'. In *Ironic victory: Liberalism in post-apartheid South Africa*, edited by R.W. Johnson and D. Welsh. Oxford University Press: Cape Town, p. 166.

34. I am grateful to Dr Carolina Dekker-Suransky from the University of Humanistics Study in Utrecht for sharing this observation.

35. See Thompson, J.J. 1993. 'Women, welfare and college: The impact of higher education on economic well-being'. *Affilia*, 8(4): 425–441; and Butler, S.S., and Deprez, L. 2002. 'Something worth fighting for: Higher education for women on welfare'. *Affilia*, 17(1): 30–54.

36. Barron, L. Facebook post, 6 October 2016.

37. Fitzgerald, P., and Seale, O. 2016. 'Between a rock and a hard place: University management and the #FeesMustFall campaign'. In *Fees must fall: Student revolt, decolonisation and governance in South Africa*, edited by S. Booysen. Wits University Press: Johannesburg, p. 243.

38. Van den Berg, L., and Raubenheimer, J. 2016. 'Food insecurity among students at the University of the Free State, South Africa'. *South African Journal of Clinical Nutrition*, 28(4). Published online 31 May. http://www.tandfonline.com/doi/ abs/10.1080/16070658.2015.11734556.

Chapter 9

1. For a critique of embedded journalism, see Tuotso, K. 2008. 'The "grunt truth" of embedded journalism: The new media/military relationship'. *Stanford Journal of International Relations*, 10(1): 20–31.

2. Coronel, S., Coll, S., and Kravitz, D. 2015. '*Rolling Stone*'s investigation: "A failure that was avoidable"'. *Columbia Journalism Review*, 5 April. http://www.cjr.org/investigation/rolling_stone_investigation.php.

3. See, among others, Siegel, M.L. (ed.). 2009. *Race to injustice: Lessons learned from the Duke lacrosse rape case*. Carolina Academic Press: Durham, North Carolina; Taylor, S., and Johnson, K.C. 2007. *Until proven innocent: Political correctness and the shameful injustices of the Duke lacrosse rape case*. Carolina Academic Press: Durham, North Carolina; Coleman Jr, J.E., Davis, A., Gerhardt, M., Johnson, K.C., Lidsky, L., and Wasserman, H.M. 2009. 'The phases and faces of the Duke lacrosse controversy: A conversation'. *Seton Hall Journal of Sports and Entertainment Law*, 19(1): 181–220. http://scholarship.law.duke.edu/cgi/viewcontent.cgi?article=3056&context=faculty_scholarship.

4. Ham, M.K. 2016. 'Fantastic lies: 10 appalling moments from the Duke lacrosse case'. *The Federalist*, 16 March. http://thefederalist.com/2016/03/16/fantastic-lies-10-appalling-moments-from-the-duke-lacrosse-case/.

5. For the basic information on this story, I draw on the excellent review of the media failure in this case by Coronel, S., Coll, S., and Kravitz, D. 2015. '*Rolling Stone*'s investigation: "A failure that was avoidable"'. *Columbia Journalism Review*, 5 April. http://www.cjr.org/investigation/rolling_stone_investigation.php.

6. Ibid.

7. Ibid.

8. See Chapter 12, 'The intimate observer', in my book Jansen, J.D. 2015. *Leading for change: Race, intimacy and leadership on divided university campuses*. Routledge: London.

9. From Max du Preez's Facebook page, 24 June 2015.

10. Mehta, L., and Movik, S. 2010. *Shit matters: The potential of community-led total sanitation*. Practical Action Publishing: Rugby, UK.

11. Conradie, E. 2014. 'From land reform to poo protesting: Some theological reflections on the ecological repercussions of economic inequality'. *Scriptura*, 113: 1–16, 7. See also Robins, S. 2014. 'Poo wars as matter out of place: "Toilets for Africa" in Cape Town. *Anthropology Today*, 30(1): 2–3.

12. Dawson, M.C. 2012. 'Protest, performance and politics: The use of "nano-media" in social media activism in South Africa'. *Journal of Applied Theatre and Performance*, 17(3): 321–345, 321.

13. Turnage, A.K. 2009. 'Scene, act and the tragic frame in the Duke rape case'. *Southern Communication Journal*, 74(2): 151–156.

14. Strauss, H. 2014. 'Spectacles of promise and disappointment: Political emotion and quotidian aesthetics in video installations by Berni Searle and Zanele

Muholi'. *Safundi: The Journal of South African and American Studies,* 15(4): 471–495, 471.

15. Vallabhjee, D. 2016. 'Wits student Sarah Mokwebo on why she went topless and how it changed the protest'. *Marie Claire,* 6 October. http://www.marieclaire. co.za/mc-recommends/wits-student-sarah-mokwebo-went-topless-changed -protest.

16. Title of new book by Duncan, J. 2016. *Protest nation: The right to protest in South Africa.* University of KwaZulu-Natal Press: Pietermartizburg.

17. Seekings, J., and Nattrass, N. 2015. *Policy, politics and poverty in South Africa.* Palgrave Macmillan: London, p. 236.

18. Turnage, A.K. 2009. 'Scene, act and the tragic frame in the Duke rape case'. *Southern Communication Journal,* 74(2): 151–156.

19. Cottle, S. 2009. *Mediatized conflict: Developments in media and conflict studies.* Open University Press: London, pp. 45–46.

20. Eyewitness News (EWN). 2015. 'The year of the student'. http://ewn.co.za/ Features/year-of-the-student#/.

21. Munsamy, R. 2015. 'The 2015 person of the year: The student'. *Daily Maverick,* 14 December. http://www.dailymaverick.co.za/article/2015-12-14-2015 -south-african-person-of-the-year-the-student/#.V_2D8aMaIqQ.

22. Hyman, A. 2016. 'Student in court for life-threatening campus blaze'. *The Times,* 13 October. http://www.timeslive.co.za/local/2016/10/13/ Student-in-court-for-life-threatening-campus-blaze.

23. I borrow the term from Seekings, J., and Nattrass, N. 2015. *Policy, politics and poverty in South Africa.* Palgrave Macmillan: London, p. 238.

24. Luescher, T., Loader, L., and Mugume, T. 2016. '#FeesMustFall: An internet-age student movement in South Africa and the case of the University of the Free State'. *Politikon,* 4 October. DOI: 10.1080/02589346.2016.1238644.

25. Oxlund, B. 2016. '#EverythingMustFall: The use of social media and violent protests in the current wave of student riots in South Africa'. *Anthropology Now,* 4 October. http://anthronow.com/in-print/everythingmustfall.

26. In April 2015, then SRC president Dlamini expressed his admiration for Hitler's charisma and organisational skills, a statement he would not retract. Naidoo, R. 2015. 'SRC president says: "I love Hitler"'. *Wits Vuvuzela* (student newspaper), 27 April. http://witsvuvuzela.com/2015/04/27/src-president-says-i-love-hitler/.

27. Oxlund, B. 2016. '#EverythingMustFall: The use of social media and violent protests in the current wave of student riots in South Africa'. *Anthropology Now,* 4 October. http://anthronow.com/in-print/everythingmustfall.

28. Ngidi, N., Mtshixa, C., Diga, K., Mbarathi N., and May, J. 2016. '"Asijiki" and the capacity to aspire through social media: The #FeesMustFall movement as an anti-poverty activism in South Africa'. *Proceedings of the Eighth International Conference on Information and Communication Technologies and Development (ICTD '16).* Article No. 15. ACM Publications: New York. DOI 10.1145/ 2909609.2909654.

29. Ibid.
30. Bosch, T. 2016. 'Twitter activism and youth in South Africa: The case of #RhodesMustFall'. *Information, Communication & Society*, 20(2). DOI: 10.1080/1369118X.2016.1162829.
31. LaRiviere, K., Snider, J., Stromberg, A., and O'Meara, K. 2012. 'Protest: Critical lessons of using digital media for social change'. *About Campus* (July–August): 10–17. http://www.education.umd.edu/Academics/Faculty/Bios/facData/CHSE/komeara/LaRiviere_et_al_2012.pdf.
32. Ronson, J. 2015. 'How one stupid tweet blew up Justine Sacco's life'. *New York Times Magazine*, 12 February. https://www.nytimes.com/2015/02/15/magazine/how-one-stupid-tweet-ruined-justine-saccos-life.html?_r=0.
33. For a US example, see Gardner, L. 2016. 'How presidents try to stay ahead of the social-media outrage machine'. *Chronicle of Higher Education*, 63(7): A18–a22.
34. Van der Merwe, M. 2016. '#FeesMustFall, Cape Town: The week the line was crossed'. *Daily Maverick*, 13 October. http://www.dailymaverick.co.za/article/2016-10-13-feesmustfall-cape-town-the-week-the-line-was-crossed/#.V__D7aMaIqQ.
35. Coovadia, I. 2016. 'UCT: The silence of things not being attempted'. *GroundUp*, 13 October. http://www.groundup.org.za/article/uct-silence-things-not-even-being-attempted/.
36. February, J. 2016. 'It is the age of unreason. It is the age of impunity'. *Daily Maverick*, 19 October. http://firstthing.dailymaverick.co.za/article?id=80943#.V__BrKMaIqQ.
37. Makhanya, M. 2016. 'Stop the war on knowledge'. *City Press*, 30 August.
38. Poplak, R. 2016. 'Trainspotter: Adam Habib – the rock, the hard place, and the cruel beauty of an uncaring universe'. *Daily Maverick*, 4 October. http://www.dailymaverick.co.za/article/2016-10-04-trainspotter-adam-habib-the-rock-the-hard-place-and-the-cruel-beauty-of-an-uncaring-universe/#.V__SoqMaIqQ.

Chapter 10

1. For example, see Osha, S. 2016. 'The image of Cecil John Rhodes'. In *#RhodesMustFall: Nibbling at resilient colonialism in South Africa*, edited by F.B. Nyamnjoh. Langaa Research and Publishing Common Initiative Group: Bamenda, Cameroon, p. 280.
2. Mbwette, T.S.A., and Ishumi, A.G.M. (eds). 2000. *Managing university crises*. Dar es Salaam University Press: Dar es Salaam, p. 7.
3. Ibid., p. 9.
4. Ibid., p. 135.
5. Ibid., p. 33.
6. Ibid., pp. 35, 34.
7. Once dubbed the Harvard of Africa, Makerere University is often cited as a cautionary tale about what happens in the post-colonial university when

governments interfere, protests turn violent, and funding declines. See, for example, Seremba, Y. 2012. 'The rise and fall of Makerere University'. *Campus Journal*, 19 April. http://campusjournal.ug/index.php/special-report/ investigation/457-the-rise-and-fall-of-makerere-university.

8.   The Commission of Inquiry into Higher Education and Training – often referred to in shorthand as the Fees Commission – was established by President Zuma to investigate the feasibility of free higher education in South Africa. Headed by Judge Jonathan Arthur Heher, the commission of three persons convened public hearings for stakeholders such as students and vice-chancellors to make presentations that would address the vexed question of university fees.

9.   Fitzgerald, P., and Seale, O. 2016. 'Between a rock and a hard place: University management and the #FeesMustFall campaign'. In *Fees must fall: Student revolt, decolonisation and governance in South Africa*, edited by S. Booysen. Wits University Press: Johannesburg, p. 238.

10. See Mdaka, Y. 2016. 'Rhodes University close to financial crisis'. *Destiny*, 15 July. http://www.destinyconnect.com/2016/07/15/rhodes-university-close-financial -crisis/. See also: Staff writer. 2016. 'Top South African university is facing financial crisis: DA'. *Business Tech*, 14 July. http://businesstech.co.za/news/ finance/130092/top-south-african-university-is-facing-a-financial-crisis-da/.

11. Jansen, J.D. 2004. 'Accounting for autonomy'. The 41st TB Davie Memorial Lecture on Academic Freedom, University of Cape Town, 26 August. http:// www.repository.up.ac.za/bitstream/handle/2263/157/Jansen%20(2004)a .pdf?sequence=3.

12. Hall, M., et al. (n.d.) 'Academic freedom and institutional autonomy: Views from the University of Cape Town'. http://www.che.ac.za/sites/default/files/ publications/d000173_11_UCT_1_cover.pdf.

13. Coetzer, P. 2013. 'Higher education institutions' autonomy under threat: Amendment Act open to constitutional challenge'. *Leadership*, 11 June. http:// www.leadershiponline.co.za/articles/higher-education-institutions-autonomy -under-threat-7462.html.

14. From statement by a government spokesman in response to criticism of the Bill, cited in Jenvey, N. 2012. 'New legislation is a blow to university autonomy'. *University World News*, Issue no. 251, 9 December. http://www. universityworldnews.com/article.php?story=20121207163547738.

15. See, among others, Cloete, N. 2013. 'A new look at demographic transformation: Comments on Govinder et al.' *South African Journal of Science*, 110(1/2): 1–4. http://sajs.co.za/sites/default/files/publications/pdf/Cloete_Commentary.pdf.

16. Africa Network expert panel. 2014. 'Why are there so few black professors in South Africa?' *The Guardian*, 6 October. https://www.theguardian.com/ world/2014/oct/06/south-africa-race-black-professors. See also Mangu, X. 2014. '10 steps to develop black professors'. *City Press*, 20 July. http://www. news24.com/Archives/City-Press/10-steps-to-develop-black-professors -20150429; and Mangcu, X. 2014. 'Ripping the veil off UCT's whiter shades of

pale'. *Sunday Times*, 6 July. https://www.uct.ac.za/usr/news/2014/Ripping%20 the%20veil%20off%20UCTs%20whiter%20shades%20of%20pale.pdf.

17. ASSAf. 2013. 'ASSAf commentary on the proposed National Institute on Humanities and Social Sciences (NIHSS)'. http://www.assaf.org.za/ASSAf-Commentary-on-the-proposed-National-Institute-on-Humanities-and-Social-Sciences.pdf.

18. Ensor, P. 2012. 'Whose "way forward" for the humanities is it anyway?' *Mail & Guardian*, 4 May. http://mg.co.za/article/2012-05-04-whose-way-forward -for-the-humanities-is-it-anyway.

19. Wong, A. 2015. 'The renaissance of student activism'. *The Atlantic*, 21 May. http://www.theatlantic.com/education/archive/2015/05/the-renaissance-of -student-activism/393749/. See also Fairbanks, E. 2015. 'The global face of student protest'. *The New York Times*, 13 December. http://www.nytimes. com/2015/12/13/opinion/the-global-face-of-student-protest.html?_r=0; and Hall, M. 2016. 'South African student protests have lessons for all universities'. *The Guardian*, 3 March. https://www.theguardian.com/higher-education -network/2016/mar/03/south-africas-student-protests-have-lessons -for-all-universities.

20. Solty, I. 2012. 'Canada's "Maple Spring": From the Quebec student strike to the movement against neoliberalism'. *Socialist Project*, 31 December. http://www. rosalux-nyc.org/canadas-maple-spring/.

21. Fitzgerald, P., and Seale, O. 2016. 'Between a rock and a hard place: University management and the #FeesMustFall campaign'. In *Fees must fall: Student revolt, decolonisation and governance in South Africa*, edited by S. Booysen. Wits University Press: Johannesburg, p. 242.

22. Meyer, D.S. 2014. *The politics of protests: Student movements in America*, 2nd edition. Oxford University Press: Oxford, p. 6.

23. Ndlovu-Gatsheni, S.J. 2011. 'The logic of violence in Africa'. Ferguson Centre for African and Asian Studies Working Paper No. 02, p. 2. http://www.open.ac.uk/ Arts/ferguson-centre/working-papers/working-paper-2.pdf.

24. All of these examples, and more, are familiar to South Africans from the hearings of the Truth and Reconciliation Commission.

25. 'Boipatong massacre – 17 June 1992'. *South African History Online*. http://www. sahistory.org.za/topic/boipatong-massacre-17-june-1992.

26. 'Bisho massacre 1992'. *South African History Online*. http://www.sahistory.org. za/article/bisho-massacre-1992.

27. 'Thembisile "Chris" Hani'. *South African History Online*. http://www.sahistory. org.za/people/thembisile-chris-hani.

28. Statement by the then ANC Youth League president Julius Malema. See Independent Online. 2008. ' "We will kill for Zuma" '. *IOL*, 17 June. http://www. iol.co.za/news/politics/we-will-kill-for-zuma-404646.

29. Statement by current ANC Youth League president (2016–) Collen Maine to struggle veterans. See Savides, M. 2016. 'Watch: ANCYL calls MK veterans to

take up arms for Zuma' (video). *Times Live*, 15 October. http://www.timeslive.
co.za/politics/2016/10/15/Watch-ANCYL-calls-MK-Veterans-to-take
-up-arms-for-Zuma.

30.   Booysens, S. (ed.). 2016. *Fees must fall: Student revolt, decolonisation and
governance in South Africa*. Wits University Press: Johannesburg, p. 329.

31.   Mamdani, M. 2011. *When victims become killers*. Princeton University Press:
Princeton, New Jersey, p. 12.

32.   Mamdani interpreting Fanon on the subject of violence. Ibid., p. 10.

33.   I am grateful to another Fellow at the Center for Advanced Studies in the
Behavioral Sciences at Stanford University, the Belgian scholar Batja Gomes
Mesquita, for pointing me in the direction of this literature. See Tripp, T.M., et
al. 2002. 'Poetic injustice or petty jealousy? The aesthetics of revenge'.
Organizational Behaviour and Human Decision Processes, 89: 966–984; Cota-
McKinley, A.L., et al. 2001. 'Vengeance: Effects of gender, age, and religious
background'. *Aggressive Behavior*, 27(5): 343–350; Schumann, K., and Ross, M.
2010. 'The benefits, costs, and paradox of revenge'. *Social & Personality
Psychology*, 4(12): 1193–1205; Gollwitzer, M., and Denzler, M. 2009. 'What
makes revenge sweet?' *Journal of Experimental Social Psychology*, 45(4): 840–
844; and Frijda, N.H. 1994. 'The Lex Talionis: On vengeance'. In *Emotions:
Essays on emotion theory*, edited by S.H.M van Goozen et al. Lawrence Erlbaum
Associates: Hillsdale, New Jersey.

34.   Mamdani, M. 2011. *When victims become killers*. Princeton University Press:
Princeton, New Jersey, p. 13.

35.   This is a question I first posed in the TB Davie Memorial Lecture on Academic
Freedom at UCT on 26 August 2004, and to which I responded as follows: 'It
cannot be when a government decree declares some final date by which a
university shuts down; or when a large institution engulfs and extinguishes the
identity of a smaller one; or when new signage goes up declaring an imagined
community. Nor can it be said that a university exists simply because it goes
through the routines of graduation ceremonies or that it registers another
"intake" of students or even that it teaches them. A university ceases to exist
when the intellectual project no longer defines its identity, infuses its curriculum,
energises its scholars and inspires its students.'

36.   Baldwin, J. 1993. *The fire next time*. Vintage Books (Random House): New York.

Index

welfare
    responsibilities and expectations 172-183
    university and academic project 191-193
    welfarisation of SA universities 9-10,
       172-193
welfarisation, of SA universities 9-10, 172-193
Wilson, W 24
Wits, *see* University of the Witwatersrand
WSU, *see* Walter Sisulu University

Y
Yale University (Connecticut) 24

Z
Zimbabwe 49, 51-52, 155, 162, 228, 244-245
Zuma, Jacob 29, 92, 107

About the author

Prof Jonathan Jansen is a leading South African educationist, commen-
tator and the author of several books including the best-selling *Letters to
My Children*. He is the former vice-chancellor of the University of the
Free State, where he earned a reputation for transformation and a deep
commitment to reconciliation. He is married with two children.